W9-BZM-301

REAL ESTATE PROSPECTING

STRATEGIES FOR FARMING YOUR MARKETS

2nd Edition

JOYCE L. CAUGHMAN

**Real Estate
Education Company**
a division of Dearborn Financial Publishing, Inc.

While a great deal of care has been taken to provide accurate and current information, the ideas, suggestions, general principles and conclusions presented in this text are subject to local, state and federal laws and regulations, court cases and any revisions of same. The reader is thus urged to consult legal counsel regarding any points of law—this publication should not be used as a substitute for competent legal advice.

Publisher: Kathleen A. Welton
Associate Editor: Karen A. Christensen
Managing Editor: Jack L. Kiburz
Editorial Assistant: Kristen G. Landreth
Cover Design: Vito de Pinto

94 95 96 10 9 8 7 6 5 4 3 2 1

Library of Congress Cataloging-in-Publication Data

Caughman, Joyce L.
    Real estate prospecting : strategies for farming your markets /
Joyce L. Caughman.—2nd ed.
        p.   cm.
    Includes bibliographical references and index.
    ISBN 0-7931-0945-0
    1. Real estate listings. 2. Real estate business. I. Title.
HD1382.6.C38   1994
    333.33—dc20   94-13448
                                                                         CIP

Contents

Acknowledgments

Grateful acknowledgment is made to the following for permission to reprint copyrighted materials:

REALTORS® National Marketing Institute of the National Association of REALTORS® for excerpts from the book, *Recruiting Sales Associates,* by Ken Reyhons, CRB, CRS. © 1986 by the REALTORS® National Marketing Institute.

Hall Institute of Real Estate, Inc., for excerpts from the book, *The Service Road to Success,* © 1974 by The Hall Institute of Real Estate, Inc.

Jacobson Corporation, Miami, FL, for excerpts from the book, *Cultivating Your Listing Farm,* by Alan W. Jacobson and Jack L. Gale. © 1977 by Alan W. Jacobson and Jack L. Gale, revised © 1986.

Kennedy International Productions, San Clemente, CA, for excerpts from the book, *How To List and Sell in the Nineties,* by Danielle Kennedy. © 1990 by Prentice Hall.

Calculated Industries, Inc., for excerpts from the book, *Successful Farming—By Mail,* by Steve Kennedy. © 1987 by Calculated Industries, Inc.

Kricket Publications for excerpts from the book, Real Estate Farming: Campaign for $uccess, by P.J. Thompson. © 1985 by Pauline J. Thompson.

JayDee Publishing Company for excerpts from the book, *The Farming Manual,* by David R. Stipp and Robert D. Underwood. © 1978 by JayDee Publishing Company.

The Real Estate Professional for excerpts from an article, "Selling Yourself Through Your Marketing Plan," by Carole Kelby. © 1988, 1989 by Wellesley Publications, Inc.

Hank Trisler of The Hank Trisler Company, San Jose, CA, for excerpts from an article appearing in *The Real Estate Professional* entitled, "A Fine Old Whine." © 1990. All rights reserved. May not be reprinted without permission.

Real Estate Business for excerpts from an article, "Prospecting Made More Manageable," by Lou Pretto; "How To Get More Profits with Response Advertising," by Daniel Gooder Richard; and "Understanding the Fear of Prospecting," by Dick Wilson. © 1988, 1989 by the REALTORS® National Marketing Institute; "Oh, What a Relief It Is," by Randall K. Eager. © 1989 by the Real Estate Brokerage/Real Estate Sales RB/RS Council of the REALTORS® National Marketing Institute. All rights reserved. Reprinted with permission.

Rufus S. Lusk and Son, Inc., for sample pages from its Real Estate Sales Directories. © 1989 by Rufus S. Lusk and Son, Inc.

NTC Business Books, a division of NTC Publishing Group, 4255 West Touhy Avenue, Lincolnwood, IL 60646–1975 for excerpt from *Successful Direct Marketing Methods,* Fourth Edition, by Bob Stone (Stone's seven-step formula for direct mail). © 1989 by Bob Stone.

ATCOM, Inc., for excerpts from *Real Estate Insider Weekly Newsletter.* © 1987.

Broderbund Software, San Rafael, CA, for computer graphics used throughout, created by Print Shop software.

Computer Digest, Clark Publishing Company, Arlington, VA, for excerpts from the article "True Confessions of a Laptop Convert," by Patricia Kirby.

Impact Farming, Real Estate Edition, Carlsbad, CA, for use of advertising copy appearing in *REALTOR News®.*

Cole Publications, Lincoln, NE, for permission to quote material regarding its programs, Smart Agent, EasyList, *Cole Directories* and its real estate listing form. © 1994. All rights reserved. May not be reprinted without permission.

Cole Publications and Information Services for permission to reprint "This Is It!" real estate listing form. Reprinted by permission of Cole Publications and Information Services, division of Metro Mail. All rights reserved.

Training Unlimited, Boise, ID, and Ann Honda for permission to reprint the personal brochure response written by Tim Cowles and distributed by Ann Honda. © 1993. All rights reserved.

Advo, Inc., Windsor, CT, for allowing reprinting of "Penetrate Your Markets." © 1993. All rights reserved.

Realty Tools, Inc., for use of the listing presentation material that accompanies its computer software program. May not be reprinted without specific permission of the company.

Paul Christian, Taylorsville, NC, for reprints of material from Paul Christian's Ghost Writers. © 1991. All rights reserved. May not be reprinted in whole or in part without permission of the publisher.

Realty World Corporation for reproduction of copyrighted promotional material provided by the company for the use of its agents. © 1993. This material is the property of the Realty World Corporation and is reprinted with its permission. It may not be reprinted in whole or in part without Realty World Corporation consent.

Long and Foster, REALTORS®, for permission to reproduce a brochure entitled "Our Marketing Process" and a newsletter entitled *The Plum Line.* © 1993. All rights reserved. May not be reprinted without permission of Long & Foster, REALTORS®.

PC World for permission to reprint "Double-Duty: 486 Notebooks," written by Bryan Hastings and Dan Miller, taken from the July 1993 issue. All rights reserved.

PC Novice for permission to reprint material. Used with permission of PC Novice—for subscription information, call 800-848-1478.

REALTOR News®, for allowing reprint of excerpts from an article "New-Fax-on-Demand" program available to REALTORS® (not available to the general public), appearing in the week of July 5, 1993. © 1993 by the National Association of REALTORS®.

RS News Briefs, a publication of the Residential Sales Council, Vol. 7, No. 4, for permission to reprint "The New Pres Kit Makes Personal Promotions a Snap." © 1993. All rights reserved by REALTORS® National Marketing Institute.

John L. Scott for permission to reprint copyrighted material: John L. Scott Coloring Contest to John L. Scott, Inc., REALTORS®, Washington.

John Gerrety for permission to reprint his newsletter. Reprinted with permission of John Gerrety, Gerrety and Bragg, REALTORS®. All rights reserved.

Real Estate Today® for excerpts from the following articles: "New Frontiers of Farming," by Jack Gale and Alan Jacobson. Reprinted from the March 1989 issue of *Real Estate Today*® by permission of the National Association of REALTORS®. © 1989. All rights reserved.

"Wheels of Success," by Carl K. Clayton. Reprinted from the April 1989 issue of *Real Estate Today*® by permission of the National Association of REALTORS®. © 1989. All rights reserved. "The Listing Farm," by Merlin B. Coslick. Reprinted from the March/April 1978 issue of *Real Estate Today*® by permission of the National Association of REALTORS®. © 1978. All rights reserved. "Produce Your Own Flyers," by Noel G. Hinde. Reprinted from the March 1987 issue of *Real Estate Today*® by permission of the National Association of REALTORS®. © 1987. All rights reserved. "Which Is the Right Hat for You?" by Laurene K. Janik. Reprinted from the September 1988 issue of *Real Estate Today*® by

Preface

Change is the challenge of our times. The culture of real estate, no less than other cultures of our society, has been hit by "future shock." Real estate salespersons who have thrived in less complicated times find themselves foundering in today's environment: Reactive is inadequate; proactive is the wave of the future. Waiting for business is out; penetrating your markets is in.

Present conditions make farming the ideal prospecting vehicle. In the real estate industry the term *farming* means the cultivation of a specific terrain in the same way that one would work a plot of land: tilling, planting, fertilizing, weeding and finally reaping the harvest of listings and sales.

Just as the farmer carefully selects a fertile tract capable of producing a good crop, so, too, do real estate agents carefully select their fields of endeavor.

As the farmer must work energetically, efficiently and persistently through all kinds of weather so the crops will ripen and mature, in order to reap the full rewards of the harvest, so must real estate agents who expect a bountiful crop persist to the end of the season.

Unfortunately, many of them do not persevere, even at their broker's urging, and the turnover in real estate listing farms is detrimental to the company image and frustrating to the agent.

Many brokers realize that concentrating an all-out effort on a defined area is proving to be the most efficient and effective method of operation for real estate salespeople and for the brokerage itself.

The problem for brokers and branch office managers has been to put these would-be farmers in possession of an action plan for the methodical development of the farm and accomplish their other tasks as well. It is a full-time job to keep a group of farmers from floundering or becoming discouraged by the seemingly endless amount of time and work necessary to reap the benefit of the process.

It helps tremendously if a broker has a company plan such as those outlined in Chapter 2.

A company blueprint, plus a guide to agent competence, would prevent so many newcomers from falling by the wayside and wasting all their efforts, money and time, as well as that of the real estate broker.

What has been wanting is a simple, clear, well-organized, action-oriented manual of farming—a "how-to" and "what-to-do-and-when" book that managers could use to train new agents or that newcomers to farming could pick up and put into practice without further instruction.

In this book, *Real Estate Prospecting: Strategies for Farming Your Markets,* real estate salespeople will find specific timetables for actions every step of the way. Selection, size, location and type of farm area are important decisions that are basic to the success of the project. Agents often make these decisions without sufficient guidance. It would be ideal if the broker or branch manager had time to use this book to lead the agents by the hand all the way through the process.

Another choice would be to use the 12 chapters of the book as a series of training sessions that the company trainer could use as a transition from the formal education program of the company to the actual training in the field.

If none of these options is available, however, this book covers all the elements of farming in logical sequence. A minimum of orientation and follow-up should be necessary. Most agents will be able to pick up the book and *go!*

Setting up farm maps and records can be so complicated and time-consuming under some existing farming systems that this may discourage agents from the whole undertaking. This book provides simple yet adequate planning and reporting systems.

The latest generation of farmers is well into the computer world, and the use of the personal computer in the listing farm puts the scientific farmer millennia ahead of the mule farmer.

Farming, especially by computer, has many dimensions in addition to the geographic farm. This book explores many avenues, such as farming for referrals among clients and customers as well as among top agents, spheres of influence and interest groups, professions, ethnic groups, bird dogs and other networks.

Among the many invaluable farming tools listed in "Resources," Appendix A, are two marvelously simple software programs, Smart

Agent and EasyList. Smart Agent contains 100 ready-to-use letters, plus the capability to create your own personal letter-writing campaigns and direct mail pieces. EasyList, a compatible computer program by Cole Publications and Information Systems, makes compiling records a snap, since you can copy the names, addresses and telephone numbers of everyone in the farm area into your records with one keystroke.

Competition among brokers is fierce in some areas, and familiarity with time-honored farming methods is useful, but creativity in devising new marketing techniques is even more vital. This book attempts to encourage imaginative ideas for offering service to the homeowner and for keeping the agent and company name before the homeowner in a consistent, yet diplomatic, manner.

PART 1

The Service Road to Success

Farming: A Systematic Way of Prospecting

Why Farm: A Professional Strategy for Success

Successful real estate salespeople have been farming for years. Some of them are not even aware that they are farming. As far as they are concerned, they are just helping the people in their neighborhood. That is the essence of farming.

In spite of the phenomenal success of farming as a concentrated professional strategy for success, hardly any other method of operation meets with more resistance. No doubt it requires sustained, systematic work.

Today's real estate climate, however, is such that the old, relaxed, reactive game plan no longer works. There is a new breed of real estate salesperson out there, making incredible sums of money, embracing change, acting, not just reacting. The new salesperson knows that waiting for business is out, and penetrating markets is the road to success. This salesperson is not afraid of computers and heeds the advice that anyone who turns away from computers will soon be out of business. Survivors adapt!

The new salesperson has learned three important skills:

1. How to use personal marketing to make the phone ring
2. How to become the real estate specialist of his or her market area

3. How to simplify life with today's technology

Many real estate brokers and managers have learned that business will not get better until the agents do and are insisting that their agents farm.

Research across the United States has convinced me that a lot of real estate firms have not yet completely comprehended the productive possibilities of farming. I found three levels of commitment to farming.

1. None. These firms rely on cold calling and traditional prospecting: "If you want to farm, go ahead. You're on your own."
2. Cooperative. These companies support and encourage the individual salesperson: "We'll help you do it."
3. Promotion department in charge: "You pay for it, and we'll keep it rolling."

Which system would best fit you depends a great deal on your talent, personality and stage of development as a real estate practitioner.

Independent, go-getter types with a lot of creativity and drive are probably just as well off on their own.

Most real estate salespeople would benefit by some cooperation from their companies. Some firms provide company postcards, newsletters and other materials. Some pay postage and other costs. Some provide a lot of guidance in the planning stage (see Chapter 2).

Frantically busy superstars are probably best served by a company farming program that does not require too much of their valuable time. Many superstars thrive best with a direct mail campaign, in addition to the follow-up of past customers and clients.

Beginners, however, could use a little help. To that end, I have written this book.

Why Farming Works: Persistence and Consistency

A startling advertisement recently began appearing in one of the real estate tabloids, arousing a lot of curiosity.

I STOPPED SELLING REAL ESTATE.
You can achieve financial security in
24 months by doing the same.

Advertising his book, *Impact Farming,* the author wrote: "I stopped selling real estate and began to sell myself. Only 24 months later, my referral business alone amounted to $62,428."

Less dramatically, Merlin B. Coslick, writing in *Real Estate Today*®, attributes farmers' success this way: "The salesperson who lists consistently has the edge in this business. . . . Like a probing radar sweep, he consistently combs his listing farm, sifting, prodding, questioning, checking, learns the territory—acting like a pro. He never wonders how to spend his day. . . . A ringing phone isn't his day—it is just part of it."

In his book, *Recruiting Sales Associates,* Ken Reyhons writes that "of all the people coming into real estate brokerage, 68 percent are completely out of business in five years. Most of them are gone within the first year."

Won't Work?

The most common reason cited for failure was "won't work." "Even badly trained agents can be successful—if they work," Reyhons says. "Brilliant salespeople can fail, if they don't work."

Why don't they work? Many reasons are given, but in most cases it is because nobody tells them precisely what to do and because they have no self-discipline. Reyhons, again, says, "It takes a great deal of self-discipline to be successful in real estate—to establish a plan of action, and then follow it to successful completion." This is especially true when there is no initial guidance and supervision.

Farming works because of the cumulative effects of persistence and consistency. It requires an investment of time before you can reap the benefits. Think of this as compounding an investment. For example, $2,000 invested every year for 30 years in an IRA becomes a million dollars. An investment in time, likewise, leads to proportionately expanding rewards.

For one thing, when you invest in a planned farming program you have the whole industry working for you. When you concentrate on listing you control the market because you control the source of merchandise. Most new agents concentrate on sales and are on their own. No one else is working for them. They do not realize the compounding effect and become discouraged.

Farming Is Marketing Yourself

Even brilliant, entrepreneurial salespeople who loathe routine and abominate recordkeeping find they have to do a certain amount of farming—no matter what they call it—because it is practically impossible to reach the top without maintaining contact with your sphere of influence on a regular basis, which is a form of farming.

Farming is simply a systematic way of prospecting. Prospecting is the key to success in any type of selling. When you farm, you concentrate your efforts on a specific spot. When you drive a stake into your garden, you first whittle the stake to a fine point, because pressure applied to a small area provides much more penetration than the same force spread over a large area. The same principle applies to real estate farming: If you spread yourself too thin, you will not make the same impression.

The Numbers Game

David Stipp and Robert Underwood, in *The Farming Manual,* explain the arithmetic of farming:

> According to the national average, one out of every five families moves each year. In addition, statistics indicate that on the average, each family moves every five years. . . . Success in real estate requires patience and perseverance. Consider these facts: It takes 100 cold calls to get ten interviews; ten interviews to get four listing appointments; and four listing appointments to get two listings.
>
> If you set your individual goals at two listings per month, the pure mathematics indicate that you must make 100 new cold-canvass calls during the month. A systematic method of farming provides a *clearly defined framework* within which to work.

These numbers do not even take into consideration that in a well-run farm it is not long before *none* of these calls are *cold* calls. Therefore, the chances multiply over time.

Name, Reputation, Confidence and Trust

The farming process ensures the confidence of all who come in contact with a farmer—confidence in their expertise and their concern for the welfare of others.

As the farmer, through experience and study, truly becomes the area real estate specialist, an inner sense of self-confidence develops. The farmer begins to believe that the person who deals with him or her is indeed lucky. This belief is transmitted to the customers and clients the farmer serves. And trust, as everyone knows, is the foremost ingredient of closing. Trusting a friend and neighbor is child's play when compared to trusting a stranger. The whole environment changes. Not only is it easier to make money, but it is ever so much more pleasant and relaxed than to be constantly dealing with strangers, many of whom make it quite clear that they are suspicious.

I remember once, many years ago, telling some of my sales associates about a couple of prospective big-city buyers with whom I was dealing. "What amazes me," I said, "is that when I was teaching public school, no one ever questioned my integrity. I have not changed one iota. Yet some of the people I deal with now seem to feel I have no right to resent crude slurs on my veracity."

In your farm, all this mistrust seems to melt away as people perceive your genuine interest in helping them reach their goals.

The Service Road to Success

In 1974, Hall Institute of Real Estate of Hanover, Massachusetts, published the most extraordinary treatise on service. It was the second volume of a series called *CARES (Coordinated Approach to Real Estate Studies)*. It was written 15 years before the discovery, by Tom Peters and other management consultants, of service as the secret of business success. In those days, it was taken for granted that the ingredients of business success consisted of ruthlessness, greed and cleverness. It is only recently that new theories of success, based upon the principle of real service and honesty, have surfaced. And it was not until those theories had been proven effective by a number of successful firms such as Mary Kay Cosmetics that people began to believe in empathy and service as the secrets of success.

In real estate "value-oriented" selling, "nonmanipulative selling" and "integrity selling" are just now making their tentative bid for attention.

The second volume of the *CARES* series was entitled *The Service Road to Success*. It asserted that "service begins where duty ends," and called the secret ingredient "and then some," which meant going the extra mile. In fact, it was frankly identified as "sacrifice," a very unpopular idea at the time, ridiculed by cynics far and wide.

Instead of trying to sell your prospects what you were trying to get rid of, the Hall Institute publication advised real estate sales associates to "determine your clients' problems and needs through intelligent and persistent questioning, coupled with your undivided attention to the answers received, the nuances of these answers, or the attitudes they reflect. It will be possible for you to better understand your clients' physical, emotional, economic, social and ego problems and needs."

Then what?

"Many of us expect too much credit for performing our duty," the Hall Institute publication states. "A far nobler purpose is required to achieve success. Duty is mere obligation. Service involves sacrifice. Successful men and women in any field do not like to do the unpleasant things anymore than do failures. The unsuccessful are satisfied with what limited results they can get without sacrifice."

Sound pretty grim? The fact of the matter is that it turns out to be inspiring. To give service above and beyond the call of duty is to be heroic. To be heroic is exhilarating.

To be heroic also pays like crazy.

Says the Hall Institute publication: "As a consequence of professional service (which reflects a commitment surpassing duty) you may be certain that you, by name, will be recommended voluntarily, enthusiastically and continually by your sellers" (and buyers and everyone else) "to all in their spheres of influence who may now, or in the future, require the services of a professionally competent and personally interested and committed real estate agent. When you have, with diligence, protected and promoted your sellers' interest, as their agent, they will in turn serve as your agent, voluntarily, and without compensation."

There you have it—the secret of the success of farming. Farming is the perfect framework within which to demonstrate your willingness to go the extra mile and take the "service road to success."

Leadership:
A Company Approach

The real estate company and the sales associate may have different concepts of the purpose of the farming program. The firm may approach the project as a method of developing its image as a progressive, professional, service-minded and competent concern, while the individual salesperson may see farming as the key to personal success or to controlling the type of clientele he or she wishes to serve.

In any case, mutual goals always must be kept in mind. If the program is to succeed, it must be designed with consideration of the needs of both. A good farming plan coordinates and synchronizes the activities of the whole office team, leaving room for individual creativity but clearly defining areas of responsibility.

Planning for Production

Maximum production of a real estate branch office requires, like everything else, a *plan*. Many offices are relatively successful without a plan, but we are talking about *maximum production*. The first step a company must take is to establish its goals. If the goal is a congenial, relaxed office that affords a modest income for a low-keyed, social-minded owner, then a fairly loose program should be sufficient.

The range of systematic planning engaged in across the country runs the gamut from none to total. One branch manager of a national company, whom I interviewed in San Luis Obispo, California, simply responded to my questions with, "Farming? What's that?" He really did not seem to understand what farming entailed and commented repeatedly, "We do a lot of cold calling." I didn't bother to point out the advantages of "hot calling."

At the other end of the scale, Grace J. Perkins, of Fox and Carskadon in San Francisco, has such a well-planned and well-executed company farming system that all her agents have to do is pick up the telephone to start the process moving in their own bailiwick (and pay for it, of course, or at least part of it).

Being Number One

If the goals are highly competitive and the broker yearns to be number one, then a centralized farming program, originating at the top, with clear, well-conceived, well-orchestrated planning is hard to beat.

I saw this firsthand at Long & Foster, REALTORS®, an independent brokerage firm in the Washington, D.C./Baltimore, Maryland, corridor that has expanded from a two-person office formed in suburban Virginia just over 20 years ago to a firm with more than 140 branch offices at last check.

This firm has an Agent Marketing Services Group that concentrates on the tools needed by agents to generate activity for themselves. Current products include *Homenotes*®, the company real estate newsletter, *Target*® and "FotoCard" mailing services and other sales aids.

Realty World produces an inventive "Just Listed" brochure that hangs on a prospective buyer's doorknob (Figure 2.1). Representatives periodically visit offices to describe the broad range of services offered to agents. Obviously, these kinds of services are tremendous recruiting tools for the firm as well as invaluable services to their agents.

A Farming Plan

A farming plan begins with a definition of the service area of the office or firm. The service area differs slightly from the market area, for individual salespeople can sell homes over a very large area, but there is a limit to the distance from which a listing can be properly serviced.

The importance of this distinction is underscored by Hall Institute of Real Estate's book, *The Service Road to Success:* "Reputations are

FIGURE 2.1 "Just Listed" Brochure and Door Hanger

WALK RIGHT IN
AND
MAKE YOURSELF
AT HOME:

Date: _____

Time: _____

Place: _____

I'd like to welcome you and your friends to preview this home. When you visit our open house, I'll be available to show you all the fine features. I'll answer your questions on any real estate matters, such as property values and sales activity in your area. I look forward to meeting you soon.

JUST
LISTED

*The right agent
makes all the difference
in the world.*®

REALTY WORLD

YOUR NEIGHBORS AT:

MADE A VERY
SMART MOVE.

When your neighbors decided to sell their property, they chose a REALTY WORLD® agent. As you can see, they got results. That's because I'm backed by some of the most advanced marketing systems in the business. So, I can attract buyers interested in homes just like yours.

If you're thinking about buying or selling – or just want to know what your property is worth in today's market – please give me a call. It's one of the best moves you can make.

Source: Reprinted with permission of Realty World® Corporation.

built and sustained primarily on the quality of service promised and delivered."

Within the service area designated by a firm, target areas should be identified and each sales associate should be given or encouraged to choose an area of responsibility that can be handled efficiently.

The centralized company program acts as a framework within which the individual agent can be and is encouraged to be creative.

The Statistics of Real Estate

The statistics of real estate form the basis for success in farming. The arithmetic is quite simple. If you know how many families move each year, how often each family moves, how many calls it takes to get an interview and how many interviews to make a listing appointment, then you know persistency and consistency are bound to produce results.

An experienced farmer who keeps records can predict with uncanny accuracy how many new calls he or she must make each month to produce the number of listings that is needed to reach his or her goal, given the farmer's level of listing skill.

If the company has provided the farmer with the framework within which to establish a systematic method of operation and a specific market area in which to concentrate his or her efforts, then the farmer will be put on the right track to success.

Many real estate salespeople fail because they do not have the initiative and the burning desire it takes to constantly devise ways to success. These same people, if given a specific program and consistently encouraged to carry it out, will become extremely successful. This is especially true if the manager of the company farm program is good at reading his or her people. Each individual sales associate operates at a particular level of competence that is usually tied to personal self-esteem. Goals have to be realistic for the person who has to carry them out. Only he or she knows what is realistic.

Hank Trisler, a training and management consultant in San Jose, California, takes a very hard stand on this. He says: "People don't want to prospect? Get some new people. You can't change people. You can't motivate others, but you can certainly replace them." In today's market, it is absolutely crucial to the success of a company that every agent have a planned program of systematized prospecting. He warns managers not to let the tail wag the dog right into failure. "Stay in control of your company so it doesn't control you."

Setting Goals

Agents must be helped to set their own goals, for only they know what price they are willing to pay for success.

It is a mistake for an agent to attempt too much or too little in the beginning. The catch is to determine what is too much or too little territory for the particular agent or the circumstances. Some sales associates might be better off not farming a geographic area at all; they may do better farming waterfront properties or spot lots, agricultural land, high rises, commercial properties or their own spheres of influence depending on their individual tendencies. It is important for managers to be sensitive to the capabilities and inclinations of the individual sales associates and allow them as much room for their creativity as they need within the framework of the program. Some will need more guidance than others.

Farming is a long-range program for prospecting that should be thoughtfully conceived and carefully developed. Studies show that the average real estate farm requires six months of work before it really begins to produce satisfactorily. After it begins producing, it should provide the farmer with 20 percent of the listings in the farm in the second year, 50 percent in the third year and up to 75 percent in future years.

Sustaining the Farmer Until Harvesttime

Meanwhile, the sales associates must feed themselves and their families. Unless the farm program is being inaugurated among a group of agents who already are established, some provision must be made to help the farmers sustain themselves until their farms reach maturity. Many farmers fall by the wayside because they cannot afford to wait. This aspect of farming should be resolved from the outset.

New farmers can start a small, expandable plot and work in some other real estate endeavor (rentals, for example) that will produce more immediate income until they are in a position to devote more time to farming. The fastest way to generate income is to hold open houses for experienced sales associates who have too many listings to be able to hold them all open. Knowing good open-house techniques will be a lifesaver (see Chapter 11). It is important to encourage new sales associates to take floor duty, but here again, agents must learn how to make the most of this opportunity. Sitting next to an expert for a few days could mean the difference between agony and ease for a new salesperson. Newcomers should be helped to early financial rewards while building the foundations for successful lifetime careers. It will be worth the extra effort for brokers and branch managers.

Designing the Company Farming Program

Designing the company farming program depends on the area and on the resources of the company. Farming an extensive geographic area may require different or additional approaches from those employed in a more restricted area because the customer profile may differ within the same service area. Large orbits, for example, may require more advertising and promotional resources from the firm and more diversity in marketing: service by a television or a local radio station or by a particular newspaper to support the diversity of the various neighborhoods within the overall company target area. This situation applies primarily to large companies with many branch offices covering a huge territory.

Regardless of the approach to farming that seems best for the situation of a particular firm or office, three basic considerations should be borne in mind: the company and/or office goals; the nature of the competition; and the compatibility of the individual sales associate to his or her expected responsibility.

Two Farming Plans

Two typical company farming plans that I came across in research around the country were those of Fox and Carskadon, Better Homes and Gardens in San Francisco and The Prudential Real Estate in Sacramento.

Prudential's program, as implemented by Les Boomer, is described in Chapter 8.

The Fox and Carskadon program was designed to provide busy, successful, experienced agents with a company farming service. The program is implemented by a direct mail firm overseen by the company's marketing director, and features a monthly newsletter; an estate magazine three times a year; *Your Guide to Homes,* a color publication showing company listings that is sent to 860,000 people in seven counties; and an oversized multipurpose postcard with the agent's picture. A historical homes calendar and other promotional items are in the works. Agents can order the program by phone or fax and participate in the personalized part to the tune of 80 percent of its cost. The turnaround time is five days.

Independent Contractors: Common Law or Statutory

Agents have protected areas, that is, they cannot farm in another agent's farm, but they can list or sell individual homes in it. Most companies do not have protected farms; anyone is free to farm anywhere. Independent contractor status can affect this decision. Interesting enough, the 1982 federal tax law changed the extent that management can control the actions of salespeople who are statutory independent contractors. Common law, which prevails in states that have not enacted legislation that matches the federal legislation, may prevent managers from controlling how salespeople work or when or where they work. An article in *Real Estate Today*® called "Which Is the Right Hat for You?" discusses this topic in detail; every manager should have a copy of it (See "Resources," Appendix A). If you plan to have protected farms or to bar salespeople from working in their preferred areas, you must look into this aspect. It also affects what you can or cannot require agents to do. Agents at Fox and Carskadon voted for protected farms. Farm follow-up is up to the individual agent. Many walk the neighborhood, give out gifts and handouts and take part in neighborhood projects. They use the telephone to see if letters, magazines, brochures or premiums sent out by the firm were received.

Several East Coast managers with whom I spoke simply obtain a commitment to farming from new sales recruits when they associate with them (Figure 2.2). These offices have been very successful with this approach.

At Fox and Carskadon, each agent is expected to work three farms: a personal farm, a client farm and a geographic farm.

Agents can give letters to the manager to post or fax to the mailing house. The turnaround time is five days. The salespeople are encouraged to be creative, but *quality* is the byword. Their goal is to be called in their farm for a competitive market analysis as often as possible. New agents can add a farm from the office farming map. It is city farming, which is an intimidating idea to many salespeople in other parts of the country. It apparently poses no problem for Fox and Carskadon in San Francisco. This office confines its activities to the northern area of the city. Another Fox and Carskadon office handles the southern region. In the office there is a map of the territory, with colored pins representing activity in individual farms. In his article "A Fine Old Whine," Hank Trisler emphasizes the importance of each agent having a clear prospecting plan and commitment to following it. Real estate owners and managers must understand the basic truth of the saying, The market won't improve until the salespeople do. The salespeople won't improve until they learn that prospecting is the name of the game. While there is no doubt of the truth of his contention that managers must insist upon agents' performance standards, management consultants in other fields

FIGURE 2.2   Commitment Letter

Date:

To: Sales associates joining _____
                                        Company name
Topic: Commitment to Success

It is well known in the business world that successful people
are those who have the self-discipline to perform the tasks
that their competitors shirk. In real estate, the problem
frequently is that salespeople either do not know what these
tasks are, or they have not formed the habit of doing them.

_____ agrees to provide a transition
Company name

period in which training and guidance will be offered free on
the condition that you accomplish the following requirements:

1. Complete all the company training classes before entering
   the branch office training program.
2. Preview 20 company listings prior to assignment of floor
   duty, and ten houses per week thereafter.
3. Keep all assigned floor duty, be on time and ready to
   answer calls. No outgoing calls will be made during floor
   duty.
4. Acknowledge that floor time is earned based on attendance
   at sales meetings and house tours, plus production plus
   ability to handle busy phones.
5. Attend weekly branch office training sessions and complete
   all assignments within that week.
6. FARM AT LEAST 350 HOMES PER MONTH.
7. Take and work all rental calls whenever possible.
8. Hold open two houses per month, or more.
9. When not holding open house on weekends, visit open houses
   in an assigned market area and turn in a report form.
10. Demonstrate knowledge of the company market area and the
    local listing inventory of the competition.
11. Contact at least one FSBO in your own farm area and at
    least two expired listings in the company market area per
    month.
12. Work with trainer/manager/assigned agent during your first
    five transactions. You must be accompanied by an
    experienced person on listing or contact presentation or
    settlement until skilled.
13. Until earnings reach $_____ you must:
    • Attend all sales meetings.
    • Go on house tour.
    • Work in the sales office a minimum of half a day, every
      weekday.
14. In order to be considered for permanent affiliation, you
    must have listed at least one house and had at least one
    successful transaction in the previous six months'
    transition period.

FIGURE 2.2 (Continued)

```
Acknowledgment:
I have a copy of the transition program for new agents and I
understand that if I diligently pursue these activities, I will
receive support and assistance in gaining the experience needed
to become a successful real estate salesperson.

A review of agent's progress will be held regularly with the
trainer and manager. If, at the end of six months, it is
determined that the agent has not followed the program
conscientiously or has not had a completed transaction, a
counseling session will be held to evaluate whether termination
of association should be considered.


_____        _____
Date                          Associate's signature


                              _____
                              Manager's signature


                              _____
                              Trainer's signature
```

are not always aware of the constrictions put on managers who manage independent contractors rather than employees.

City Farming

Although many agents assume that farming doesn't work in big cities, farmers in at least three cities are doing extraordinarily well: San Francisco, Sacramento and the District of Columbia. In Brookland, a Washington, D.C., neighborhood, farmer John Gerrety of Gerrety and Bragg has been doing an incredible job. Note the content and tone of a section of his newsletter (Figure 2.3), developed to encourage city dwellers who might otherwise hesitate to tackle a whole city. This reaction, of course, is understandable, given that the District of Columbia is made up of 66 neighborhoods where houses range in price from under $50,000 to the millions (Figure 2.4). While John Gerrety did not use the company newsletter even when he had access to one, preferring a more personal approach he did take advantage of a strong company farming program that supported every phase of the farming process, paid all the postage and provided optional mailing services. When the large company moved its branch office out of his market area, Gerrety

FIGURE 2.3   Gerrety Newsletter

Another, smaller-scale, but perhaps **CELEBRATE** just-as-fun festival will be taking place **OUR NEIGHBORHOOD!** all day Saturday Sept 19th, sponsored by Families United of Brookland. Games, baked goods, fun, arts and crafts, and good times are planned. Everyone is invited to come and enjoy the afternoon! Activities will take place on Lawrence street between 12th and 14th streets. For further info call Anna Cole 635-0929, Ivy Pope 526-0184 or David Bennet 526-4406. **SEE YOU THERE !**

Help! Help! Again! I need an assistant! You have been good to me over the past few years and I need help to keep up with all the calls and requests that you've been sending my way! I'm looking for an energetic, conscientious person to work with me for about 20 hours each week for now (maybe more, later) running errands (should have own car) answering some calls and taking care of short tasks. I would need this person for the most part during flexible business hours rather than on weekends or at night. The pay is good and no typing skill is required - just a smile on your face and a good head on your shoulders! Ideally this person would be interested in eventually obtaining a real estate license and could benefit from this experience of working at my office. If you know someone who could use the part time work, please have them call!

Congratulations and Best Wishes to Algetha Quander on her 75th Birthday! Those who know Algetha know of all the many wonderful volunteer services she has given our community over the years. On Saturday evening September 19th she will be honored with a special dinner by the Advisory Board of Christian Communities Group Homes (CCGH), one of the organizations she dearly serves. For the past seven years CCGH has been helping our community by providing caring and supportive shared-homes for needy senior citizens (many from our own neighborhood). Presently 18 seniors, living together as families, are cared for in 3 large homes at 18th and Evarts St. N.E., one of which is staffed 24 hours a day! According to Mary Ann Welter, President of the CCGH Advisory Board, Algetha has been a major force behind the success of the group homes since its inception and we congratulate her on her 75th and thank her and the CCGH for their ongoing examples of worthy community service! For more information on the honorary dinner or on the good works of the CCGH call Mrs. Welter at CCGH (832-1149) or at home (832-8138).

The Rental Scene

Are you a tenant or a landlord? Are you thinking of becoming one? I have come across a very well put together booklet which concisely explains, in plain English, many of the Do's and Don'ts, rights and responsibilities of landlords and tenants in D.C. This can be especially important when it comes to raising rents, expiring leases, the sale of the rental property, etc. The booklet, "Guide to Rental Housing in the District of Columbia" is unfortunately no longer in print, but I have xerox copies to share with you if you're interested. Just call or fill out and send in the enclosed Business Reply Card today!

In a recent previous newsletter we noted that a good number of shops along the West side of 12th street from the corner of Monroe through Stanley's Five and Dime was sold earlier this year. According to the Brookland Tour Committee, the Newton Theater has also been sold. The Purchaser of these properties is reportedly a Texas firm by the name of Jenko, but has a manager or developer-partner in nearby Bethesda called the Relm Corporation. Tentative

- MORE -

FIGURE 2.3   (Continued)

plans are said to include a new Peoples in the theater, with the current Peoples being converted to a hospital supply store. A chain department store may take the place of Stanley's or, if plans and negotiations develop between the Relm Corporation and the Brookland Community Cooperative Association (BCCA) we may see a long needed full-line grocery/food cooperative in our "downtown" Brookland. Wouldn't that be nice!

By the way, membership in the BCCA and the Brookland Tour Committee is always open to all, as well as in the Brookland Neighborhood Civic Association and ANC (Advisory Neighborhood Commission). These (among others) are great organizations to get involved with to keep up with what's going on in our community as well as to meet new and friendly faces. Why not join today! Call for information and further details anytime!

Recent Sales ...

Listed below are some homes in the area which have recently come under contract or which have settled. Settled prices are actual prices; Under Contract prices are "asking" or List Prices and may differ from the actual prices, but this is not known until the property goes to settlement.   Block addresses are shown but feel free to call to inquire of the specifics of any of these transactions:

SETTLED			UNDER CONTRACT		
Address By Block #	Bedrms/Baths	Price	Address By Block #	Bedrms/Baths	Asking
3800 Block 13th St.	3BR/1½BA	$108,000	1400 Block Newton St.	4BR/3BA	$129,000
1200 Block Perry St.	4BR/2½BA	175,000	1200 Block Jackson St.	3BR/1BA	79,900
3900 Block 13th St.	2BR/1BA	105,000	1800 Block Monroe St.	4BR/1BA	93,000
1200 Block Kearney St.	3BR/1BA	100,000	1500 Block Otis St.	3BR/1BA	119,950
1600 Block Otis St.	3BR/1BA	99,500	800 Block Taylor St.	3BR/2BA	87,000
1700 Block Allison St.	3BR/1BA	135,999	1300 Block Franklin St.	3BR/2BA	95,000
4100 Block 13th Pl.	3BR/1BA	110,000	3000 Block 17th St.	3BR/2BA	62,950
1400 Block Hamlin St.	6BR/4BA	83,500	1000 Block Taussig Pl.	3BR/2BA	128,500
4000 Block 13th St.	4BR/2BA	115,900			
1200 Block Irving St.	4BR/2BA	109,000			
3000 Block 7th (Condo)	1BR/1BA	48,000			
3000 Block 14th St.	4-Unit Apt Hs	95,000			

If anyone is interested, there is a cozy starter home at 1827 Jackson St. N.E. 3BR/1BA on the market for only $77,900 with large yard. Also available are 1019 Quincy Court - a 2BR/2½BA super modern luxury Townhome ($109,900) and 1031 Michigan Ave - a 1BR modern apartment style condominium in a beautifully maintained building (The Perrington) Unit #301, asking only $58,950! Please call if interested in any of these and pass the word! And for your information, two other fine homes are on the market in the 1300 Block of Jackson St. and the 1200 Block of Franklin St. - asking $92,500 and 79,900 respectively.

See You Soon!

Support Your Local Brookland Businesses...

AND COMMUNITY ASSOCIATIONS!

FIGURE 2.3   Gerrety Newsletter (Continued)

Brookland Centennial Festival Committee

Slowe School Demountable
14th and Irving Streets, NE
Washington, D.C. 20017
(202) 635-6565

Preliminary

Brookland Centennial Festival

September 25, 26 and 27, 1987

Preliminary Schedule of Events

Friday, September 25th: CONTACT PERSON *

Brookland Exhibit Opening - Brooks Mansion (7:00 p.m.)

"Early Brookland" Panel Discussion - Brooks Mansion (7:30 p.m.) ···· JOHN FEELEY

★ Centennial Ball - St. Anthony's Parish Hall (9:00 p.m.) .... PAUL WASHINGTON

Saturday, September 26th:

Centennial Mile Race - 12th Street (10:00 a.m.) .... BRIAN FLOWERS

Parade along 12th Street (11:00 a.m.) .... BOB ARTISST

Walking and Van-Driven Tours of Brookland (All day)

Brookland Exhibit - Brooks Mansion (All day) ···· JOHN FEELEY

Brookland Centennial Proclamation
Greetings from Dignitaries - 12th Street (12:00 - 1:00 p.m.)

Band and Stage Shows - 12th Street (1:00 p.m. - 7:00 p.m.) .... JULIA PARKS

Gospel Choirs - 12th Street (TBA) .... IDA JACKSON

Brookland Archeological Project Exhibit & Presentation .... JOHN FEELEY
Brooks Mansion (TBA)

Sunday, September 27th:

Walking and Van-Driven Tours of Brookland (All day)

Brookland Exhibit - Brooks Mansion (All day) ···· JOHN FEELEY

Be Sure to Get your Reservation in Now! — * Call 635-6565 and leave message if
Contact Person is not in.

Sponsoring Organizations
Advisory Neighborhood Commission, 5A • Brookland Civic Association • Brookland Tour Committee
Brookland Community Cooperative Association • Families United of Brookland

FIGURE 2.4   District of Columbia City Neighborhood Map

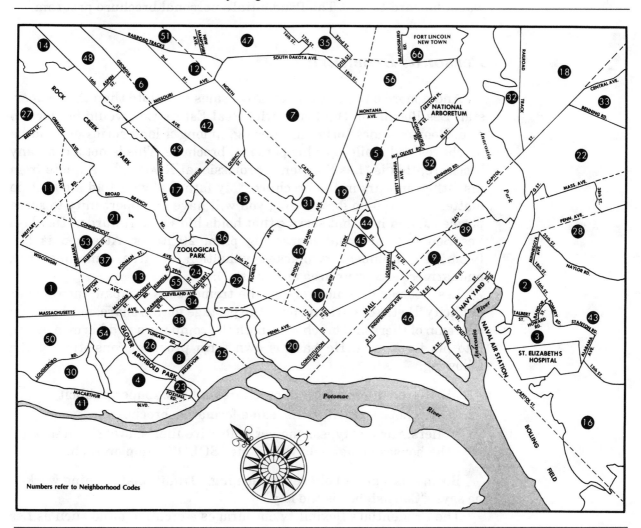

Source: Reprinted with permission of Rufus S. Lusk Co.

was so well entrenched that he was able to open his own company, hardly skipping a beat.

Cooperative Company Farming Programs

Most national franchises provide a variety of promotional material for their agents to use in prospecting. Many have approved suppliers for magnet cards, sports schedules, plastic bags and pens, all with the franchise logo. Some, like Century 21, have catalogs containing every imaginable promotional item. Others, like The Prudential, leave much more up to the ingenuity of the individual sales associate, although it would be hard to beat The Prudential's personal brochure program.

Personal Brochure

And a more energetic and creative sales associate than their superstar, Les Boomer of the Prudential Real Estate Co., would be hard to find. Boomer's most original offering, among a long series of creative brochures and mailers, is his personal brochure. This is not a company brochure; this is "Les Boomer, a professional REALTOR®." A quote from his father appears in the brochure: "My father always told me that no matter what you do for a living, you will have an opportunity to serve people . . . and it is that service that holds life's true rewards." Inside is Les Boomer's personal marketing plan: 20 items. Attached is Les Boomer's complimentary market evaluation (not free, complimentary, and farmers are "your area specialists").

Les Boomer does not rely on the tremendous company newspaper publicity. He takes part and pays the postage for his share, but he keeps a stream of fliers and brochures, both the company's and his own, going into his farm area. He has his own farm program consisting of the following:

1. Self-promotion: personal brochure and newspaper publicity
2. Open houses: invitations, same format as brochure
3. Fliers: various types; one very effective flier shows pictures of all the houses he has sold with a big "SOLD" stamp on each.

Boomer is a great believer in farming. "Traditional farming works," he says. "Consistency is the key."

The Prudential's flexibility encourages a creative mind such as Les Boomer's. The company works with its agents to farm the company service area and gives the individual agent a lot of freedom to use personal creativity. Several of the sales associates in the same office with Les Boomer send their own newsletters instead of using the one provided by the company, which demonstrates a good example of a loose, cooperative program (Figure 2.5).

Prototype Branch-Office Farming Program

A more structured branch-office farming program that might be adapted to your local situation is outlined in the following story of the development of an actual program.

This particular office is located in a waterfront community, which is also the state capital and a tourist center. It contains a large historic

FIGURE 2.5 Personal Brochure

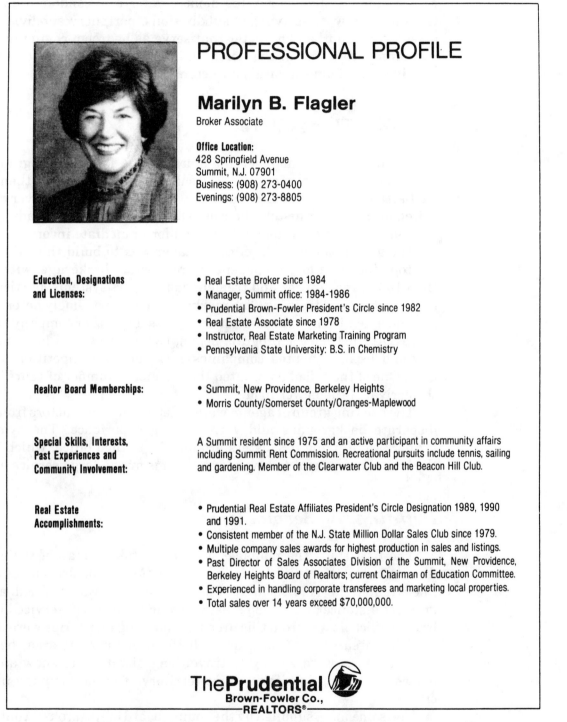

PROFESSIONAL PROFILE

Marilyn B. Flagler
Broker Associate

Office Location:
428 Springfield Avenue
Summit, N.J. 07901
Business: (908) 273-0400
Evenings: (908) 273-8805

Education, Designations and Licenses:
- Real Estate Broker since 1984
- Manager, Summit office: 1984-1986
- Prudential Brown-Fowler President's Circle since 1982
- Real Estate Associate since 1978
- Instructor, Real Estate Marketing Training Program
- Pennsylvania State University: B.S. in Chemistry

Realtor Board Memberships:
- Summit, New Providence, Berkeley Heights
- Morris County/Somerset County/Oranges-Maplewood

Special Skills, Interests, Past Experiences and Community Involvement:
A Summit resident since 1975 and an active participant in community affairs including Summit Rent Commission. Recreational pursuits include tennis, sailing and gardening. Member of the Clearwater Club and the Beacon Hill Club.

Real Estate Accomplishments:
- Prudential Real Estate Affiliates President's Circle Designation 1989, 1990 and 1991.
- Consistent member of the N.J. State Million Dollar Sales Club since 1979.
- Multiple company sales awards for highest production in sales and listings.
- Past Director of Sales Associates Division of the Summit, New Providence, Berkeley Heights Board of Realtors; current Chairman of Education Committee.
- Experienced in handling corporate transferees and marketing local properties.
- Total sales over 14 years exceed $70,000,000.

The Prudential
Brown-Fowler Co.,
REALTORS®

■ Summit: (908) 273-0400, FAX (908) 273-7464   ■ New Providence: (908) 464-5200; FAX (908) 464-1133
■ Basking Ridge: (908) 766-5666; FAX (908) 766-1975   ■ Corporate Relocation: (908) 464-5200; FAX (908) 464-1133
An Independently Owned and Operated Member of The Prudential Real Estate Affiliates, Inc. and ©1992 The Prudential Real Estate Affiliates, Inc.

Source: Reprinted with permission of Marilyn B. Flagler.

section and is surrounded by small waterfront communities on the myriad coves and creeks. Much recent development of diverse kinds has occurred: resort and year-round homes, waterfront condominiums and town houses, water-privileged subdivisions, periphery subdivisions of essentially suburban character that serve as bedroom communities to two large cities, one in the north and one in the south, and outlying subdivisions of almost rural character.

The Way Things Were

When the sales manager inaugurated the farming program, the office had a large cast of experienced sales associates, some of them with well-established specialties, such as waterfront properties, very high-priced properties or historic houses. The office also had a steady trickle of agents entering the field with a need for immediate income.

The goal of the branch-office manager was to build this office into the top office in a large independent real estate brokerage, with more than 100 branch offices and tremendous support systems, particularly in marketing and training. The market area was extremely heterogeneous and extended into the market areas of several other company branch offices. At the time the program began, two or three very large nationally and locally oriented companies also were in competition for the area. One of these had dominated the area for a number of years before the arrival of the newer firm.

The existing group of agents were independent contractors from very disparate backgrounds and with varying experience. The available farmers were living in clusters around the branch office, which is not the best arrangement to cover target farms over a large service area.

Defining the Service Area

The first thing the manager did was to take a map of the county distributed by the Multiple Listing Service (MLS) and draw a heavy red line around the service area. The *service* area was defined as the greatest distance over which a listing could be properly serviced by the branch office. It was from this area that farming territories were drawn up. This area did not coincide with the office *market* area, because certain agents were willing to travel long distances to show and sell homes, extending into the service territory of other company branch offices.

The same map, supplied by the county board of REALTORS®, contained a list of the subdivisions or neighborhoods with their map coordinates. Within the designated service area, 400 housing subdivisions could be identified.

Analyzing the Sales Staff

The manager then took a list of sales associates affiliated with the branch office at that time and marked each name and address with the appropriate map coordinates. She had about 100 agents, of whom 60 were contributing 75 percent of the business.

In determining the service area, the manager took into consideration whether she already had sales agents in the communities around the outer rim and if she did have an agent living or working in an area at some distance from the office, she debated whether it would be feasible to service a listing from the branch.

The War Room

In a small room, which she was using for training, she hung a large bulletin board with a huge map of the service area. She called this the "war room." On the map she placed pins representing each of the agents on the office roster in the subdivision in which they lived.

It became immediately apparent that huge gaps existed in the service area, where there were no sales associates near enough to farm the area. On the other hand, some communities had two or three company representatives living in them. Unaware of the uneven distribution of her agents and because she had such a large complement of sales associates on board, she had not been actively recruiting new agents.

The manager saw at once that targeted recruiting would be necessary if she were to capture the target farms and cover the service area.

This fact became immediately obvious to the agents as well and she could hear an undercurrent of rumbling in the room.

Work Where You Live

At this point a "Work Where You Live" recruiting campaign was proposed, using target cards to the blank areas. Resistance to any plan that entails adding new agents often stems from the experienced agents' fear of competition. The first thing a manager must make clear is that the more good listers an office has, the more opportunity there is to sell in-house. Most firms award a bonus for the sale of office listings. If a good lister is affiliated with a competitive broker, the net result for the sales associates would be a reduced commission on all that salesperson's offerings. It would be preferable to have the good lister on one's own team.

Market Share

The second step is for the manager or broker to overcome the feeling among agents that there is only a fixed amount of business, that taking on more agents will result in less income for those already on board. Everyone must understand that what the company desires is increased market share—so greatly increased that present sales associates would not be handicapped, but rather would be enhanced.

A good way to express this concept visually is with a pie chart showing the present market share as a pie divided into pieces representing the present split among agents. Then, superimposed over the small pie, show a larger pie, reflecting market-share goals, with the pie now split among the projected number of sales associates. This way, they can see at a glance that under the new farming program everyone's share will be proportionately larger (Figure 2.6).

Even though most accept the concept, it needs continual reinforcement to prevent the negative thinkers from influencing the neutral thinker and to constantly provide the positive thinkers with ammunition to carry the project along with their teammates. Good management is often a case of getting everyone on the team. There are always, however, a few highly independent and often highly productive people who march to that different drummer. They respond best to leniency, being allowed to "do their own thing." Luckily, most of them do not care what the rest do so long as they receive appreciation and recognition.

Once it was established that in order to increase market share it was necessary to recruit in the areas where there was no one who could or was willing to farm, the manager decided that Val-Pak, a national co-op direct mail advertising system that spotlights selected areas, would be a good medium for getting the company name into the target areas and for recruiting new agents in those areas at the same time. (Later on, when intense farming spread company-wide, the marketing department hired a firm to do all direct mail, including farming.)

Selective Recruiting

The branch manager knew that it would take some time to recruit and train new agents and to get them into the field. In the interim, her plan was to distribute literature, such as the company farm newsletter, "Houses Wanted" and "Work Where You Live" recruiting brochures in the barren areas. The response from these mailings then could be shared among the agents close enough to service them. Agents were given a generous recruiting bonus for each new salesperson they referred to the company. This practice encouraged the existing salespeople to follow up recruiting leads.

FIGURE 2.6   Pie Chart

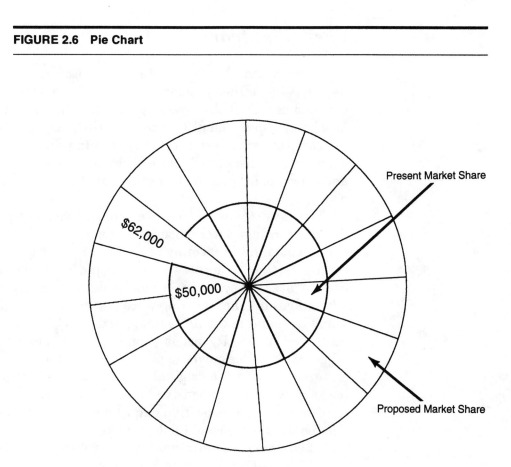

Ground Rules

Ground rules were established, first by discussion, then by vote. Because the agents were common-law independent contractors, there were no hard-and-fast company rules on how or where an agent could work. The firm company policy was that no sales associate could own a territory; that is, he or she could not keep other agents from farming it. Nor could the company prevent a sales associate from farming the area of his or her own choice or insist that every sales associate farm a territory. The only thing the company could do was extract a commitment to farm from new recruits and encourage the veterans to try farming.

It became obvious to everyone in the group that they would all be more successful farmers if a cooperative effort were made to distribute the territories "logically" among the salespeople.

The Farm Team

A "farm team" was selected to referee the word *logically,* which usually was defined as meaning located as close as possible to agents' own homes unless they were specializing in certain categories, such as new homes, investment homes, historic homes and so on. If someone in the company was now effectively farming an area, a new farmer obviously would have a much more difficult time becoming established there and consequently might be better advised to choose another neighborhood.

The farm team met once a month (wearing red bandannas) and farming strategies were discussed. Agents were encouraged to fill in the empty spots in the farming area. There was a great deal of latitude in farm selection. Where two salespeople were particularly keen on a certain area, they were encouraged to farm as a team. The many advantages of team farming were discussed at length. There also were many husband and wife teams, particularly in condominium developments or inner city areas. Some salespeople were looking for two adjacent areas for move-up purposes—starter homes plus a more affluent area to move the original buyers into as their families and pocketbooks grew. Large expensive homes and luxury condominiums made a natural duo for prospective empty nesters and retirees. Several small subdivisions were combined to make a farm of sufficient size pay off, with 200 homes the minimum size because the company paid farmers postage costs on third-class bulk-rate mailings. (Two hundred pieces is the minimum bundle for third-class bulk rates.) A maximum beginning farm of 500 homes was suggested.

Certain areas were eliminated for various reasons: another branch office had the area well covered, the houses were situated too far apart to make farming profitable and so on. Certain areas outside the determined range (15 miles) were included because no other office was covering them and an experienced sales associate resided there. Any agents who wished would be assigned these areas as "passive" farms where literature was the main contact. In areas near the office, some sales associates already were farming. Green pins on the war room map denoted active farmers.

Different Strokes for Different Folks

The manager then sat down with her list of agents and analyzed each one. Some were "old dogs," to whom it would be hard to teach new tricks. Many now were working very effectively in accordance with their main interests: some specialized in new homes; some in condominiums; some in their own spheres of influence, such as among the local political figures and state legislators; some in educational circles, both state and county; some in concert with other company branch agents in ocean-resort areas; and several in commercial or industrial real estate. The manager decided that she would leave certain salespeople in place.

Research

Research was conducted on the subdivisions, starting with the largest and most important. It was possible to pull out of the computer, for each subdivision, the addresses of houses sold within the past year, as well as those now on the market. These printouts provided information, such as the price and style of the houses, whether they were waterfront, water-view or water-privilege and so on. It was more difficult to establish the exact number of homes in each subdivision. Further research would be needed. The company owned a set of tax books, tax maps and a microfiche system of locating houses in each tax area. Computer printouts of a minimum of four subdivisions could be purchased from the tax assessor's office. This is an efficient but costly method. There are companies that make computer programs for this purpose such as Cole Publications and Information Service's EasyList, which lists owners by ZIP code. Real estate offices could purchase an office program and parcel the names out to the agents for their farms. Otherwise, agents can find the names in cross directories produced by Rufus S. Lusk and Son Company; Real Estate Data, Inc. (REDI); and Cole.

Brainstorming

Brainstorming with the farm team resulted in a decision to work in six concentric circles outward from the branch office. Subdivision maps were obtained for each subdivision in the targeted circle. Tax maps, zoning maps and maps from private industry were found. The concentric-circle idea worked well, because, naturally, a larger concentration of salespeople already were living in areas closer to the office.

The team tentatively designated the salespeople as farmers in subdivisions in which they were living, using yellow pins. A few were spotted in outlying territories. At this point it was clear that some reinforcement of the system would be necessary to gain the needed cooperation. Some agents, of course, fight any change and the manager already had decided to leave them alone. The office as a whole was doing very well and there was no reason to disturb people who already were succeeding. The problem was to convince the average and the newer sales associates that the new system would work as well for them as the existing system had for the old pros.

The branch manager began to work on a presentation to the whole office on the advantages of a coordinated branch-office farming plan. To this end, she developed the outline in Figure 2.7. The branch office cited

---

FIGURE 2.7   Objectives of Branch-Office Farming Plan

OBJECTIVES OF
CENTRALIZED FARMING PROGRAM

I. Advantages to the firm:

  A. To provide a continuous impact of new listings with an equally consistent opportunity for sales turnover;

  B. To ensure regular, systematic contact with the service area in order to accomplish this objective;

  C. To provide a vehicle for bringing the company and the individual agent closer to the community; and

  D. To develop the company image as a progressive, competent and professional enterprise.

II. Advantages to the sales associate:

  A. To provide a permanent framework for finding buyers and sellers;

  B. To develop an efficient listing/selling cycle with the least expense and effort;

  C. To promote the local "farmer" by establishing a system that regularly disseminates information designed to secure the confidence of clients and friends and establish the name, reputation and expertise of the salesperson;

  D. To allow agents to target specific populations by income bracket, interest area, educational background, community groups, etc.;

  E. To provide an opportunity to take advantage of the ratios of real estate arithmetic;

  F. To provide an outlet for individual innovation, initiative, imagination and creativity in promoting the services offered as individuals, branch office and company; and

  G. To capitalize on the fallout from a program that coordinates and synchronizes the efforts of the entire real estate team to the benefit of all the individuals on the team.

in this example overtook the number-one office in a new area against very stiff competition.

There is hardly anything a small broker or branch manager can do to achieve maximum production as effectively as to implement a well-conceived and well-executed farming plan. This involves the four basic managerial skills needed by a real estate broker or manager: recruiting; training and retaining sales associates; and product marketing. For other tips for successful planning, see Figure 2.8. The plan acts as an engine to keep all the parts running in harmony.

FIGURE 2.8   Farming Plan Tips

PLAN YOUR WORK (and Work Your Plan)

Good advice . . . but often ignored.

Without a farming plan, you are at sea and might as well take up fishing!

- Give first *priority* to planning because it is possible to ruin yourself in your farm area if you get off on the wrong foot.

- Pick a *place* to plan. Somehow the planning juices run faster when you have a definite area to work on your plans.

- Have a *regular* planning time. If you are an early bird and like to plan at dawn before the family is up or a night owl wide awake after everyone else is snoring away, establish an hour on a regular basis: daily, weekly, whatever.

- Plans should reflect *goals,* so the goals must come first. Keep these goals firmly in mind when you are planning. Goals can be in terms of total income, dollar-volume sales, a certain number of listings or sales or contacts.

KISS (Keep It Simple, Sugar).

Plans should be clear and easy to follow.

- Don't plow more than you can cultivate. Be *realistic* about how much time and energy you have.

- Be *flexible.* If you find as you go that your plans are not working out—you hoped to telephone 40 people a day, but 20 is all you can manage—readjust your plans to fit the realities.

- After the plan fits you and you are happy with it, then *stick* with it.

- At regular intervals reevaluate your plan to suit changing circumstances. Make sure your original plan is still the best one you can devise.

- If you are not achieving the results you hoped for, sit down and write a major revision. Do not drift on without any plan. Just make sure it works.

3

On Your Own: Plan Your Work and Work Your Plan

Plan Your Work

Planning is making choices. After you have read this book, you will have enough information about the various alternatives to be able to make choices to suit yourself. Do not let the abundance of ideas confuse you. Just pick out the method of operation that suits your personality and talent. Study the various planning tools in this chapter before you make any decisions. Happy farming is like a good cocktail: It requires the right mix of ingredients. If you do not like alcohol, then mix a Virtuous Mary instead of a Bloody Mary. The basic ingredients of farming are mail, telephoning and personal visits. How you integrate them into the whole farm program has a lot to do with your harvest.

Your first chore is to organize your farm records so that you can keep track of what is going on. This is a chore that is so off-putting to certain real estate veterans that they refuse to get into farming at all. In general, good salespeople rarely are patient with paperwork. People who are, rarely make top salespeople. So it is important for you to make recordkeeping as streamlined as possible.

The job of organizing a farm is time-consuming, but once it is done, it is done. It can be kept up with a little routine housekeeping once a week to bring records up-to-date.

Let us imagine that you have decided to go into farming in a big way. (There is no other way. Going into farming in a small way is like being a little bit pregnant—nine months of labor and nothing to show for it.)

What should you do?

Step 1: Select the type of farm.

Geographic

Do you intend to focus on single-family residences, condominium projects, exceptional homes (costing more than a million dollars), historic homes, waterfront properties, horse farms, investment properties, commercial properties?

Spheres of influence

Will your clients be doctors, attorneys, educators, sports figures, entertainers, entrepreneurs and various other target groups; past clients and customers; or influential people in the farm community?

Sphere-of-Influence Farming

This is the type of farming Dan Richard of the Gooder Company calls "hydroponic farming," named after the practice of growing vegetables without soil. This is an especially appropriate expression when farming for buyers in large high-rise buildings or apartment complexes. The *Apartment Shoppers Guides* are a good source of apartment buildings to canvass. Renters also are moving in and out of condominiums, especially those originally built for investors to rent out.

If you choose a sphere-of-influence farm or a target farm, your main concern is going to be the collection of telephone numbers and addresses. Keeping in touch with former clients, friends and other acquaintances means making a minimum of four contacts a year.

Vary the approach. The initial approach probably should be by telephone, just chatting about your mutual interest. With garden-club members, you might mention a new type of gladiolus called *Impressive,* which is hardy as far north as Canada and may be left in the ground year after year to form a small grove of beautiful light pink glads touched with deep rose. By the way, did you hear the news about some local real estate event?

Send holiday cards, particularly at Thanksgiving. Produce them on your computer if you can. Another appropriate greeting card is an anniversary card sent on the date a customer bought a house from you.

Once a year send a calendar, particularly an activity calendar or birth-day calendar highlighting birthdates of the homeowner's family members (Figure 3.1), complete with your name and telephone number, of course, and your credits such as Certified Residential Specialist if you hold the designation. If you don't, you can use a slogan like, "your real estate specialist." Send postcards from vacation, mentioning family members or the dog or personal events to let homeowners know they are not just dollar signs in your head.

Farming by target group is easy with a computer prospect management system. You can sort in your farm by group: senior citizens, civic association members, garden club members or whomever, and send special interest bulletins or targeted mailings to narrow categories of people, which will give you much greater response than broad generalized mailings. Not only is this kind of prospecting more fun, but the quality of the mailings in terms of their real interest and use to the recipient is far superior than are nontargeted pieces.

The same approach works with any group. Recently, a broker told me about one of his agents who was the REALTOR® of choice for all the local chiropractors!

If you think your former customers might be outgrowing the home you sold them, start sending them open-house invitations. Or send a newsletter or useful information on how to fight their tax assessment. If you are terribly busy, another alternative is to join one of the follow-up companies to do this for you—not as effective as personal follow-up, but far better than no follow-through at all.

Geographic Farming

Step 2. Determine the size and location of your farm.

Unless you plan to conduct a passive farm effort (direct mail with no personal follow-up), you should start with 200 to 500 homes—no more, except when you already are a farming pro. You can enlarge your farm later. Multiply the turnover rate by the average commission on homes in various areas to arrive at potential income from each. Unless there is a good reason not to, choose the area you live in. Your reception will be warmer.

FIGURE 3.1   Birthday Calendar

Step 3. Collect the information you need to set up your farm records.

- Obtain a detailed map of the area.

- Get subdivision plats of the area, reduced to as many 8½"× 11"pages as necessary.
- If your farm area is not in a subdivision, get county parcel plats from the courthouse.
- Obtain the names of all the homeowners in your farm from county or city courthouses or from the tax assessor's office. You can compile a list by hand from the assessment rolls or you can buy field book pages for about $1 each or in some areas you can buy computer printouts of subdivisions (1,000 or more names) for less than $100. These printouts are worth their weight in gold because of all the useful information they contain: legal descriptions, all owners' names and addresses (including absentee owners and lot owners), tax assessments, improvements and lot sizes. Some private companies, such as Lusk and REDI, have tax assessment records on microfiche, which you can photocopy from the microfiche machine. This service provides transparencies broken down into street sequence, owner's-name sequence, subdivision-name sequence and property-map sequence, so that you can look them up by whichever sequence you happen to know: agricultural/commercial/industrial properties by owner's name, the latter by land-use code or subdivision or by property map, or absentee owners by name or by subdivision.

These transparencies show the tax account number, so you can check taxes with the treasurer's office, the owner's name and the mailing address, including the home address of owners not occupying the property. Also included are the premise address; map number-grid-parcel; liber/folio; plat/bk/page; and section/blk/lot where used. All these make it possible to locate the property on county or city tax or zoning records or county courthouse property records. (Sometimes the price and date of the last sale is listed—a very valuable piece of information for farmers.) The assessor's estimate of the fair-market value of the improvements, if any, and the assessed value are all given, along with the year of assessment. Find out where all this information is kept in your area. A sample of a Lusk microfiche transparency is shown in Figure 3.2. If it is not available through the sources listed above and your own company does not provide it in your office, does the local board of REALTORS® have it, or does the public library? This kind of information is useful not only for listing and selling property, but it is vital to you because it demonstrates a high degree of professionalism on your part to be able to come up with the answers quickly when people ask you questions. The main ingredients of professionalism are knowledge and competence. It is not necessary to be excessively slick and businesslike to be professional. You can be as folksy as the territory demands, but you also must be knowledgeable.

FIGURE 3.2   Microfiche Copy

Sample of Lusk's Charles County Microfiche

6540 ACADEMY DR   1. STREET SEQUENCE

COUNTY DISTRICT# ACCOUNT# MAP# GRID# PARCEL# SUBDIVISION	OWNER'S NAME AND MAILING ADDRESS FORMER OWNER TAX EXEMPT CATEGORY	PREMISE ADDRESS (DIR) OWNER OCCUPIED LAND USE LAND AREA LEGAL DESCRIPTION (SEC/BLK/LOT)	YEAR BUILT HOUSE TYPE BLDG MATERIAL QUAL CONSTRUCTION # STORIES/BSMT SQ FT 1ST FLOOR	LAST SALE SALE PRICE LIBER/FOLIO HOW CONVEYED MORTGAGE PRIOR SALE SALE PRICE LIBER/FOLIO HOW CONVEYED	LAND FCV IMPR FCV TOTAL FCV ASS'D VALUE LAST RE-ASS'D
COUNTY#: 05 DISTR.#: 3 ACCT#:111253 MAP#: 10 GRID#: 21 PRCL#: 234 ACADEMY HILL	WHEATLEY, ROBERT L & MARIE P 6540 ACADEMY DR OWINGS, MD 20736 KAINE INC	6540 ACADEMY DR OWINGS 20736 OWNER OCCUPIED (R)RESIDENTIAL LAND AREA: 2.418 ACRES IMPS LT 5 SEC 2 6540 ACADEMY DR ACADEMY HILL (2/ / 5)	1986 STANDARD UNIT WOOD OR STUCCO GRADE 4 1 1/2 STY W/BSMT 1ST: 1,280 SQFT	11/25/86 $140,000 386/ 832 PRIVATE SALE $140,000 335/ 134	$36,965 $117,325 $154,290 $62,650 1986
COUNTY#: 05 DISTR.#: 3 ACCT#:111334 MAP#: 10 GRID#: 21 PRCL#: 234 ACADEMY HILL	RYAN, PATRICIA A & MICHAEL E 6541 ACADEMY DR OWINGS, MD 20736 KAINE INC	6541 ACADEMY DR OWINGS 20736 OWNER OCCUPIED (R)RESIDENTIAL LAND AREA: 1.001 ACRES IMPS LT 11 SEC 2 6541 ACADEMY DR ACADEMY HILL (2/ / 11)	1986 STANDARD UNIT WOOD OR STUCCO GRADE 4 2 STORIES W/BSMT 1ST: 992 SQFT	10/21/86 $145,000 382/ 606 PRIVATE SALE $135,000 335/ 134	$27,000 $97,135 $124,135 $50,490 1986
COUNTY#: 05 DISTR.#: 3 ACCT#:111261 MAP#: 10 GRID#: 21 PRCL#: 234 ACADEMY HILL	KAINE, ROBERT BROOKE & KAREN MARIE 6550 ACADEMY DR OWINGS, MD 20736 KAINE INC	6550 ACADEMY DR OWINGS 20736 OWNER OCCUPIED (R)RESIDENTIAL LAND AREA: 5.758 ACRES IMPS LT 6 SEC 2 6550 ACADEMY DR ACADEMY HILL (2/ / 6)	1986 STANDARD UNIT WOOD OR STUCCO GRADE 5 2 1/2 STY W/BSMT 1ST: 1,576 SQFT	6/13/86 $155,250 369/ 36 PRIVATE SALE 335/ 134	$44,515 $204,100 $248,615 $100,780 1986
COUNTY#: 05 DISTR.#: 3 ACCT#:111326 MAP#: 10 GRID#: 21 PRCL#: 234 ACADEMY HILL	BOUTAUGH, WINSTON G & NANCY J 6551 ACADEMY DR OWINGS, MD 20736 KAINE INC	6551 ACADEMY DR OWINGS 20736 OWNER OCCUPIED (R)RESIDENTIAL LAND AREA: 2.000 ACRES IMPS LT 10 SEC 2 6551 ACADEMY DR ACADEMY HILL (2/ / 10)	1986 STANDARD UNIT WOOD OR STUCCO GRADE 4 2 STORIES W/BSMT 1ST: 1,437 SQFT	10/28/86 $135,000 383/ 460 PRIVATE SALE $100,000 335/ 134	$30,500 $115,670 $146,170 $60,270 1986
COUNTY#: 05 DISTR.#: 3 ACCT#:111288 MAP#: 10 GRID#: 21 PRCL#: 234 ACADEMY HILL	KAINE INC PO BOX 419 HUNTINGTOWN, MD 20639	6560 ACADEMY DR (R)RESIDENTIAL LAND AREA: 2.823 ACRES LT 7 SEC 2 6560 ACADEMY DR ACADEMY HILL (2/ / 7)		335/ 134	$31,380 UNIMPR $31,380 $12,820 1986

Source: Reprinted with permission of Rufus S. Lusk Co.

Additional Information

- In addition to the microfiche, Lusk also offers computer and manual systems for researching past sales, including financing, tax and other valuable information.
- You can determine the age of the house by asking the tax assessor for the amount of the first tax payment and the date.
- Addresses and telephone numbers can be found in reverse telephone directories put out by the local telephone company and by some private cross directories such as those produced by Stewart, Haines and Cole. For a sample listing from the Haines directory, see Figure 3.3.
- Local boards of REALTORS® and title companies also keep up-to-date real estate records. Homeowners' associations are other sources. In your local library you may find an assortment of books that are useful, such as the *City Directory, Cole's Directory* and others. Ask your librarian to help you. I have found them willing to dig deeply.

FIGURE 3.3 Haines Directory

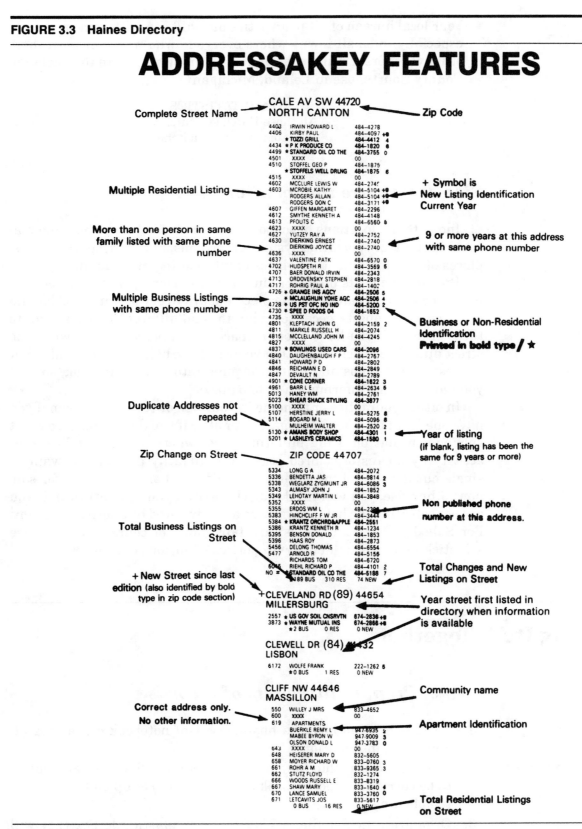

ADDRESSAKEY FEATURES

■ Your local bureau of vital statistics may aid you with some research, especially in small towns where everyone who was ever born there still lives there. I still am fascinated by the sign I saw in the Leelanau County Courthouse in Leland, Michigan:

VITAL STATISTICS
All those Hatched, Matched,
Unlatched and Dispatched

Step 4. Prepare the location map.

Indicate the locations of schools, recreation facilities, shopping plazas or malls, transportation systems, museums, libraries, sports arenas, places of worship and other places of interest in your community.

Prepare the parts of your reduced subdivisions plat or the sections if it is too large to handle in one piece. I mark every unimproved lot and every leased property because I plan to send different types of mail to these groups. If you have enough space and time, you could write the street number on each lot, so that you will have both the legal and street address. These maps and plats are going into your farm book, so that you have all your information in one place.

In either your office or at home in your den or recreation room if you have one (or in the basement, garage or attic if you don't), mount a giant subdivision plat on a big bulletin board, where you can indicate all activity by means of colored stick pins. Identify groups you want to single out for special promotions and also all homes that are for sale now; otherwise, you will need a disclaimer on your literature that you are not soliciting the listings of those already listed by another company. For Sale By Owners (FSBOs) are fair game, of course. You can use self-sticking labels to identify properties of various categories.

Putting It All Together

Step 5. Prepare three sets of records.

1. Prepare a "farm book," a huge loose-leaf notebook containing all your farm information.
2. Buy a 7″× 5″portable file folder, an accordion folder small enough to be carried in a pocketbook or briefcase or set up on the desk for telephoning.
3. Organize a tickler file, a 7″× 5″wood or plastic file box that will remind you of what you need to do each day (Figure 3.4). Many computer software packages allow you to do the same thing.

FIGURE 3.4   Tickler File

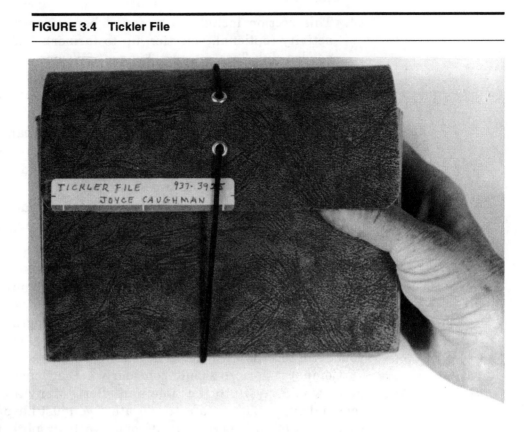

You will be happy to hear that I have devised a form that can be used in all three files. You make it just once and run two copies. The copies fold up into sections and fit into the two small files. That way, wherever you are, you have your records.

The Farm Book

This book should be divided into seven basic sections:

1. Include maps and plats in the first section.
2. Your farm roster goes here. If you are going to farm actively, you must obtain the name and address of every owner in your area. Include a page for each homeowner by street number and name. They can be filed by street or alphabetically, or both, whichever suits your plans best.
3. Add homeowners' names by subject group and street (selection of group depends on your plans): owner-occupants, renters, absentee lot owners, absentee single-family owners, commercial owners and recreational property owners in waterfront, view, lakefront, golf, tennis, retirement communities.

4. This section includes a roster of homeowners by neighborhood activity (optional, selection up to farmer): PTA, senior citizens, garden club, Toastmasters, League of Women Voters, women's club, Lions, Moose, Elks, Masons, Rotary, Kiwanis, political clubs, chamber of commerce; junior chamber, ACLU and card and game groups (bingo, bridge, canasta, Scrabble® and chess).

5. Include your monthly farm letters here: first year, 12 monthly farm letters; second year, 12 suggested options for newsletters.

6. Keep your annual farm goal, monthly goals and monthly inventory of farming activities in this section.

7. Keep your calendar of monthly mailings, calendar of monthly telephoning, calendar of monthly home visiting and blank daily planning lists here.

If all this seems like a lot of work, it is. To make it work, you need to keep your eye on your plan; for other tips, see Figure 3.5. Some of the work is avoidable. Computer buffs can save tons of work by keeping all their records on computer. A Coles information program called EasyList that you can import into your computer program allows you to enter all your farm records with one keystroke.

Computer novices should consider whether learning to use a computer would be worth the time and effort. Many are what they call "menu-driven." This means to operate it you just have to make choices from a list of options (menu). It comes with simplified instructions, a glossary, a tutorial and an on-line manual. It should not set you back two or three months while you are learning. With the new computer prices it should not set you back an arm and a leg to buy either.

If you cannot afford the time or money for a computer, you could start out with manual records and learn as you go, converting to computer records when you have mastered the language and stockpiled the cost.

While successful salespeople are rarely technically minded and may back off from coming into the technological era, let me remind you again that farming is *befriending*. The point of all this is to develop a loyal following of satisfied and grateful neighbors and friends who, incidentally, will make you exactly as much money as you deserve.

Work Your Plan

The first part of your planning involved putting together the records. To help you with this is a calendar of actions for you to take each day. At the end of 30 days you should be well on your way to having your farm systems in place.

The second part of your planning should have entailed some deep thought about how you plan to operate your farm. The series of planning

---

FIGURE 3.5   Tips for Making Your Farming Plan a Reality

Plan Your Work (AND WORK YOUR PLAN)

The second part is the most difficult part.

Many grandiose plans are filed and forgotten. Keep your eye on your plan. Put it on a bulletin board or under a plastic sheet on your desk calendar, where you can:

- *Refer* to it constantly. Put sticky notes on it to indicate future changes or outstanding successes. Scribble all over it if you want to.

- *Keep records*—save everything pertinent to your success.

- Being the boss doesn't mean you can loaf around waiting for the spirit to move you. You will do much better if you have a *regular work pattern.* Plan it to suit your temperament, but plan it.

- *Learn the territory.* Becoming the real estate specialist entails knowing everything about real estate and the people in your farm. You will be asked questions about anything and everything.

- *Keep studying*—workshops, seminars, sales meetings, real estate articles and books. Never let the customers know more about the subject than you do.

- Be service-minded—nobody cares what you know *until they know that you care.*

- Act *enthusiastic,* even on your down days. What goes around comes around. The power of positive thinking is uncanny. Take another look at your plan if things are a little tough.

- Keep reaching for your goals. Stick to your plan. Keep your plan in action. Working your plan means figuring out *how* to make the *what* work out.

FIGURE 3.6   The Four Seasons of Farming

It helps to know that there are four seasons of farming:

1. Winter: getting acquainted
2. Spring: building trust
3. Summer: becoming the neighborhood
                    real estate specialist
4. Autumn: the harvest

---

pages found throughout the book conform to the four seasons of farming pattern of progression of objectives (see Figure 3.6). For the sake of discussion, let's say that your plan is pretty much as follows:

1. Send out a friendly introductory letter to all.
2. Stop by within a week and leave on every doorknob a door hanger with your picture, name and company printed on it.
3. Follow up any number of ways. You could visit each neighbor street by street, giving out something like a calendar or a refrigerator magnet of your card.

Many computer programs allow you to print out the names, addresses and telephone numbers street by street, to make canvassing easier. You can also divide up the area into target groups and call on one group at a time, providing each pertinent information.

Well, you certainly have your work cut out for you. What are you waiting for? Start working on that introductory letter: It is your first foot forward and it has to be right.

Just keep plugging away on your plan, one item at a time. If you have an action plan for the year and activity calendars for each month and you are filling in your daily farming sheets from them, you should be chugging right along.

Don't make the mistake of expecting results too soon. It is the cumulative effect of all you do that finally sprouts. What would you think of a tomato farmer who sat in the field all day waiting for the tomato to grow? This could be a mighty long wait, with a mighty frustrated farmer.

The best thing for you to do right now, after you have done all you can in your farm, is to take floor duty (opportunity time or whatever they call it where you live) and sell a house. Or ask some busy veteran salesperson if you can hold an open house for him or her and then sell it! Or sell one of the people who came to the open house in your farm and get the ball rolling. If there is a house in your farm listed by another broker, concentrate on getting it sold. Call your whole list of prospects, your whole sphere of influence and find a buyer for that house. Nothing could get you off to a better start than to be the one to sell any house in your farm. Work out a two-year schedule like the one in Figure 3.7.

FIGURE 3.7   Planning Schedule Year Two: Integrated Mail, Telephone and Person-to-Person Campaign

Month	Letter	Enclosure	Telephone Follow-Up	In Person
Jan	Town map	New Year's card		Questionnaire/survey
Feb	Newsletter	Valentine's Day card	Did you send back completed questionnaire?	
Mar	Tax survivors' letter	St. Patrick's Day card		
Apr	Resort properties' and investors' letter	Kid's coloring contest sheet		Pass out seeds
May	Newsletter	Mother's Day card		
June	Good-news letter	Father's Day card Plastic doorknob bags to return completed questionnaires		Pick up plastic bags returning questionnaires
July	Fight tax-assessments letter		Who needs help?	
Aug	Newsletter	Flier: Home protection while on vacation		
Sept	Letter: home improvements that pay off	Smile stickers		
Oct	Frequent questions and answers on real estate			Pass out next year's calendar
Nov	Newsletter	Turkey raffle tickets (free)		Drawing at community center
Dec	Christmas letter	Real estate activity summary		

PART 2

Prospect Management and Strategies

The Computer Revolution

Easy Street

Computers simplify virtually every aspect of farming. Most salespeople are reasonably familiar with computers because most busy real estate boards in the country now provide computer Multiple Listing Services (MLS). Most small companies that do not have an MLS computer terminal in their office do own an office computer to which their salespeople have access. No one running a business today can afford to be without a computer to organize and analyze information.

Granted, some REALTORS® have not taken advantage of their MLS terminals to reach their dollar potential and a few approach the terminal as if it might bite. I am sympathetic to this viewpoint because I resisted the cold, robotlike angle of computers and artificial computerspeak. Gradually it was borne in on me that real estate agents, even more than other businesspeople, need the capacity for prospect management, customer management and direct mail, and for printing cards, letters, labels and envelopes. Once converted, though, like any convert I am one of the computer's most enthusiastic supporters; not, however, to the point of those at the other end of the fervency spectrum who are so addicted to the computer that they cannot find time to list or sell.

Once you get into the computer dimension, it is fascinating. You can perform incredible things with it. It is easy, however, to become too involved in the computer world. The trick is to use computers to save yourself time and to bring yourself into the cutting edge of professionalism, without losing your human dimension.

Selecting a Farm

The first vital step in farming is to select a farm. This step brings you into immediate confrontation with the computer. From your board MLS main computer, you must pull out comparable sales from several previous years and all those listings now on the market in the areas you are considering for a farm. In addition to the number of "solds" and listings in these areas, you must analyze the potential farm areas carefully to determine:

1. What is the average sales price? Add all the prices of houses sold the past year and divide by the number of sales.
2. What is the turnover ratio? Divide the number of sales by the number of homes. Do this for the past three years to determine the trend.
3. What is your possible market share? Using 25 percent for the second year and 75 percent for the final years, calculate the number of listings you can expect to attain.
4. What is your potential income? Based on the average sales price, the turnover and your market share, plus your commission split, figure out your potential income for each area.
5. Is the area being farmed now? Rank the brokers according to the number of sales to find out if one broker is dominating the area.
6. Who is your competition? Check to see if that domination is produced by one particular salesperson. If the salesperson is from your own company, you might decide to pick another area.
7. How successful is your competition? If the farmer is a competitor, you might want to investigate just how deeply entrenched the person is and whether it would be worth the fight. Remember, no strong person is immune to personality clashes and, particularly if this is your home turf, do not be afraid to challenge your competition if you decide this is the farm you want.
8. Is the market trend in the area up or down? (See Number 2.) You want an area that is on the rise, not one that is deteriorating, unless you plan to specialize in "fixer-uppers" or rehabs.
9. Is the farm manageable? Obviously, a farm with an annual turnover of 15 houses with an average sales price of $300,000 would be easier to manage than one with 120 houses with an average price

of $60,000. A farm in which you live is easier to manage than one 15 miles away.

10. Are the homeowners compatible with your perspective? A farm in which the homeowners are similar to you will be easier for you to work than one where you have nothing in common with the people. You may want to pick an area of homes with the same price range as your own home. There are, however, some very empathetic, flexible salespeople who can get along anywhere.

Commission Splits

One thing that will greatly affect your potential income in your farm is how you split the commissions on sales in your farm.

Naturally, you cannot expect to sell all your own listings, but you can aspire to a healthy share, especially if you concentrate on it. The commission split factor is discussed in Chapter 11. Open houses are the best way to get a listing/selling cycle going in your farm.

The second year, try setting a goal of selling at least one-third of your own listings. Ultimately, you should strive for two-thirds in your own farm.

There are two ways to go about selecting a farm:

1. Set an income goal and determine what size farm would be required to reach your goal. Find a farm area that satisfies your income needs or possibly farm two areas.
2. Farm where you live or nearby and accept the income available from an efficient farm operation. In the latter case, you may need to supplement your farm income with income from sales in other areas.

Turnover in some areas may be so low that you may have to increase farm size to compensate. If this happens, you will have to concentrate on good farm management to handle the load. Remember also that even if you concentrate most of your efforts in a farm, the farm is not the sole source of income. As much as 50 percent of your income may result from general brokerage sales.

For example, you want to make at least $20,000 from your farm the second year and $100,000 in your target year. The turnover ratio in your area is averaging about 6 percent. You can realistically aspire to a 25 percent market share the second year and 60 percent in the target year (the year when your farm reaches maturity). An average sales price in your region for a good subdivision or parcel of your choice is running about $100,000, with some at $80,000 and some at $120,000.

How big a farm do you need?

In the three potential farm areas analyzed later in this book, average commissions to the farm agent are about 2 percent per home listed. The exact figure depends on the commission rate and the proportion of commission splits you have, of course. But let's use 2 percent.

1. In order to earn $20,000 at 2 percent, you would need a dollar volume of $1,000,000 ($20,000 divided by .02 = $1,000,000).
2. If the houses were selling for $100,000 (average sales price), you would need to sell ten houses ($1,000,000 divided by $100,000 = 10).
3. If your market share is 25 percent, then the total number of houses you would have to sell would be 40 (10 divided by .25 = 40).
4. If the turnover is 6 percent, and that equals 40 homes sold, then the farm must contain 667 homes to provide you with $20,000 (40 divided by .06 = 666.66).

Now you must determine if that size farm will provide you with $100,000 in your target year. Your projection is for 60 percent of the market share, with split commissions on no more than one-third of your listings.

1. To earn $100,000 at .02, you would need a dollar volume of $5,000,000 ($100,000 divided by .02 = $5,000,000).
2. If houses are selling for $100,000, you must sell 50 ($5,000,000 divided by $100,000 = 50).
3. With your market share of 60 percent, you would have to sell 83 homes (50 divided by .60 = 83).
4. With turnover at 6 percent, you would need 1,383 homes (83 divided by .06 = 1,383).

In other words, you would have to double the size of your farm in the ensuing two or three years. When choosing a farm, you would need to consider an area where you could easily add 200 to 300 homes a year. You must search the computer for an area where 80 or more homes were sold during the previous year.

Is there any other way you could increase your income in the target year? You could increase your market share. Would 75 percent be an attainable goal? You could increase your commission by raising the commission rate on your listings. Commissions are negotiable and you are worth more. What about the turnover rate? Is there a "hot" subdivision where the market trend is rapidly rising sales? Why not choose a subdivision of higher-priced homes with at least an equal turnover rate?

Analyzing Areas Under Consideration for a Farm

Suppose you are in a large suburban area or a city where the variety in price range is extreme. How do you decide what mix to choose?

	Area A	Area B	Area C
Average sales price	$100,000	$60,000	$300,000
Average commission rate	.06	.07	.05
Average total commission	$6,000	$4,200	$15,000
Number of homes	400	466	300
Number of homes sold last year	40	70	15
Turnover ratio	10%	15%	5%

Analyzing Area A	Second Year	Target Year
Homes sold × market share	40 × 25%	40 × 75%
Market share × split ratio	10 × .666	30 × .333
Number of homes sold (split commission)	7	10
Number of homes sold (full commission)	3	20
Total average commission less split with broker	6%–3%	6%–3%
Salesperson (full commission)	.03	.03
Salesperson (split commission)	.015	.015
Number of homes sold (split commission)	7 × .015 = .105	10 × .01 =.15
Number of homes sold (full commission)	3 × .03 = .09	20 × .03 = .6
Average commission divided by number sold	.195 ÷ 10	.75 ÷ 30
Average commission	.0195	.025
Number of homes sold × average price	10 × $100,000 =	30 × $100,000 =
Dollar volume × average commission	$1,000,000 × .0195 =	$3,000,000 × .025 =
Farm income	$19,500	$75,000

Analyzing Area B	Second Year	Target Year
Homes sold × market share	70 × 25%	70 × 75%
Market share × split ratio	18 × .666	53 × .333
Number of homes sold (split commission)	11	18
Number of homes sold (full commission)	7	35
Total average commission less split with broker	7%–3½%	7%–3½%
Salesperson (full commission)	.035	.035
Salesperson (split commission)	.0176	.0175
Number of homes sold (split commission)	11 × .0175 = .1925	18 × .0175 = .315
Number of homes sold (full commission)	7 × .035 = .245	35 × .035 = 1.225
Average commission divided by number sold	.4375 ÷ 18	1.54 ÷ 53
Average commission	.024	.029
Number of homes sold × average price	18 × $60,000 =	53 × $60,000 =
Dollar volume × average commission	$1,080,000 ö .024 =	$3,180,000 × .029 =
Farm income	$25,920	$92,220

Analyzing Area C	Second Year	Target Year
Homes sold × market share	15 × 25%	15 × 75%
Market share × split ratio	4 × .666	11 × .333
Number of homes sold (split commission)	3	4

Number of homes sold (full commission)	1	7
Total average commission less split with broker	5%–2.5%	5%–2.5%
Salesperson (full commission)	.025	.025
Salesperson (split commission)	.0125	.0125
Number of homes sold (split commission)	3 × .0125 = .0375	4 × .0125 = .05
Number of homes sold (full commission)	1 × .025 = .025	7 × .025 = .175
Average commission divided by number sold	.0625 ÷ 4	.225 ÷ 11
Average commission	.0156	.0205
Number of homes sold × average price	4 × $300,000 =	11 × $300,000 =
Dollar volume × average commission	$1,200,000 × .0156 =	$300,000 × .0205 =
Farm income	$18,729	$67,650

Prices, market share, commissions charged and gross commission split all affect your income goal, to say nothing of your selling skills. Remember, a real estate salesperson should not become so engrossed in the mechanics that he or she neglects basic selling and people skills.

Organizing Your Farm

There is no question that the organizational part of farming is very intimidating to many people-oriented personalities. They would rather spend their precious time with people than with things. Quite rightly so: The only time you are making money is when you are eyeball to eyeball with the customer or client—listing or selling.

The great part about using the computer to keep farm records is that the efficiency of a good farm recordkeeping system is vastly improved with the computer programs now available. It is well worth the price in dollars to free up your time to spend with your prospects.

Starting right from the very beginning with farm research, in most places today you have a choice between manual methods and computer methods.

You can pore laboriously over tax records, Lusk directories and other data, hand-copying from these materials or photocopying from the microfiche if you have one in your office. Much easier is a trip to the assessment office where you can order a computer printout of approximately 1,000 names. In Annapolis, Maryland, the cost is approximately $85. In some places in the nation you can get this information on a computer disk that you insert directly into your own computer system. In Sacramento, California, Les Boomer subscribes to a service of a company called MetroScan, which sends him a computer disk updating the tax rolls monthly. Courthouse Records of Colorado identifies absentee owners in each subdivision in selected areas. See "Resources" in Appendix A at the end of the book. You can access up to 500,000 properties on a single compact disk—great for covering an office's entire market area. Cole's EasyList program allows you to input onto your

Smart Agent disk, if you have one, all the names, addresses, and phone numbers of your farm no matter what its size: by community, county, rural route, ZIP code or whatever you want. If you own or plan to buy another computer program for mailing, check the compatibility with Cole's EasyList. You may be able to use it.

Once you have this information in your computer you can use it for any task, from farm contacts to mail campaigns. If you do not have access to a computer, you will have to hand-copy the information onto index cards or onto the pages of your farm loose-leaf notebook, as explained in Chapter 3.

There is no comparison between manual and computer list maintenance. For example, the post office always is changing carrier routes. When this happened recently in my area, it took me less than 20 minutes to change my entire farm of 350 names.

Computer Farming Programs

As real estate came into the computer age, a great variety of computer programs became available. The REALTORS® National Marketing Institute (RNMI) responded by making a computer applications course available. Test marketing revealed a 100 percent acceptance level from test participants. More than 63 percent of 2,500 REALTORS® surveyed nationwide had reacted positively to the idea of a computer course and an *RS News Brief* poll showed that 90 percent of Certified Residential Specialists (CRSs) reacted positively to the idea. According to Randall K. Eager, CRS, CRB, writing in a *Real Estate Business* article entitled "Oh! What a Relief It Is," "More than one-third of those responding were sales agents who had never even touched a computer."

The popularity of the RNMI Residential Sales Council's Computer Applications Course, RS206, since its inception—and especially its wholesale acceptance by top producers like CRSs and what I call "the new breed" who have latched onto technology in general—indicate that within the next few years those who continue to resist the wave of the future will be pulled even further out to sea by the undertow. Survivors adapt. They embrace change. This is being felt in every industry all over the world. A list of software programs that range in price from more than $600 down to less than $100 is featured in "Resources," Appendix A.

Smart Agent

After testing a number of these programs in my own farm, I am now using Smart Agent. This program is geared to allow you to do either active or passive farming: community involvement or direct mail. You have the choice of either a full record or only a mailing label. You can browse through your records and in just a few minutes identify a group of prospects, select from among 100 letters written by the author of this book, personalize the letter, print it, print an address label and before you know it you have a mailing all ready to go. You can create custom letters; edit by name, address or carrier route; delete files; and search farm files by target group, street, subdivision or ZIP code.

You can divide your farm into a number of groups: owner-occupants, absentee owners, lot owners, absentee lot owners, waterfront properties, investors and senior citizens; and by clubs, such as garden clubs, political clubs, church groups and others. Within the group function, the possibilities are infinite. You can target special mailings to any group. You can contact people in your farm by group as well as by street or if you are looking for a split-level for a customer, you can canvass split-levels only.

The print menu in this program allows you to mail automatically a monthly farming letter, printing address labels or continuous envelopes or postcards. This program also lets you print a farm record for each homeowner that you can keep in a farm book or print on an index card (they come in continuous form, too) to slip into your pocket as you walk your farm or put on your desk for follow-up on the telephone.

Smart Agent has its own simple (but, therefore, somewhat limited) word-processing program. Anyone who can type, using even the hunt-and-peck method, should be able to fathom this word-processing program with minimum, if any, instruction, plus a little experimenting to get used to its quirks.

For Beginners

When I compare learning Smart Agent word processing to learning early versions of word-processing programs such as WordStar and WordPerfect, I have to wonder at its simplicity. The main problem I have with most computer programs is a question of personal memory. I use "information overload" as an excuse for my own memory problems. Whatever the cause, I find learning most computer programs involves, for me, at least, writing down every important function in a logical manner, so that I can find it when I need it. None of this is necessary with this program. It is just a matter of diving in and starting to use it.

Some of these software programs are, like Smart Agent, "menu-driven." A menu is simply a list setting out the choices of things you can do with the program. You pick from this list of options by highlighting the one you desire.

This is ever so much easier than memorizing a lot of system commands. Multiple-choice computing may one day supersede the present preference for character commands popularized mostly by the IBM clones and the availability of software for the IBM compatible computers. *PC Novice,* a monthly magazine written in plain English (see "Resources," Appendix A), calls the use of icons (tiny on-screen pictures), menu bars, mouse (a hand-held device through which you can select on-screen options) and trackball, a similar device that doesn't have to be moved by the arm (and therefore does not give the user something like tennis elbow) "the style of computing for the future."

The advent of Microsoft Windows certainly advanced this prediction. Windows is particularly good for those who want to do a farm newsletter on their own computer. At last check, Microsoft Publishing only cost about $100. It has ready-made templates, which take the design skill out of it; you just choose the format that best suits the kind of newsletter you want to do. You can insert graphics from a number of programs like Smart Pics by Lotus, or Print Shop by Broderbund. It is so easy to do that one user told me her nine-year-old niece knocked out a two-page "kidletter" in a couple of hours.

Windows itself is one of three basic choices for people struggling with the task of buying a brand-new computer system. The Disk Operating System (DOS), Microsoft Windows or Apple Macintosh are the three major choices. Since I use the DOS and Windows, I will focus on their programs and applications. Windows sits on top of the DOS system and provides access to multiple applications simultaneously. Each application (word processing, drawing, a clock, calendar or calculator) operates in its own "window." You can move easily from one to the other. You have a "file manager" to organize files and directories. A directory is similar to a book's table of contents. Directories in Windows can be opened one by one by clicking the mouse on the appropriate icon and peering inside the selected application.

Some programs, like Smart Agent, allow you to use either the arrows on your computer or a mouse or trackball to select options.

If at anytime you are unsure of what to do, you have directions at the bottom of the screen or you can use the F1 key to bring up a "help" menu, actually a window that contains instructions.

For the complete neophyte, the one-third of you who have never even touched a computer, pick a program that has written plain English instruction on how to get started. If a tutorial is included with the disk, it will take you through the whole program once and familiarize you with how it all works. Sometimes, as in Smart Agent, there is a functions index where you locate the function immediately in the computer manual section that explains how to do anything from writing a new letter to printing a label or removing a record. If there is no glossary of the computer terms used in the on-line computer manual, buy one in a computer store so you can follow the technical instructions.

As *PC Novice* points out, "No matter how many icons and buttons [or how many simplified instructions or help screens], computing will still be more difficult than crossing the street."

And well worth the effort: Computers allow agents to work smarter instead of harder. Computers increase your efficiency and allow you to become more productive. In other words, they help you *earn more money*.

An example is the many different letters or messages, covering a variety of situations stored within good farming programs and how easily you can insert any others you wish. You also can use letters provided as a starting point and alter them to suit any situation. The short messages lend themselves well to postcards, which are available on continuous forms for a dot-matrix printer.

If you are new to computers, you should be aware that a certain amount of experimentation, imagination and flexibility are necessary. Play around with the program until you master it.

Besides *DOS for Dummies, PC Novice* and your own computer manual, Egghead and other computer stores also have computer instructions on video to run on your VCR with pertinent information about using a computer, knowledge that might make you feel more confident (see "Resources," Appendix A, for other suggestions).

Cultivating Your Farm

Your own creativity is the only restriction on the range of material that is possible to produce with a computer.

Whichever program you buy should allow you to print out address labels, envelopes, postcards, index cards, letters and all kinds of messages.

With the addition of a graphics program, you can produce your own letterheads, fliers, newsletter inserts, bulletins, booklets and all types of inexpensive paper gifts, such as bookmarks, calendars, lists of important telephone numbers, sports schedules, information bulletins and maps as well as greeting cards for all occasions. Print Shop, Print Magic and a number of other programs provide extra disks of pictures and type fonts to use on all kinds of printed products. The graphics are similar to the clip art now being used for newsletters by many agents. One caveat is that computer graphics often are copyrighted, so they cannot be used in publishing without permission. Most of the computer graphics in this book are from Print Shop and are used with permission.

One limitation of these graphics programs is that they are difficult to incorporate with text, so that they can be used for letterhead, fliers, banners, etc., but if you want to use them in the body of newsletters, be sure the graphics software you purchase can be merged with the operating system you are using. Until recently, computer programs were so expensive and complicated that cut-and-paste was easier. Even then it was possible to write a letter on 8½″ × 11″ paper and print an extremely simple short newsletter in a straightforward manner. This is the kind of folksy, noncommercial newsletter that is popular in small towns and rural areas.

Most word-processing programs offer a multicolumn format; however, you may be better off with a graphic artist preparing a "board" for you, which will give you a permanent format for your newsletter. Then on your word processor, write your text in one long, thin column. Cut and paste it onto your board. Fit in your graphics wherever they add spice.

These can be real estate–related clip art or pictures from the graphics library of a computer publishing program, printed out, cut and pasted in like clip art. First Publishers provides a good library.

Market Analysis

All the work that you perform in your farm leads up to one thing: earning a commission. For this you need listings and sales. A number of programs are available that help to harvest your crop.

One of these, Toolkit, a market analysis system, offered by Realty Tools, Inc., can create an 11-part listing presentation package (Figure 4.1).

This Toolkit competitive marketing analysis (CMA) package makes an impressive presentation tool. Everything recommended by big hitters such as Carole Kelby, such as your marketing plan, is included, plus an analysis of the current market and a rundown of company services.

Keep in mind, however, that as used in a listing farm, the competitive market analysis is much more than a listing presentation tool. Most of the homeowners requesting a competitive market analysis are asking for this information for future use. There are two hidden traps for farmers: One is the tendency to use an inappropriately hard-sell approach that will work against the farmer's overall objective of a friendly, ongoing relationship with neighbors; the other is the tendency to forget the whole thing when it appears the homeowner is not "serious," i.e., not ready. It is important that farmers take the long view of prospecting. One reason some agents fail at farming is their tendency to be impatient and shortsighted.

The farmer, therefore, should emphasize that in order to be valid, a competitive market report must be timely. The farmer who uses a computer CMA can make it clear that he or she stands ready to produce one at the drop of a hoe. When he or she gives or sends out certificates, the certificates should state prominently that *the offer is good indefinitely and the certificate can be used more than once.*

The capability to produce one of these market analyses at will makes life easier for the agent. Two or three computers are available that give you the essential data to put into the program as long as you have access to a telephone outlet. These computers hook into the MLS main computer. This is the main reason to consider one of the very small notebook-

FIGURE 4.1 Features of Toolkit Program

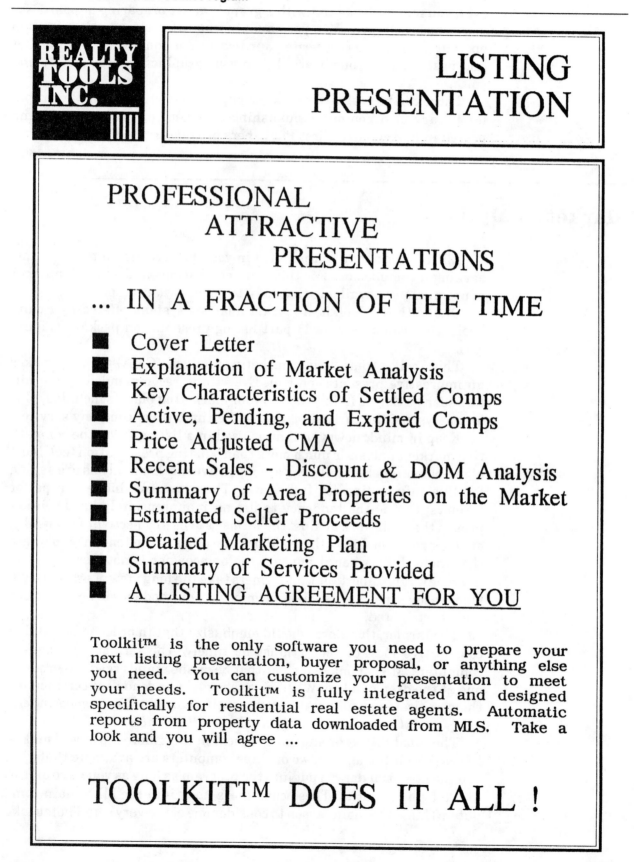

REALTY TOOLS INC.

LISTING PRESENTATION

PROFESSIONAL
ATTRACTIVE
PRESENTATIONS

... IN A FRACTION OF THE TIME

- Cover Letter
- Explanation of Market Analysis
- Key Characteristics of Settled Comps
- Active, Pending, and Expired Comps
- Price Adjusted CMA
- Recent Sales - Discount & DOM Analysis
- Summary of Area Properties on the Market
- Estimated Seller Proceeds
- Detailed Marketing Plan
- Summary of Services Provided
- A LISTING AGREEMENT FOR YOU

Toolkit™ is the only software you need to prepare your next listing presentation, buyer proposal, or anything else you need. You can customize your presentation to meet your needs. Toolkit™ is fully integrated and designed specifically for residential real estate agents. Automatic reports from property data downloaded from MLS. Take a look and you will agree ...

TOOLKIT™ DOES IT ALL !

type laptop computers. Such a notebook, combined with a lightweight ink-jet printer, provides complete portability. Computers such as the Moore Personal Terminal allow you to transfer all of the MLS information into your own home or portable terminal so you can produce the market analysis on the spot on the homeowners' premises. How is that for impressive?

In addition, three large financial data bases can provide you with immediate information about financing, including prequalification, loan selection, loan application and loan approval. Especially powerful is the ability to tap into a computerized mortgage data-base service that gives you the information you need to evaluate the best mortgage "deal" for your buyers' specific circumstances—particularly potent if you are trying to compare ARMs.

Speed is a factor, too. Citicorp started a program that qualified homebuyers in as little as 15 minutes by running applicants' financial profiles through a new in-house computer program. Now most mortgage brokers can do the same. Some take the loan application directly into the computer and if the buyer has the necessary information, he or she can get instant pre-approval.

Your ability to come up with financial data instantly and on-the-scene will be convincing evidence to people in your farm that you are on the cutting edge, especially if you live in a technologically advanced area full of computer aces.

Customer Management

Most impressive of all are programs that allow you to calculate loan payments, determine buyer loan qualifications and create amortization schedules, home-investment analyses, variable interest-rate payments and appreciation tables. One agent ran an advertisement in a local homes magazine that read, "My portable terminal will provide you with a personal, private consultation in your own home."

A number of programs offer a sales record menu that allows complete customer management, including a method of calculating settlement dates instantly to suit buyer, seller and all the parties. It also can automatically keep track of listing expiration dates.

My feeling is that during this whole discussion of state-of-the-art real estate practice, the windmills of your mind have been calculating costs. The $64,000 question is: "Will it pay off?" Not if you are just puttering around in the garden, hoping to produce a tulip or two. For those looking for a bumper crop, it already has paid off a number of trailblazers across the nation. This is the difference between farming with a mule and with the latest farm machinery.

A Computer Farming System

1. A personal computer (possibly laptop) and a decent printer (The computer should use 3½-inch disks, not 5¼-inch disks.)
2. Farm record software
3. Customer management software
4. Competitive market analysis software
5. Graphics software
6. Word-processing software
7. Owner information software
8. Continuous-feed letterheads, envelopes, address labels, postcards, index cards, etc.
9. Modem to MLS or data banks and telemarketing
10. The right attitude; this is a skill, like playing the piano.

Choosing Software

Software is the name given to the programs that allow you to carry out the functions you wish to do. If you want to write letters and information bulletins for your farm, for example, then you need a word-processing software program. If you are a computer genius and want to publish a very professional newsletter, you could buy a desktop publishing program such as Ventura Publisher or Pagemaker.

My advice is be very careful about getting involved in desktop publishing unless you are using a Macintosh or Windows and choose a very simple program like Microsoft Publisher. Too much time and aggravation is involved in a really sophisticated system for anyone who plans to be a real estate agent rather than a publisher.

There is a wonderful alternative to doing desktop publishing yourself. First, call a local desktop publishing service. Most large metropolitan areas now have them, and some small and medium towns do, too. Find out which word-processing programs are compatible to desktop publishing. If you have one of these, simply type out your articles for the newsletter without any special treatment at all. Give the disk to the service bureau, which will format the text. Most of them have proofreaders who will edit out the worst mistakes, too. They will help you with an attractive layout and then supply you with camera-ready copy that you can either photocopy or send to your printer. This saves a lot of time and money in equipment. It also gives you a professional-looking document.

Some companies have gone one step further such as Graphics, Etc., in Washington, D.C., by combining desktop publishing and printing. They will take your raw copy and art, convert it and print it all in one operation for less than what the two-step process would cost you. It is also a tremendous time-saver, to say nothing of saving the cost of desktop publishing programs and the grief of learning them.

Some of the software programs that you want may work on any computer; some may not. Some of your activities may work on any printer; again, some may not. For instance, laser printers turn out letter-quality work, but they do not take continuous-feed paper, address labels, envelopes, index cards or postcards.

Miracle of miracles, Vertisoft Systems, Inc., has come up with a program called Emulaser that, for less than $50, will upgrade your printer to the highest quality laser printer, and has more than 70 scalable fonts and prints in bold and italic, plus graphics and color. The company claims that your printed output will look so good that everyone will think it came from a $3,000 PostScript laser printer.

Decide what you plan to do *before* you buy the hardware. Many programs are available only for IBM-compatible computers, that is, an IBM computer or any of a number of IBM clones.

These programs will not work on a Macintosh. On the other hand, certain wonderful desktop publishing programs will work only on Macintosh. Some are full-fledged Windows software, specifically designed for MS-Windows and also have Macintosh versions. Macs are particularly good for producing jobs with a lot of great artwork. Some, like Realty Systems' map software, which prints high quality uncluttered maps that would be great farm handouts, work only with DOS.

Once you know what you plan to do with your computer and what programs do it best, then you can look into the hardware.

Choosing Hardware

A great many computers are available that do a perfectly good job and that will not require you to take out an equity loan on your home. An article on buying computers, which appeared in the *Baltimore Sun,* advised a buyer "to go down to Klone Kloset, a local store that makes its own PCs and buy one of their inexpensive knockouts." The writer, Michael Himowitz, was quite serious. "It really doesn't matter what kind of IBM-compatible you buy; they all do the job," he says. As he told his nervous friend, "After the warranty expires, you may have more trouble getting a brand-name computer fixed than you will have with a no-name clone!" Sound hard to believe? Well, there is a logical reason for this. The generic clone is made from off-the-shelf components that can be replaced by generic parts if anything goes wrong. Anyone can fix it.

A word of warning when you buy a new computer: *PC World's* "market place" recently quoted a survey of PC buyers by Channel

Marketing Corporation that found that within six months of purchase, more than 60 percent of buyers lamented that they hadn't bought more expansion space and memory. Channel President David Goldstein recommends buying as much RAM and hard-drive space as you can afford. A good time to buy big is when there is a hard-disk price war on (check local dealers).

Many types of computers are available: giant mainframe computers used by Fortune-500 companies, with lots of little satellite computers hooked into them; bulky personal computers and their bulky printers and other attachments that require huge desk areas; and a whole new rash of laptop computers that the latest issue of *Computer Digest* called "power computing with a handle."

A Few Words about Operating Systems

The main difference between IBM compatibles and Apple computers is the operating system. By far the most common is DOS, the system used by IBM. Apple computers use an operating system called System 7. Microsoft Windows, while not a true operating system, differs from both in that it sits on top of the DOS operating system, but acts more like a Mac. The way the operating system affects the user is called "interface," which describes how the user communicates with the operating system. With command-driven interfaces like DOS, the user had to learn a lot of character commands, somewhat like learning a foreign language. Menu-driven interfaces are easier because all you have to do is pull down menus with the mouse. Newer versions of DOS have something called a DOS shell, which allows users to choose which way they wish to operate. Old-timers will probably continue to use commands, while newcomers will find the shell much easier because it allows the user to skip memorized commands and work from multiple-choice menus.

Before the advent of Windows, many users were torn between the friendliness of Mac and the need for IBM compatibility. The sudden popularity of Windows may be attributed in part to the merging of these two characteristics. MS-DOS and PC-DOS will run the same application programs as Windows. Microsoft claims that most applications are still written for MS-DOS. Some other DOS systems, like DR-DOS, are not compatible with Windows.

The other factor (besides what you plan to use your computer for) is cost. Says *PC Novice:* "If cost is a priority, you can't beat an inexpensive operating system with a command-driven interface. Luckily, computers have never been cheaper." According to *PC Novice,* "if you are weighing your options, wondering whether to buy a PC, now's the time to do it." *PC Novice* is a good place to start when considering exactly what to do. Articles in this premium edition include "Buying Your First PC," "Beginner's Guide to Troubleshooting," "Setting Up Your Computer" and everything else you need to know. It wasn't written for kindergartners, but it is in plain English.

Back to Hardware

The feeling of joy expressed by Macintosh users is best illustrated by Patricia Kirby in "True Confessions of a Laptop Convert": "Oh, freedom! Had there been a Macintosh laptop, I would have chosen it, even though I needed IBM compatibility. It would have been possible to work around the compatibility issue with attachments. But alas, there is no Macintosh laptop at the moment and probably won't be for a long time to come."

Actually, three years later, there are seven different Macintosh laptops! The whole range of laptops has mushroomed. Says *PC World* in its issue featuring mobile computing: "The latest wave of portable wonders comes replete with 486-level chips, rich color displays and roomy hard drives, and they can match or exceed the power of many of today's desktops." In fact, suggests *PC World*, "If you need to use Windows and all your applications at home and on the road, consider using a notebook as your only computer." *PC World*, by the way, is an excellent source of information about purchasing computer products of all kinds. One recent issue contained a 40-page guide to mobile computing (see "Resources," Appendix A).

"Although notebook monitors and keyboards are smaller and more cramped than their desktop counterparts, nearly all notebooks, as laptops are now called, have connectors that you can plug into desktop monitors and full-size keyboards when you get home," says *PC World*.

For a real estate salesperson, the best of all possible worlds probably would be a Macintosh in the home office with a Hewlett-Packard Series II printer and an IBM-compatible laptop in the car with a continuous-feed portable printer. Most of us learned long ago that the best of all possible worlds is the impossible dream and that you have to learn to choose.

One solution is to rent a computer for a special use. In most large cities, you can now find computer rentals almost as easily as car rentals. This keeps you from desperation if your computer breaks down in the middle of your newsletter.

Once the computer franchises get going you may be able to rent a computer in almost any part of the country for as long as you need it for a specific job, or to try out new systems. One of the scary parts of buying a computer is your inability to get a real feel for it until you have already made an irrevocable decision. Rental computers would eliminate this problem.

A Complete Farming Package

You can put together a complete computer farming package in a laptop computer with a 20-meg hard disk. In case you do not have the slightest clue to what that is, it is a very desirable feature that allows you to store your programs *in* the computer, instead of having to constantly load them in with "floppy disks." Use a battery that snaps on, which means you do not have to plug into an electric socket for three hours.

A communications modem allows you to get through into your MLS computer system at your local board of REALTORS® whenever you have access to a telephone. It will also let you dial out to another computer for financial and other information.

Your portable office can be completed with two items of software: Smart Agent or a similar contact management program plus ToolKit or a market analysis program like it.

If you want to use the same system for portable and desktop you can add word processing and a graphics program to your hard disk to gain a powerhouse system. For sales managers and trainers, include a video-cassette recorder training tape and attach an overhead projector ($1,100 extra). Use it in training, seminars and in the field at open houses, for example.

Two programs, called, fascinatingly, Brooklyn Bridge and Fast Wire, permit you to move information from an existing computer with the older standard 5¼-inch disk onto the hard disk of your laptop (which uses the newer 3½-inch disk) without having to laboriously "input" (computerese for *type*). The whole works, including computer, battery, modem, hard disk, 3½-inch drive and the two software programs, would cost somewhere in the neighborhood of $3,000, including an ink-jet portable printer that weighs about four pounds and sacrifices some quality for portability. (Prices are subject to change—up or down.)

A computer program can be set up for office farming, on location, using a hard disk, that would allow an unlimited number of agents to farm from one office. This could be done with each agent using his or her key data disk at about $40 apiece. Using a 3½-inch disk, each agent with two backup disks could have a 2,000-home farm. The old 5¼-inch disk would have limited the agent to 480 homes and multiple backup disks to accommodate farm data.

A small-office prospecting system using a personal computer designed by Lou Pretto, president of Business Computer Consultants for the Board of Realty Information Systems in Pensacola, Florida, recently was described in *Real Estate Business* magazine:

> For sales associates who always start out with high resolve to see ten or twenty new people a week, then fall by the wayside after a few good weeks, a computer may be just what they need.

How can a computer help? It creates a system that makes it very easy for the sales associate to prospect and follow up. Second, it keeps the sales cycle moving, and third, it forces the associate to stick to the system.

Sales trainers have been saying for years that successful people are those who perform the boring tasks that unsuccessful people don't want to do. *Boring* usually means repetitive. Here's what Randall K. Eager says about repetition in his article regarding prospecting and personal referral systems:

> [Success] depends on a systematic method based on spaced repetition, in other words an organized system used over and over again. The major mistake most agents make with their prospecting methods is the *lack of continuity and repetition*. Part of this is due to a lack of organization. Enter the computer. The computer can perform those repetitive functions over and over again.

Once you have set it up, you can forget it.

Printers

The range of prices and the performance of printers is much greater than the range for computers, from the lowliest dot-matrix through ink-jet to laser printers that cost a fortune and do a job that is comparable to a good lithograph-house product (called letter quality). Printers used for desktop publishing are at the top of the scale.

What do you need? That depends on what you are trying to do. Do you need a color printer? If you are planning to send out greeting cards in your farm area or produce color fliers or banners, you may. Epson manufactures an excellent color printer.

Running off 350 greeting cards or fliers for your farm or producing a four-color newsletter probably is too time-consuming and causes too much wear and tear on your printer. You usually are better off using an instant-print service. You can design and produce camera-ready copy, but the printing at copy centers and instant printers is so inexpensive these days that it is usually easier and cheaper to send your printing to them.

Get some good advice on printers and then go to the computer store and try them out. You can see for yourself the difference between letter-quality and lesser-quality printers. Try to balance quality and price to arrive at a compromise.

The ink-jet printer has received a lot of publicity, but since the advent of the improved dot-matrix 24-pin printer, dot-matrix printers are the printer of choice for most home users. They are inexpensive, relatively fast and great for graphics.

Lightweight portable ink-jet printers are ideal, though, for use with notebook computers out in the field. Ink jets are now extremely popular because they produce near-laser quality for near–dot-matrix prices, but they are slow as molasses. Laser printers prices have come down, too. At last count there were ten or more excellent laser printers for less than $1,000. Lasers produce the highest quality output, but they can't print carbons, business forms or wide spreadsheets, and they aren't as good for colored fliers, banners, posters and do-it-yourself simple newsletters as the old-fashioned speedy, inexpensive dot matrix. A good dot-matrix printer with an Emulaser now will give you a letter-quality job. Don't forget to look at the Emulaser if what you want is quality and the flexibility of a dot-matrix printer.

As in the case of all hardware choices, your selection depends on what you plan to do with the printer. What are your priorities? Is quality, speed, flexibility, cost, silence or something else more important to you?

You might want to consider a second printer of another type to keep at the office or at home if you can afford it.

The Epson LQ 800 is a very high quality printer at a reasonable price and has good ratings in consumer magazines.

Regarding ink-jet printers' performance: Their main attribute is that they are virtually soundless. The quality is no better than a good dot-matrix printer and sometimes worse, and the special paper needed costs more than twice as much as ordinary paper and has a grayish cast to it. If you want one, you might consider an ink-jet portable printer, Diconix, which, although only about the size of a book, has some excellent features.

Laser printers' costs usually rule them out for all but the most exacting jobs. For real estate people, the fact that most do not use continuous-feed paper is an even greater limitation. If you are rich and can afford two printers, make one of them the Hewlett-Packard Laser Series II.

If you can only afford one printer, the dot-matrix printer is the most versatile printer on the market, according to Jack Segal, printer product manager at Citizen America, quoted in *PC Novice*.

Be sure the printer you choose is compatible with the computers you plan to buy and with your software. Everything you encounter in real estate training today makes it more obvious that it won't be long until real estate practitioners who refuse to come into this generation by taking advantage of modern technology such as car phones, voice mail, fax machines and computers will be as obsolete as dinosaurs.

Time is money. Knowing that you are only making money when you are in plain sight of a prospect, aim to keep your computer learning time to a minimum. The time you devote to becoming acquainted with the program will be well worth it later in both time and money. Of course, time *is* money to a real estate professional.

For those who would like more information, there are books, magazines, catalogs and articles galore. Try Omega Press, *Computer Digest,* Dynamic Graphics, *Information World* and others listed in "Resources" in Appendix A.

There also is a Time-Life series called *Understanding Computers*. Attending a basic computer seminar at your local community college would be helpful, too, if you have time.

Another thought is a "user's group." In case this seems like a waste of your precious time, remember computer users buy houses, too, and who can they trust?

People who understand computerese!

Farming by Mail: Direct Mail

Phantom farming is what some people in the industry call mailing to a target or geographic area without any personal follow-up. Others call it passive farming. Whatever you call it, what it amounts to is plain, old-fashioned direct mail.

If this is what you are doing or plan to do, you should be aware that it is direct mail because you need to follow the basic principles of direct mail campaigns—time-tested and proven techniques for achieving an acceptable response rate.

The approach is entirely different from that you use in *active* farming, where your objective is to become personally involved in the life of the community.

For active farming you need to make yourself known through a series of folksy or friendly, service-minded communications.

Junk Mail

My research indicates that the vast majority of today's farmers are doing some version of direct mail and failing to get sufficient response to make it worthwhile to continue. Much of this mail is sporadic—useless junk mail. It is giving farming a bad name, both from the recipient's viewpoint and from the farmer's viewpoint.

What is junk mail? The answer lies in the eye of the beholder. If the receiver views the mail as a useless nuisance, it is considered junk.

The recipient of an article on how to fight your tax assessment, for example, or what the new sewer system cost projection is would not feel he or she was receiving junk mail. If homeowners were planning to sell their house, they would not feel an offer of a free market analysis was junk mail; neighbors who considered themselves permanent residents of the town in which they were born would.

To be effective, a mailing must be suited to its objective. If the objective is for the agent to be perceived as the neighborhood real estate specialist, every mailing must reflect that objective.

In any case, it must follow the time-honored principles of direct mail. A strong direct mail campaign should evoke a response of no less than 1 percent, according to direct mail experts. Mail 300 pieces and you should acquire at least three responses. That may not seem like much, but if you were able to turn one of those responses into a listing or a sale in your farm, your mailing would be a success.

For direct mail, following the time-honored principles of the direct mail industry, you need the traditional mail-out package consisting of the following:

1. A sales letter containing an offer they can't refuse, typically about four pages long, but possibly eight to ten pages long (as long as is needed to tell your story)
2. An envelope in which the letter is inserted, folded so that the headline (yes, headline) faces the sealed side so that it is the first thing the recipient spots
3. A response card that is easy to complete and states your offer clearly
4. A brochure, bulletin or additional insert that describes the offer as temptingly as possible (a testimonial can be used)
5. A free gift, or, an offer of a free gift, a prize or a premium . . . a "sweetener" of some kind

If a direct mail campaign does not invoke a response of 1 to 3 percent, the reason may be either that your offer is too weak or it is not well presented. You may not really have written a *sales* letter.

On the other hand, an active farming campaign (notice the word *campaign*—no hit-or-miss mailings, please) with telephone or personal follow-up or both can result in a 15 or 20 percent response. This will make you rich. Tired, maybe, but rich.

Tom Schiffer of Albuquerque, owner of Schiffer/Sinclair, a Gallery of Homes affiliate, calls himself a "born farmer." Here is a man who came out of a retail sales background with a lot of experience in marketing and applied his marketing know-how to a new business. Last time we checked, he was running almost 300 percent ahead of his nearest competitor in his market area. A big believer in postcards, Schiffer keeps the cards flowing like honey. I myself prefer letters, but a lot depends on the message.

The Gooder Group has a new postcard prospecting program called "Newscards." Dan Richards, president of the Gooder Group, asks: "What looks like a postcard, works like a newsletter, and can keep agent farming costs low?" Since these are available in both double-card and triple-card formats, there is room for a significant message.

One agent source of information valuable to your farm prospects is "Fax-on-Demand," a new member service of the National Association of REALTORS®, initiated by its REALTOR® Library, which provides access to public-policy issue summaries, news releases to the media and brief updates on current topics. Using a touch-tone telephone you can call anytime and select the information you want from a menu of available options. When you have made your selection, you key in your fax number. Within moments, the information requested will come across your fax machine. The service, not available to the general public, is free to members of the National Association of REALTORS®. It would be a good policy never to send out a mailing that did not have a valuable tidbit of information included someplace.

Whatever farming tool you use, Tom Schiffer's advice is to construct a schedule and stick to it like glue. A consistent program like Schiffer's over a period of time will bring market dominance. Many agents never accomplish this result because they send an occasional card or write a friendly letter every once in a while with no response trigger and with only a feeble follow-up effort or none. Figure 5.1 shows an example of a year-long schedule of biweekly mailings.

The difference between the direct mail approach and the personal approach is demonstrated clearly in two books on farming (see "Resources," Appendix A). One is called *Successful Farming—By Mail,* written by Steve Kennedy. This book is jammed with information about how to do direct mail professionally, how to write a sales letter and all about the U.S. Postal Service. It is a great book for the passive farmer.

The other recommended book is called *Real Estate Farming: Campaign for $uccess,* by P.J. Thompson. The best feature of this book is its letter-writing campaign. The book provides a series of sample letters to send out monthly in your farm—holiday letters, friendly letters, service-oriented letters and letters for every occasion. To produce results, these letters are intended to be followed up. They do not have the basic structure of a letter intended for direct mail only: no hook, no premium, no offer and no appeal to fear, greed, guilt or exclusivity. They are just nice, friendly "getting-to-know-you letters." Taken together, they form a wonderful basis for a lifetime community friendship. Each letter has a theme and each opens up the imagination to devise other themes. This is a great book for the active farmer.

FIGURE 5.1   Sample Direct Mail Schedule

418 Third Street, SW • Taylorsville, NC 28681 • 1/800-234-1481

Paul Christian's
GHOST ᐁᐁ
WRITERS   *Practical hints for scheduling a direct mail program*

Wednesday - 14 Day Mailing Cycle

January	1 [2] 3 4 5 6 7 8 9 10 11 12 13 14 15 [16] 17 18 19 20 21 22 23 24 25 26 27 28 29 [30] 31
February	1 2 3 4 5 6 7 8 9 10 11 12 [13] 14 15 16 17 18 19 20 21 22 23 24 25 26 [27] 28
March	1 2 3 4 5 6 7 8 9 10 11 12 [13] 14 15 16 17 18 19 20 21 22 23 24 25 26 [27] 28 29 30 31
April	1 2 3 4 5 6 7 8 9 [10] 11 12 13 14 15 16 17 18 19 20 21 22 23 [24] 25 26 27 28 29 30
May	1 2 3 4 5 6 7 [8] 9 10 11 12 13 14 15 16 17 18 19 20 21 [22] 23 24 25 26 27 28 29 30 31
June	1 2 3 4 [5] 6 7 8 9 10 11 12 13 14 15 16 17 18 [19] 20 21 22 23 24 25 26 27 28 29 30
July	1 2 [3] 4 5 6 7 8 9 10 11 12 13 14 15 16 [17] 18 19 20 21 22 23 24 25 26 27 28 29 30 [31]
August	1 2 3 4 5 6 7 8 9 10 11 12 13 [14] 15 16 17 18 19 20 21 22 23 24 25 26 27 [28] 29 30 31
September	1 2 3 4 5 6 7 8 9 10 [11] 12 13 14 15 16 17 18 19 20 21 22 23 24 [25] 26 27 28 29 30
October	1 2 3 4 5 6 7 8 [9] 10 11 12 13 14 15 16 17 18 19 20 21 22 [23] 24 25 26 27 28 29 30 31
November	1 2 3 4 5 [6] 7 8 9 10 11 12 13 14 15 16 17 18 19 [20] 21 22 23 24 25 26 27 28 29 30
December	1 2 3 [4] 5 6 7 8 9 10 11 12 13 14 15 16 17 [18] 19 20 21 22 23 24 25 26 27 28 29 30 31

Computer farming programs, such as Smart Agent, also are available to generate letters, labels and envelopes, and to keep farm records at the flick of a switch.

Smart Agent separates functions into passive and active farming so that you can use it for either direct mail only or for personal farming with follow-up (see "Resources," Appendix A).

You need to make an early decision about which way you plan to go. The vast majority of real estate agents follow the passive-farming path. In surveys I conducted across the country, with rare exceptions, only a small percentage of the sales associates in real estate offices were *actively* farming.

Active farmers, however, dominated their market areas. In one 20-agent office, a successful active farmer accounted for one-half of the dollar volume of a busy office. One new farmer accounted for a $3 million volume in her second year. Her comment was, "I'm a believer!"

One farmer in the Washington, D.C., area represented 99 percent of the listings in a farm with 4,000 people!

On the other hand, an occasional direct mail whiz has ground out 50,000 to 60,000 pieces of mail per month to become one of the top producers in the country.

It is not necessary to go it alone in choosing direct mail. A number of firms will handle the whole mailing for you. Big real estate firms sometimes provide this service to their sales associates.

Some commercial mailing companies also send out packages of assorted advertisements in one envelope to specified ZIP codes. They may offer an exclusive to each type of business and only include one real estate company per package. Val-Pak is one of these direct-marketing systems. They mail coupons that offer everything from one dollar off any large pizza to a certificate entitling you to a free investment analysis. Some, like Money Mailer, are franchises, with each office independently owned and operated. Others like Trimark are purely local. One, advertising itself as the "Largest Direct Mail Company in the Country," is called ADVO, Inc., and claims it can deliver your message into your customer's mailbox in an area as small as a ZIP code area or as large as an area with 47 million homes. The main office is located in Hartford, Connecticut.

If you plan to send personalized letters, they too can be created far in advance. Since you know the exact date on which the next letters will be sent, simply date them ahead, then take them to the post office on that date. Be sure you allow enough time for them to arrive at their destination on the appointed day. Test-mail your post office to see how long deliveries take.

When appealing to either the "FSBO" or the "expired" listing owners, work on a three- to five-day schedule. Remember these special groups will act like greased lightning once they decide to list their homes. You can't afford to hang around. Try mailing to these groups every Tuesday and Friday to maximize your chances and the use of your time.

Learn about "niche" marketing, the art of marketing yourself to a narrow, select group of prospects sharing common interests, such as military relocations, empty nesters and residential investors. Plan your campaign carefully. Real estate marketing specialist Dave Beson observes in a Paul Christian publication that top producers share a common trait. They take a long view and plan their activities at least a year in advance, including a budget for promotional expenses.

Top producers foresee the results they will achieve long before they even begin a promotion, aware of that old axiom "for every action there is an equal and opposite reaction." By planning ahead and acting on the plan, the results they achieve are automatic. The most significant difference between winners and losers (besides their earnings), says Paul Christian, is their ability to act on their plans. Above all else, *promote yourself*.

Elements of a Good Letter

Letterheads

What about letterheads? Most are too busy and distracting. Make up your own letterhead, put your own name and perhaps a small picture of yourself way over on the left side. If you need the company name on the letter, place it at the bottom in small type.

Salutation

The salutation sometimes causes headaches. Do you want a general salutation, such as Dear Neighbor or Dear Homeowner, or will a qualified salutation, such as Dear Fellow Homeowners, sound more personal and connected to you? What about Ms. for a title? Dear Mr. and Ms.? Gentlemen? Think of the implications.

Date

Should you date the letter? If you are using bulk mail this is pretty dangerous. In fact, it is better to avoid exact dates on all mailings unless it is essential. Spring, 1999, is better than an April 3 letter that arrives June 10. When using limited-time offers, say "this month," "within the next thirty days" or "this summer." Be as general as you can be.

Opener

It is hard to exaggerate the importance of the opener, which is used to "set the hook," as Steve Kennedy says. A whole series of familiar openers exists. Try collecting some of your "junk mail" and see what kinds of openers keep you reading. Are you turned on by "If you are a local lot owner . . ." or "as a homeowner in our community . . ." or does a question get to you? How about this one?

> Breathes there a man with soul so dead
> Who never to himself has said:
> "I wonder what my house is worth?"

Storytelling

Are you attracted to people who tell a story: "Last week I was talking to my neighbor on Hickory Lane and he asked . . ."

Invitation

What about issuing an invitation? "You are cordially invited to the drawing of the free raffle tickets you received in the past month's letter for a Thanksgiving turkey . . . for a spring azalea . . . to a special open house held for neighbors of Mr. and Mrs. David Burns."

Transitions

Transitions are necessary so that the trip from one paragraph to the other is not so bumpy. Your challenge is to divert the reader from the attention phase to the desire phase. The advertising world calls these transitions copy turners: "that's why, you, too, can . . ." or "here's your chance to . . ." or just plain "however."

Main Body

The main body of the letter needs skillful guidance. First of all do not be afraid of length. It is well proven that long, long letters sell. In fact, I receive a promotional piece for an investment newsletter that discusses the investment market—leading smoothly from one discovery to another—and I find myself hanging on to the usually bitter end.

KISS still means (southern version) keep it simple, Sugar. Use the present tense and use specifics instead of generalities. Avoid slogans, jargon and boasting. Employ emotion, not intellect. Connect with words and phrases and use bullets or numbers to set something important aside and call attention to it. One-sentence paragraphs will keep readers reading or using them as subheads for dense copy will sustain flagging interest.

People read letters that look good and scan smoothly. Wide margins, well-indented paragraphs, spread-out copy, set asides and insets, ragged-right margins, underlining and capitalization of important thoughts all are devices to hold attention.

Write "more" at the bottom of pages and scrawl handwritten notes in margins or underline in pen. Add a penned exclamation point. *Keep it interesting.*

Closes

Closes depend on your objective. What do you want readers to do? Okay, then tell them so. Ask for immediate action. Mention your limited time offer—"just ten more days until your right to fight your tax assessment expires. . . . Get your brochure today," limited quantity offers, "these investment booklets may not last out the week at the rate they are being gobbled up, so call for yours today. Limited quantity."

Create urgency. Use hurry-up phrases or repeat the benefit. Use a strong close.

The end is near, but the complimentary close never lends a satisfactory solution. Sincerely, how is that for originality? Sincerely yours, there's a dandy. Cordially or yours truly—too formal. Do not use anything corny, even if you are tempted. Skip flowery phrases like "Yours in anticipation of many years of devoted service." It is better just to make do with "Sincerely" and let it go at that. Sign it clearly, for people are suspicious of a person whose signature is one long squiggle—what's this person trying to hide?

Title

Title? Think up a good one if you can. The one I like best is Certified Residential Specialist, but then, not everyone is entitled to use it. Neighborhood Real Estate Specialist might work. Maybe you will decide that you *do not* need title, but what you *do* need is a P.S. This is the best-read item in the letter. Put something important in it. Express urgency, exclusivity, benefits, special offers, bonus gifts or something compelling.

P.S.

Your P.S. can be handwritten (in color is great, blue or red), but I wouldn't pay for an extra color just to have your P.S. stand out. Or maybe I would if it said something vital, for instance, "Will you marry me?"

Now that you have this letter written and printed, you are going to fold it with the copy facing out toward the sealed side of the envelope, showing the headline when the reader opens it.

A good prospect management program like Smart Agent or Real Estate Agent will address it for you, to the individual or to the Doe Family or Current Resident, in case there is some indication there has been a change of residency or to the Smith Household, if the composition of this family is somewhat baffling. In rural areas just plain "Rural Boxholder" will save you money and time. You can use envelopes or address labels attached to the mailer, whichever you like.

Ghostwriters

Are you saying to yourself, "No way, I'm a real estate salesperson, not a writer"? Well if you just cannot manage any of this, call up Paul Christian Communications and buy a series of five camera-ready farming letters or ask the company to edit your letters or customize a series of 12 monthly letters for you.

If you do not use Ghost Writer to edit your material, be sure to *have everything you send out edited* by a person whose language skills are superb. If you do not have a friend, family member or associate who can perform these tasks for you, have the work ghostwritten. Maintaining a degree of humanness and simplicity does not mean producing letters full of poor grammar, misspellings, typos and incorrect information. Very slick, professionally done letters and newsletters usually are not so effective as personally prepared but well-done ones, but they are better than the amateur production that smacks of carelessness or ignorance.

Principles of Direct Mail Letters

Before we leave direct mail letters, let me give you one example of how applying the basic principles of direct mail can change a letter (Figures 5.2 and 5.3). First we have a letter written to introduce two sales associates to an area in which they plan to conduct active farming as a team. One is an old hand, the other a newcomer. They are using a service approach, communicating some vital information out into the farm, while introducing themselves and attempting to get business.

In Figure 5.3 is a revision of the letter in accordance with the principles of direct mail expertise as expounded by Bob Stone in his book, *Successful Direct Mail Methods.*

Response Marketing

Direct Mail Campaigns That Work

What can you do to make your campaign work? First of all, you need a planned, sustained campaign.

FIGURE 5.2 Original Letter

DEAR LOT OWNER:

My name is Joyce Caughman and I live on Hickory Lane in Loch Haven. I am an Associate Broker and a Certified Residential Specialist with ABC, REALTORS®.

In the course of the sale of a lot on North Carolina Avenue to a young customer of mine, I became aware of the expenses of the lot owner since the county began installation of sewers.

Jennie Jones, a sales associate I work with in the local ABC office, had a similar experience in the sale of some lots in Ponder Cover. She realized the desirability of these lots to builders who wish to erect new homes, but had no appreciation of the complications sewer has added to lot sales until her client went through it.

Because there has been so much confusion regarding the effect on lot owners of sewer installation on the Mayo peninsula, we decided to make the attached information available to you.

Naturally, the addition of sewers will increase the desirability of your property. You may wish to hold it for future use or you may be thinking of selling soon to take advantage of the wonderful appreciation we in the water communities have realized.

Actually, you can see from the attached information that you may well be able to sell before the sewer assessment becomes due. Jennie and I and some of the other sales associates in our office have been receiving inquiries from both sellers and buyers and would like the opportunity to bring them together.

If you're interested, please call Joyce Caughman at 261-7665 (Washington line) or Jennie Jones at 266-5505 (local line). For a market evaluation or an investment property analysis, just drop the enclosed card in the mail and one of us will be glad to provide this information free of cost.

Yours sincerely,

ABC, REALTORS®.

FIGURE 5.3   Revised Letter

Headline Get attention Announce benefit	**YOUR LOT MAY BE WORTH TWICE WHAT YOU ARE THINKING . . .** The addition of sewers in our community will greatly increase the desirability of your lot.
Enlarge on benefit	Contrary to common belief in the neighborhood even if you do not now have a building permit, <u>if your lot perks</u> you can get a permit now and build now. You can sell the lot and the new owner can build NOW with septic and hookup to sewer when available.
Relay specifics	Because there has been so much confusion regarding the effect on lot owners of sewer installation on the Mayo peninsula, we have decided to make the attached information available to you. Please read it carefully.
Prove value with experience	My name is Joyce Caughman, and I live on Hickory Lane in Loch Haven. I am an Associate Broker and a Certified Residential Specialist with ABC, REALTORS®. In the course of the sale of a lot on North Carolina Avenue to a young customer of mine, I became aware of the expenses of the lot owner since sewer construction was begun. Jennie Jones, a sales associate I work with in the local office of ABC had a similar experience in the sale of some lots in Ponder Cove. She realized the desirability of these lots to builders who wish to erect new homes, but had no appreciation of the complications for the lot owner until her client went through it.
Explain loss	While you may wish to hold on for future use, if you are thinking of selling to take advantage of the wonderful appreciation we in water communities have experienced, you may be well advised to move quickly to sell before the sewer assessment becomes due.
Benefits summary	We have been receiving inquiries from both sellers and buyers and would like the opportunity to bring them together.
Incite action	An immediate market evaluation or investment-property analysis can give you the basis to make a decision that could put a considerable sum of money in your pocket. You should move while the season for septic tests is here. Interested? Please call Joyce Caughman, 261-7665 (Washington line) or Jennie Jones, 266-7665 (local line). Or just drop the enclosed card in the mailbox and one of us will be glad to provide this information to you free of any cost or obligation.

How to make it work? Do response marketing.

1. Use a *premium* (free gift or offer of one, a prize or "sweetener") Golden rule for a sweetener: Offer something of value only to the qualified prospect. A free dinner will bring you lots of prospects not in the market for your product.
2. Include a brochure or information bulletin describing the offer as temptingly as possible.
3. Include a response card, one easy to complete that clearly states the offer.

There are two kinds of offers: service offers and premium offers.

Service Offers

These are designed to convince an active prospect to ask for an appointment such as a general list of services available from Town and Country Realty, ERA's free market analysis certificate, Long and Foster's offer to do an equity evaluation, the Gooder Group's new "Agency: Straight Answers About an Agent's Role" brochure, "Home of Your Dreams" brochure by Coldwell Banker or "How To Sell Your Home for Top Dollar" by B.F. Saul.

Premium Offers

These include educational literature (knowledge as service, very popular today), such as the Gooder Group series of brochures on a range of useful topics. Paul Christian Communications also has an array of messages for various occasions. You can compile your own bulletins of local information on tax breaks, government services and specialized information of interest to specific target groups such as senior citizens, gardeners, educators and so on. The advantage of premium offers is a greater response. You find active prospects with immediate needs and future prospects who bring tomorrow's business. Domino's Pizza once sent me a mailing that contained a refrigerator magnet, which has resulted in a continuous stream of business for them ever since. I still have the house magnet of a friendly competitor, ten years later.

Premium offers don't repel people who fear being "bugged" by a salesperson. No appointment is solicited. In addition, receiving a free gift is a powerful attraction. People don't feel "taken" if they get something out of the exchange.

Simple guides for buyers, sellers and investors, which explain the workings of the industry, have proved to be dynamite real estate premiums. It is amazing how confusing the public finds real estate. Chapter 8 features a variety of promotion tools to use in mailings.

Reply Card Offer

It is hard to exaggerate the importance of a reply card offer that contains an illustration of the premium or a clear description of the service offered. Headlines and copy that *asks for response or action* from your target group is vital. If there is no postpaid response card, studies show there is no response in 50 percent of cases.

Commercial Mailings

Mailing pieces are available that use these principles: have offers targeted to qualified prospects, headers and copy that asks for action. See "Resources" in Appendix A. Val-Pak, Money Mailer and ADVO are among these. ADVO's advertising advice, *penetrate your market area,* could hardly be improved upon. The question of costs, particularly of cost per response, is discussed in Chapter 8. Something for real estate salespeople never to forget is that in real estate time is money. Depending on your own productivity, it might be less expensive to go the commercial route.

Fliers

Noel G. Hinde, director of advertising and public relations for TRI, REALTORS®, calls fliers "the fast-food-for-thought that is most effective in marketing the vast majority of single-family homes." She describes the typical flier as "photocopied or quick-printed in black ink on one side of a standard 8½" × 11" sheet of paper and mailed, hand-delivered or placed at strategically located pickup points."

Because fliers can create a strong first impression, are designed to elicit a speedy response and are easy to produce, they are the ideal vehicle. The secret to effective use of fliers is directing them to the "ideal target audience" for the house, which means it is necessary to analyze carefully exactly who might want and need this type of property and get the flier to that person, be he or she a renter, a developer, a real estate salesperson, an investor or whomever. Take advantage of local board of REALTORS® computer services that offer a search file listing characteristics of residential property being sought by other salespeople in the various member offices. You then could request a list of these salespeople and send them fliers of your listings that correspond.

Format Your Flier

Hinde suggests dividing your page into three sections: one for an attention-getting headline or grabber, the next for the message and the last for identification. You can divide the page horizontally, vertically or diagonally. She recommends a "neat uncluttered layout, a catching headline and a well-selected photo or graphic to give your flier a professional flair."

If you have a computer and one of the graphic programs such as Print Shop or Print Magic, you can turn out stunning fliers for your farm. (See the flier to FSBOs in "Copy It," Appendix C, created with Print Shop plus a word-processing program.

Other Direct Mail

Cards

Many of the large regional companies and the franchises send out a series of cards in their market areas: just listed, just sold in one day, houses needed, how much is your home worth, we helped your neighbor and others. Realty World, Century 21 and ERA provide their agents with a whole catalog of franchise materials from which to choose. Personal marketing is now so popular that most have made space for the agent's photograph on the company promotional material. Agents and branch managers alike seem to prefer these. Some companies encourage agents to send out cards. If the agents do not take advantage of the opportunity, then often the branch will send them out with the manager's name on them. This is especially true of "houses sold" cards. Usually, the agents pay for the cards, if not for the postage as well, or at least part of it. Some companies pay all postage for promotions.

Many real estate marketing firms sell very attractive and often witty real estate promotional cards; Carole Kelby and Harrison Publishing Co. offer some of the best. The Harrison cards are remarkably inventive, with one for every occasion known to real estate. I like "I'm a Residential Specialist," showing a doctor with a house. This is a good card for a real pro who is not yet a Certified Residential Specialist and can't use the CRS promotional materials. How is this for a neat "sold" card—"It seems like magic," showing a magician on the cover; then, inside, "But it is just a good real estate agent at work. Everything we touch turns to 'sold'." (By the way, these cards are in color.)

You can create cards on your computer, using continuous-card forms and a graphics program like Print Shop. Besides sending out holiday greeting cards in your farm, you can design cards and send them unsigned, to homeowners to use themselves. This is especially good for Mother's Day and Father's Day cards, and all kinds of anniversary cards. Providing the owner whose home you have just sold with "Moved to . . . " cards is an excellent settlement gift.

Kall Publication publishes a catalog chock-full of what it calls "bright ideas in residential farming" (featuring a big lightbulb on the cover). They offer a series of circulars for you to use as fliers or from which to create custom brochures. They also sell "Kall cards," and I must say that you need a certain sense of humor to enjoy these. I showed them to my husband (he has a dry sense of humor) and he thought they were amusing.

For example, one of them says: "Telling the good guys from the bad guys isn't always this easy," over a picture of guys in black hats and guys in white hats. Then, it goes on to say, "May I explain my services when you're ready to buy or sell real estate?" These cards have room on the front to personalize them with your picture.

I am thoroughly convinced that a good letter-writing campaign is the best way to break into an area. Alternating with cards or using cards on certain occasions might be good, but there is nothing like a good letter for getting your message across. A *good* letter.

If there is one thing I have learned in training thousands of salespeople, however, it is that you must work with your own strengths. If writing letters is not your cup of tea and you are spectacular on the telephone, concentrate on your area of strength. To specialize in telemarketing, buy Steve Kennedy's book, *Successful Farming—by Phone,* and go to it.

Or maybe you should buy a newsletter to distribute in your farm. For more information, see Chapter 7.

Farming by Mail:
Active Farming,
the Personal Touch

Proactive or Reactive?

Dan Richard of the Gooder Group compares passive real estate farmers with gardeners and active farmers with real farmers. Gardeners plant an annual crop and then wonder why it doesn't come up the following year. Farmers mean business. They plan, they plant, they fertilize, they cultivate and they never fail to harvest.

Letters for Real Farmers

The contrast between the phantom farmer who is never glimpsed by the majority of the readers and the serious farmer who hopes to become their bosom buddy is nowhere better illustrated than in the four starter letters advocated by Danielle Kennedy, the darling of the real estate lecture circuit and a experienced, successful salesperson (Figure 6.1).

If I had written the first letter in Figure 6.1, I would have added a few words about my knowledge and training, such as: "XYZ Realty has

FIGURE 6.1   Four Sizzling Starter Letters

Letter Number One

Good Morning—

Guess who's gone into real estate? That's right—I'm proud to
say, "I have!"

For a long time I've had a deep concern and interest in our
community. I've lived here _____ years, and during that time
I've (describe your community service, clubs joined and so on).

I know the properties here, and I have a deep pride of
ownership in our home.

Now I want to take these qualities into the active market. I
want to ask you for your trust and confidence in important real
estate matters.

Do you feel I'm worth the risk?

I hope so, because I've dedicated myself to marketing our
wonderful community to people like yourself who have my love
and respect.

Sincerely,

Source: *Breakaway,* by Danielle Kennedy, © by Tom Hopkins Champion Unlimited. Reprinted with permission.

gone to a lot of trouble to give me the information and training I need to make you proud of me."

I say this because if you announce right off the bat that you are a newcomer, you are going to have to overcome a certain reluctance people have about entrusting their lifetime savings to you. On the other hand, if you live right in this neighborhood, you can't keep your newness from being public knowledge, so you might as well deal with it. The best approach is to emphasize your training and the fact that you are willing to devote all your time to helping them, which busier agents cannot do.

Kennedy comments about letter number three, "Bear in mind, when sending out several hundred letters saying 'I'm reliable,' that you have made quite a statement about yourself.

"Get yourself organized FAST because you'll have response from that large mailing—maybe at first some of these people will only be testing

FIGURE 6.1 (Continued)

Letter Number Two

Hi Friend—

Yes, I want to call you friend, and I hope you will consider me one. Everyone needs a friend in real estate—someone you can trust with such important matters as your security and your investments.

Would you place that kind of trust and confidence in me?

You may ask, "Why should I?"

Here are a few reasons:

1. I am honest. I don't shade the truth. My word is good.
2. I am reliable. If I tell a client I'll do something, wild horses won't stop me from doing it.
3. I have time for you. Most people today are "too busy." I'm never too busy for you!
4. I'm a licensed real estate agent. This means I passed a state licensing examination that required much dedicated study.
5. I am constantly taking courses on all facets of real estate: appraisal, negotiation, financing and so on. I'm taking these courses for you—to be a better me for you.
6. I live here and have pride in and concern for our community.
7. I have dedicated myself to serving in (name the service organizations you belong to and are active in).
8. I am proud to be associated with Go-Get-Um Realty, which many people believe is the finest real estate organization in the area.
9. If you give me the chance, I promise that I'll prove that I care, and that I'm highly capable of serving your best interests.

Thank you for taking the time to read this.

Sincerely,

Tillie Newcomer

FIGURE 6.1 **Four Sizzling Starter Letters** (Continued)

Letter Number Three

```
Consider me a new friend!

How do you do?

I'm Danny Kennedy. My home is just around the bend from you on
Gridiron Drive, and I'm also a real estate counselor. Since
your neighborhood and mine is my favorite, I'm delighted to be
its specialist for (XYZ Realty).

This means that I know all the developments on real estate
listings, sales, and new neighbors here. I'm well posted on our
entire area's cultural activities, tax proposals, and school
bond issues. I also keep current on specialty shopping that's
open now or due to open soon, and on other community services
and events—from attorneys through handymen and physicians to
zoo admission hours. Please call me if you have a question you
want answered.

You might even get a good recipe or two from me now and then.
I'll be distributing scratch pads soon for your convenience.
Please consider me a friend and community professional who is
deeply committed to keeping our neighborhood one to be proud of.

Sincerely,
```

you." In other words, don't make any promises you don't plan to keep, if you want to pass that test.

Letter number four is an introductory letter or follow-up letter to be sent 60 days after letter number three is sent to your farm. Notice how Kennedy is not afraid to repeat her major themes; people have short memories.

The tone of all these letters is very personal and relaxed. It is certainly in tune with the viewpoint of Jacqui Gordon, one of the instructors in our company's initial training program, who advised a group of newcomers: "Give the impression to each family in your farm that you are working with them and them alone." Not every salesperson will be comfortable with this cozy formula, but for a warm, outgoing personality it is tailor-made and extremely effective.

For a more reserved personality, however, the four examples of introductory letters by Alan Jacobson and Jack Gale in their book, *Cultivating Your Listing Farm,* might be a better fit.

These letters are a happy medium between the impersonality of passive farmers and the intimacy of certain active farmers.

FIGURE 6.1   Four Sizzling Starter Letters (Continued)

Letter Number Four

Hi Neighbors—

Can we be friends?

A good REALTOR® who believes in the town he lives in and serves should also be considered a friend. So please think of me that way.

I am your hometown representative for the area served by Birch Street Elementary School, and I keep totally current on all properties marketed in the entire Greenpretty Valley.

I know the streets, schools, shops and churches. If you need hometown advice, you may lose out if you don't talk to me. Keeping current with our local scene is my work and what I love. Just ask my broker. I spend many hours studying and working to be a better me—for you.

Cordially

P.S. Watch for my handy notepads!

When the mailing is handled entirely by the firm, it is difficult to inject any degree of personal warmth into the letter.

The difference between a *company*-oriented introductory letter and an introductory letter oriented toward an individual agent is discussed in the *Real Estate 'Insider' Newsletter*.

In a recent issue, the editor compared two letters he had received, one from a company and one from an individual. He noted that both these letters can work well. The first letter from the sales associate, however, had two advantages over the second letter from the company. The two advantages he cited were that the first letter was personally signed and that the agent's card with both his office and his home number was enclosed. These, the editor said, "reinforce the associate's concern. The potential client will think to himself or herself, 'That salesperson must really be concerned, otherwise he [or she] would not hand out his [or her] home number.'"

The company letter spelled out the advantage of listing with the company because of its many services. The salesperson's letter explained what that individual could do to help the seller and presented seven questions that the salesperson could answer for the homeowner:

1. What is my home actually worth on the market?
2. How much equity do I have in my home that I might use?
3. Can I use this equity to obtain my goal to buy a summer home, a boat, go on vacation to that exotic land, repair the house, go into business, etc.?
4. Do I have sufficient home insurance in today's home values?
5. How can I buy a new home, sell the one I'm living in and produce the down payment if I have to wait to close on my home?
6. I want to relocate; where can I get advice?
7. And most important—I want to sell my house and need professional advice. What do I do?

One of the major difficulties encountered when a real estate firm controls the whole farming function, as some do, is that lack of personal touch. The company often thinks in terms of its own services rather than the client's needs. This view turns the farming effort into direct mail advertising—passive farming. Active farming—where the level of commitment the firm shows contains a strong element of agent involvement—is much more effective.

Even though letters may be couched in personal language, they need not be light-headed. My own approach to mailing tends to lean heavily—in today's information society—on informative articles on useful subjects in which the audience has shown an interest. Find out their interest either by employing questionnaires or by enclosing return cards to determine response.

I would use information bulletins as enclosures or premiums, and would keep the cover letter as personal (and as emotional as contrasted with intellectual) as is compatible with the sender's personality.

I believe strongly in empathy, in the ability to see from the other person's point of view. If you can do that, you always will know what to say. Different audiences—engineers versus watermen, sophisticates versus country people—require different approaches, subject matter and language. Tune in. Put yourself in their shoes and write to yourself.

Remember that a lot of the "junk" mail sent by your competitors goes right into the wastebasket because:

1. It is not unique. (Would you like a free market evaluation? Two to three received per week in some areas.)
2. It is not valuable to the recipient. (Our company is the greatest!)
3. It is too slick or too amateurish.
4. It is sporadic. (What? Yet another real estate agent? Never heard of this one.)

The easy approach is to mail a professionally prepared card, brochure or newsletter to your entire farm. The problem is that, according to David Stipps and Robert Underwood in *The Farming Manual,* "national statistics indicate that only 1 percent of such material is actually read and acted upon." "Acted upon" is the ruling phrase here. One to three percent may respond. But the first ingredient of closing is trust. Has prior trust been built? No, that is why a long campaign is necessary and why active farming generates 20 percent response, instead of 3 percent tops for direct mail. Kennedy's letters are masterpieces of trust building.

Plan a Two-Year Letter-Writing Campaign

Instead of producing the usual newsletter, try developing a two-year campaign following these suggestions:

- Compose three or four introductory letters that gradually lead from the personal to the professional.
- Start slowly and build up toward your objective of becoming perceived as the *neighborhood specialist.*
- Begin with your objective, then decide your theme and how to carry it out, and choose your gift or enclosure.
- As time goes on, give less and less attention to the personal and more and more attention to the professional.
- Vary the length of the letters. Sometimes write short snappy notes; at other times write long letters (six to eight pages) of interesting, carefully written information that leads from one revelation to another on a topic that, according to a previously sent questionnaire, is of vital interest to your neighbors (Save the Bay? Fight Your Tax Assessment! Local Tax Breaks for Senior Citizens). Slip in a card now and then.

In laying out a two-year plan, start with a carefully thought-out objective.

Year-One Letter Campaign

1. Objective: Introduce myself as a neighbor in the real estate business who has the welfare of the neighbors in mind.

Theme	Method	Enclosure
Holiday message: Happy New Year, spring fever, Thanksgiving, be my valentine—whatever fits the season	Use the season to express a desire to serve the community.	Community events calendar, forget-me-not seeds, sheet of heart stickers

2. Objective: Reintroduce myself as a neighbor in the real estate business and tell how I work.

Theme	Method	Enclosure
Local news	Explain how I work to keep abreast of local developments that affect their property values.	Community map, my picture, telephone numbers

3. Objective: Emphasize that while I am a real estate agent, I am first and foremost a friend. I am a *knowledgeable* friend, an asset everyone needs and I am available for real estate counseling in order to get them in the habit of coming to *me* when they have questions.

Theme	Method	Enclosure
Real estate news, economic trends	Use articles from the business section that forecast interest rates.	Mortgage rate card (plastic or cardboard)

4. Objective: Make it clear that I am a friend of the neighborhood, which is why I have chosen to work with a company that cares about the community as I do.

Theme	Method	Enclosure
Community service, my company's involvement and my own	Clippings or information to show service	Company brochure

5. Objective: Show that REALTORS® are really doing something for their customers and clients.

Theme	Method	Enclosure
What can you do for me (from their viewpoint)?	List services a real estate specialist can render (six frequent needs).	Home insurance needs brochure, relocation flier, blank competitive market analysis form

6. Objective: Find out enough about my neighbors' beliefs and needs to be able to reach and serve them. Raise the level of response to mailings.

Theme	*Method*	*Enclosure*
Getting to know you	Develop a question-naire that is fun and revealing.	Questionnaire return card

7. Objective: Prove that I give as well as I receive. Meet people face-to-face.

Theme	*Method*	*Enclosure*
Thanksgiving or Easter	Conduct a free raffle of a turkey or azalea, depending on the season.	Raffle tickets and flier

8. Objective: Ask for business. Identify people who are thinking of making a move of some type.

Theme	*Method*	*Enclosure*
Moving up	Explain the ramifica-tions of this maneu-ver carefully; e.g., "people have been asking . . .," "Much as your neighbors would hate to see you leave town . . ."	Coupon for a buyer's and seller's guide. Do *not* enclose guides!

9. Objective: Get listings and sales by making an appointment to conduct a competitive market analysis or a buyer qualification.

Theme	*Method*	*Enclosure*
Your house may be worth more than you think.	Timing. Try to do in January letter. Show neighborhood appreciation.	Sales activity chart showing last year versus this year; computer analysis

10. Objective: Ensure confidence in my professionalism, i.e., knowl-edge and competence.

Theme	*Method*	*Enclosure*
I am an expert; call me for real estate counseling.	Use Kennedy letter number five (Figure 6.2) or "Frequent Questions I Get and the Answers."	Make up a professional-looking booklet, "Questions and Answers."

11. Objective: Make people select me over all my competitors. Increase my percent of market share in my farm.

Theme	Method	Enclosure
I am a success.	Use Kennedy letter number five (Figure 6.2) or copies of any awards or recognition received.	Refrigerator magnet of a house with your name and telephone number on it

12. Objective: Demonstrate that I am service-minded.

Theme	Method	Enclosure
Christmas	Letter to homeowners: "Pretty decorations attract buyers," or "Take security measures, especially if going away."	Security tips, Christmas or Hanukkah cards (unsigned for them to give to someone else)

Danielle Kennedy's fifth letter (Figure 6.2) was designed to be used late during the campaign to demonstrate knowledge, optimism and success. How much later depends on how soon your success comes. Sometimes it takes a long time to get established in a community. Some communities are much friendlier than others. Some are quite standoffish. Then, too, real estate is cyclical. Wait until you have something to crow about. This may not happen until the second year. Some people get lucky during the first year and some feel lucky all the time. Kennedy says that this letter always must reflect confidence and optimism, so if you don't have both, don't send this letter. Also, if you are not comfortable with economic predictions, you may not want to venture into that area. This is a very effective letter if sent out under the right circumstances because it will take you a long way toward achieving your objective of becoming the real estate specialist in your farm.

Kennedy's fifth letter is a good January letter. It's okay to send in December or maybe after April 15. Change copy as market changes. What does it say (below the surface, that is)? Does it say, "This gushy babe is an airhead!" Maybe, to some. Or does it say, "This person understands the whole picture"?

To establish professional credibility, somewhere during the letter-writing campaign you should formulate this type of letter.

With her fifth letter, Kennedy includes a cartoon of an old man with a long, long white beard, entitled: "The man who waited for real estate to come down." This cartoon also could be called "the man who waited for interest rates to come down."

Figure 6.3 includes a form for you to use in planning your second-year letter campaign.

FIGURE 6.2 Letter Number Five

```
Hi!

Am I lucky.  Because this year I had the opportunity to serve
(  ) clients in our hometown. 19__ was a good year for owners
of real estate. The average days on the market for property in
our area was just (  ) days. The financing picture was
flexible. Interest rates were _____ at (  %) as the year
ended . . . that figure must be compared to the rapid
appreciation rate of (  ) percent. As so many astute buyers
demonstrated during the year, a person would be silly to let
the interest rate stand in the way of a sound purchase of real
estate.

The general economic trend was stable according to an article
in the Wall Street Journal dated _____.

Here are some predictions for the coming months: (Quote from
Kiplinger, Board Room Talk, Forbes, etc. Out-of-state, like
most distant prophets, newspapers carry more weight).

Building starts will be _____ the first half of the year
according to _____. A slowdown of new construction, of course,
throws additional buyers into the resale market. "Car sales
will hit _____," states the _____. "Retail sales are expected
to reach _____ and personal incomes will set new highs at
$_____" says the _____.

The outlook is that people will be spending money, and that
means that real estate will continue to be a first priority in
millions of households.

All in all, things look bright. I hope to see you during the
coming year (months). Please consider me a friend. Realtors are
the best kind—we care about your security.

Cordially,
```

Source: *Breakaway,* by Danielle Kennedy, © by Tom Hopkins Champion, Unlimited. Reprinted with permission.

Year-Two Letter Campaign

Your second-year objectives might be to keep up the momentum, do a good job and get more new business.

During the second year, concentrate on trying to provide the right mix of communication; use a combination of techniques, such as a mailer, telephone call and a personal visit. Make it all dovetail easily and naturally. Fulfill monthly objectives. Use letters to arrange follow-up telephone calls and personal visits.

FIGURE 6.3 Year-Two Letter Campaign

Planning Your Second Year of Farming

Month	Objective	Theme	Method	Enclosure
13.				
14.				
15.				
16.				
17.				
18.				
19.				
20.				
21.				
22.				
23.				
24.				

Personal visits are easier to make if you are working on a community project such as collecting for the American Heart Association, acting as den mother for a Cub Scout troop or taking part in beautification work for the garden club. If necessary, invent a project, such as a free raffle for a good cause. Volunteer for the Parent-Teacher Association and conduct a door-to-door survey. Participate in a community watch, distribute stickers.

You also can distribute a variety of general information handouts: stain-remover charts, calorie counters, first-aid pamphlets, tipping tables, garden hints—just tap your creativity.

Think of ways to help people by keeping them informed. Watch the news to discover themes for this purpose. Possible themes could include: investment in real estate (April 15); tax kit (keep good records and save); don't do anything to lose your over-55 tax break; fight your tax assessment; renting versus owning; owning a second home, careful!; make (our town) beautiful; and your home equity is your savings bank.

The advantage of these informational fliers or bulletins is that they are inexpensive to you but valuable to the recipient. Eventually, though, you should plan to spend some money on promotion in your farm. Start with something simple and inexpensive, small and lightweight. As you succeed, plow a certain percent of your yield back into the farm.

Mailouts can be enclosed with your monthly letter or mailed or passed out separately. People love to receive gifts: activity cards; picture postcards; real estate theme postcards; thank-you cards; greeting cards; fliers; invitations; congratulations; recognitions; flash cards (special hot news); charts; promotional items; maps; bookmarks; four-leaf clovers; sheets of holiday stickers containing hearts, shamrocks, holly, turkeys, pumpkins, etc.; sports schedules; entertainment schedules; or six-inch rulers or refrigerator magnets. Use your imagination and ingenuity, but keep your gifts small and light.

7

Farming by Mail: Newsletters

Farmers have three choices of newsletter available to them: do-it-yourself, ready-to-print and preprinted. The decision rests on a number of factors.

The first factor is your audience. If you live in a folksy community that needs the personal touch, then you should produce a very personal newsletter.

If you live on "High-Tech Corridor," crowded with engineers and scientists, then your newsletter should be as informative and as professional-looking as possible.

If you live somewhere in between, use a ready-to-print letter that you can personalize.

The second factor is time. A good newsletter takes a lot of time to produce. Is your time better spent listing and selling houses? Are you busier than the proverbial one-armed paperhanger? If so, putting together your own newsletter is not an efficient use of your time.

A third factor is talent. A good professional-looking newsletter requires a sense of design that is above the capabilities of most real estate agents. You also must possess excellent writing skills. In addition, you must be able to spell perfectly, know proper grammar and be able to type and you must have a fund of knowledge to keep you from making factual errors.

The fourth factor is cost. You want to reach your objective at a realistic cost. When calculating costs, consider the value of time. Measure the cost, as in any investment, in terms of probable return. There is a tremendous difference in cost between a one-page, do-it-yourself newsletter turned out on the office copier and a four-color, four-page national newsletter mailed by a newsletter service so that once you have placed your order there is nothing for you to do but wait for delivery to your farm.

Homemade Newsletters

Homemade newsletters also present three choices to the farmer. One method is to place a piece of legal-sized paper into your typewriter. Type a line across the top, paste a screened picture of yourself in the left-hand corner and use press-type letters to give it a catchy title. Add the company logo, your name and telephone number under the line. You are ready to roll. Divide the rest of the letter into two columns and start typing short paragraphs on a variety of subjects of interest to your audience, inserting catchy headings in between.

Brainstorm the Title

Get together with a few friends and relatives and solicit ideas for a title. Run a contest on your farm, if you are already farming, for a newsletter title, or just ask for suggestions, using a return card in your query.

Here are several ideas proposed in a brainstorming session I recently attended: Talk of the Town, Realty Happenings, Realty Star, Town Trumpeter, Property Pipeline, Real Estate Reporter and Realty Recorder. Using your name in a creative way also was suggested: The Wright Stuff, Joyce's Voice, Tony's Tipoffs, etc.

Now that you have settled the title question, what topics are you going to use?

Content

Recently I received one of those simple newsletters in the mail. It was nicely produced. The picture was clear and pleasant. The title was catchy. The typing was dark and readable. The paragraphs were short and concise. There were no typos, misspellings, grammatical errors or misstatements of fact.

But I searched the letter from top to bottom and could not find a single real estate topic. Religious quotation. Political statement. Recipe. Local news. Planting tips. A variety of snappy items. Real estate? Nothing.

The purpose of your letter is to convince your reader that you are the real estate specialist of the neighborhood.

Every issue, you should make sure that there is an eye-catching headline on some real estate "hot button" appearing on the cover page of your newsletter.

Follow the real estate and business section of your newspaper scouting for ideas. Read *Money Magazine, Forbes* and *The Wall Street Journal* if you can. Keep a folder of items for future use. Be careful not to break any copyright laws; you may have to rewrite or cite the source. Always give credit to the source unless your material is rephrased completely.

It might be a good idea to join the Association of Real Estate Editors. If you do, you will receive a constant stream of press releases on real estate topics to use. If you are a REALTOR®, use Fax-on-Demand.

At a certain time each year, draw up a list of real estate topics you plan to use in each of your monthly newsletters.

Twelve Real Estate Topic Suggestions for Next Year

Following are suggested topics for each month of the upcoming year:

1. How to fight your tax assessment
2. Real estate tax breaks for 19___
3. Home improvements that pay off at resale time . . . and some that do not
4. Investors: Is it the right time to buy or sell?
5. How much homeowner's insurance is the right amount?
6. How do you go about getting your senior-citizen property-tax reduction?
7. Are mortgage rates headed up or down?
8. Is a home-equity loan safe?
9. How can you move up to a better home without ending up with two mortgage payments?
10. After-sale headaches and how to avoid them
11. Who does the real estate agent represent in a transaction?
12. Tax ramifications of owning a second home

Special Features

You can break up your newsletter into regular features that appear in the same space each month. Following are some examples of departmentalizing your newsletter:

Heading	Content
The Passing Parade	Births, graduations, marriages, engagements, reunions, promotions, awards, achievements
Hail and Farewell	People moving in and out of town, going on holidays, etc.
The Bulletin Board	Announcements, upcoming events, garage and yard sales, lost pets, babysitters, items for sale, local services (kids who wash cars, cut lawns, rake leaves and other available services such as sewing and painting)
Crockpot	Recipes and menus
The Fixit Person	Household repairs: how to cut a pane of glass, how to change a washer
Playpen	Kids' news
Q & A	Real estate questions and answers
Meet Your Neighbor	Profiles of local people
Realty Roundup	A box of listings available in your neighborhood

Ask for news items. See if any of your neighbors would like to be in charge of writing a short item on a subject of interest to them, such as wildflowers of the region, local songbirds, sewing tips and so forth, either on a one-time basis or as a regular monthly item. Set a maximum number of words so that you can allot your space.

Questionnaires

Sending out a questionnaire in your farm is a good plan. One authority maintains that real estate questionnaires receive more response from farm mailing than does any other material. They automatically generate responses from people who are interested in real estate and provide you with valuable information about how to slant your newsletter to appeal to your audience.

Simply write a list of proposed topics and ask, "Would you be interested in receiving information on any of the following subjects? If so, just check the ones that interest you and turn the page inside out, seal it with a piece of cellophane tape and drop it in the mail. I will see you receive a brochure that answers your questions." On the outside of the flier, put your return address in the center and a stamp in the right-hand corner. It should have been folded in three sections when you put it in the #10 (business-size) envelope to mail to the owner, so it will be easy for them to reverse the procedure. This method will keep you from having to pick up all the questionnaires. If the whole object was to get you in the house, enclose a free return card telling the prospect to mail it and you will pick up the questionnaire. The card could have a place for their phone number so you can also get some unlisted phone numbers. Then include a P.S. with a small block next to it that says, "Call me for a time and date to pick up the questionnaire."

Be sure that you include an "other" option on the return card so that your audience can include topics you may not have thought of. Hand deliver the brochures in your farm. Use any excuse to meet the people. If no one is home, leave a little note on their door—"Sorry I missed you. Here is the information you requested. Give me a ring at (telephone number) if I can answer any questions."

Brochures and Booklets

You can buy informative booklets and brochures from companies listed in "Resources" (Appendix A), or you can make up your own. A couple of pages of accurate information with some clip art (see Figure 7.1) and good-looking headings should be enough.

Check and Double-Check

After you have completed the newsletter, ask someone you trust to proofread it. A sales associate sent me a newsletter that was on two 14-inch sheets of paper, folded in half, with one page inside the other to form a minimagazine. A saddle stapler was used to join the sheets along the fold. The farmer had gone to a lot of trouble to produce a very different newsletter. The agent's picture was appealing and the content was excellent. A business reply card was included. All in all, this was a very good, simple, do-it-yourself newsletter.

The fly in the ointment was that it contained two grammatical errors, six typos and two misspellings.

Nothing is worse for your image in your farm than producing an amateurish rag full of typos, misspellings, grammatical errors and misstatements of fact. Such a newsletter will cause a lot of damage. Unfortunately, few do-it-yourself newsletters meet the minimum standards for an effective farming tool.

To produce a simple newsletter on legal-sized paper, just fold it in three parts, seal it and mail it. No envelope is needed.

Do It Yourself

Clip and Paste

If you have the time and the talent, you can create almost professional-quality newsletters with this method.

Let's assume that you have the talent: You have an eye for design. You are a born writer. You understand proportions, you know how to do layout and your lettering is distinguished or you know how to use an art knife to apply store-bought lettering. In other words, you know how to prepare camera-ready copy for printing. You know paper sizes, how to adjust copy length and how to use a proportional wheel. Your grammar, spelling and typing are *perfect* or you know someone with these skills.

Do you have any idea how much time all this is going to consume?

Would you be better off selling or listing a house and buying the newsletter ready-made? Even if your artistic juices are flowing, wouldn't you be better off buying a ready-to-print newsletter and personalizing a segment of it?

No? You are a frustrated publisher and you are dying to start using all your great ideas. You know something? You may be an outstanding success at this!

Look at the newsletter illustrated in Figure 7.2, produced by Elizabeth Plummer of Long & Foster, REALTORS®, in Annapolis, Maryland, called "The Plum Line."

The masthead is beautiful. The design is great. The letter is clean and letter-perfect. The format is well planned so that a certain feature appears each month in the same space—real estate news, an interesting feature such as that year's Navy football schedule, a tree chart, a recipe at the top of page two (you could alternate this with a how-to repair tip), the topic of the month. Actually, this newsletter is produced by a farming team. Their slogan at the bottom of the letter says, "Dial the best. We'll do the rest." A slogan is a smashing idea, if it is a smashing slogan. This one is pretty close to smashing. The newsletter is definitely smashing. It continues: "For Real Estate Services call Elizabeth Plummer—Phyllis Reynolds, 301-266-5505 Md. Wats: 1-800-345-6787."

They claim this thoroughly professional job can be produced easily in one morning a month, once you get the hang of it.

In her book, *Real Estate Farming: Campaign for Success*, P. J. Thompson provides 18 pages of instruction on how to get the hang of this. If you plan to produce your own professional newsletter, that chapter alone is worth the price of the entire book. See "Resources," Appendix A.

Clip Art

Use clip art to liven up your letter. You can buy books of noncopyrighted pictures at local art-supply stores. You also can buy "instant art" from publishers listed in "Resources," Appendix A. Most of the graphics used in this book are computer graphics from a computer software program called Print Shop. See Figures 7.1 and 7.2 for sample clip art and how it can be used.

FIGURE 7.1 Clip Art Sample

FIGURE 7.2   The Plum Line Newsletter

Long & Foster Realtors • 2563 Forest Dr., Annapolis, Maryland 21403 • 266-5505

Dear Friends,

This certainly has been a long and very hot summer. The very thought
of football season and autumn leaves turning is like a long needed breath
of fresh air. We hope that all of you got your REDSKINS schedules in time
for the first game. (Please contact us if you can use another.) In case
you would like to see a game here in Annapolis, we've copied the NAVY
schedule below.

YOUR NEIGHBORHOOD SALES REPRESENTATIVES,

Phyllis Reynolds   *Elizabeth Plummer*

PHYLLIS REYNOLDS   &   ELIZABETH PLUMMER

Summer is almost over, and
when the temperature drops
houses begin to sell. As
we are heading into this
excellent fall market,
interest rates appear to
be heading up. Pressure
on the Fed to keep inflation
under control forced them
to bump up the discount
rate. The effect of this
increase will sift down
to the mortgage market
during the next few weeks.
Look for rates to stabilize
before the election in
November.

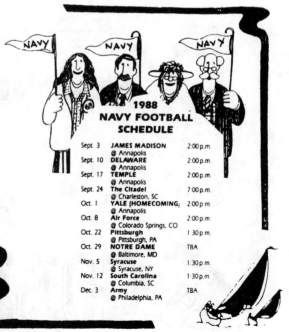

1988 NAVY FOOTBALL SCHEDULE

Sept. 3	JAMES MADISON @ Annapolis	2:00 p.m.
Sept. 10	DELAWARE @ Annapolis	2:00 p.m.
Sept. 17	TEMPLE @ Annapolis	2:00 p.m.
Sept. 24	The Citadel @ Charleston, SC	7:00 p.m.
Oct. 1	YALE (HOMECOMING) @ Annapolis	2:00 p.m.
Oct. 8	Air Force @ Colorado Springs, CO	2:00 p.m.
Oct. 22	Pittsburgh @ Pittsburgh, PA	1:30 p.m.
Oct. 29	NOTRE DAME @ Baltimore, MD	TBA
Nov. 5	Syracuse @ Syracuse, NY	1:30 p.m.
Nov. 12	South Carolina @ Columbia, SC	1:30 p.m.
Dec. 3	Army @ Philadelphia, PA	TBA

FIGURE 7.2 (Continued)

WHAT'S COOKIN'

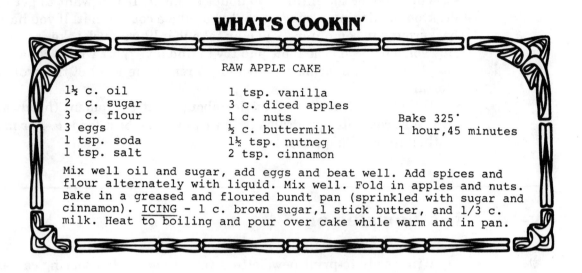

RAW APPLE CAKE

1½ c. oil	1 tsp. vanilla	
2 c. sugar	3 c. diced apples	
3 c. flour	1 c. nuts	Bake 325°
3 eggs	½ c. buttermilk	1 hour, 45 minutes
1 tsp. soda	1½ tsp. nutmeg	
1 tsp. salt	2 tsp. cinnamon	

Mix well oil and sugar, add eggs and beat well. Add spices and flour alternately with liquid. Mix well. Fold in apples and nuts. Bake in a greased and floured bundt pan (sprinkled with sugar and cinnamon). ICING - 1 c. brown sugar, 1 stick butter, and 1/3 c. milk. Heat to boiling and pour over cake while warm and in pan.

Desktop Publishing

The wave of the future. No doubt about it. If you want to get into desktop publishing, I suggest that you take a course in it. If you have a background in computers, you may take to it like a duck takes to water. Buy some books on the topic and try to find an expert who is capable of simplifying the information enough to reach the level of the ordinary mortal.

You also will need good advice about what equipment (hardware) and what computer programs (software) will be best for *you*. For more on this, reread Chapter 4.

Ready-To-Print Newsletters

With ready-to-print newsletters you are actually ordering camera-ready copy to take to your printer or copy center or to copy on your office copy machine. You can send these out just as they are. Often they are one legal-sized page or one letter-sized page printed on both sides. You can fold it up when you get it back from the printer (buy a folding machine) and either staple it or put a sticker on it and mail it out. If you fold it right, you can place the address label over the opening to keep it together and save one step. You can insert it in an envelope, of course—one more step and a few extra pence. If you are hand-addressing these newsletters, as some purists advocate, write something interesting on the outside of the envelope, such as "Peek inside, you'll be glad you did" or "Free favor inside." Or have a stamp made with a neat teaser of some kind and stamp them all. You can also buy envelopes printed with slogans. That's it, the whole ready-made process. Two- and four-page ready-to-print newsletters are also available. Newsletter Services' *Home News Digest* has a rather different and interesting shape. The page has been folded in, about three inches from one end, then folded in two, creating a mailer that is 5½″ × 8½″. I tried this with a recruiting brochure of mine, but I used colored cover stock instead of regular paper stock. It was a howling success. You could do this with your own do-it-yourself newsletter, which makes it less flimsy and more unique.

Newsletter Services also provides a four-page booklet on how to personalize a ready-to-print newsletter.

The Gooder Group offers both preprinted and ready-to-print newsletters, with several choices of each. Their best-seller, *Homeletter*, is available in either form. They also produce a series of handbooks that allow you to elicit responses from your farm by offering them in your newsletter to recipients who return the attached card. Sometimes the return card is built into the newsletter. The handbooks are substantial—20 or more pages of well-done information on selling, buying or moving. Also available are some lightweight brochures that can be tucked inside your newsletter or put in a #10 envelope along with it. The brochures cover sought-after subjects: tax reform info, easy fixups and so on. The Gooder ready-to-print letters come with complete instructions for personalizing.

Most of the other ready-to-print newsletters on the market also can be personalized. You can drop in columns of local interest on top of existing general-interest columns. The only thing you have to be careful of is that the difference in type does not make it glaringly obvious what you have done. This is where a desktop publishing capability, with various fonts, would make life easier. Newsletter Services in its newsletters uses the ITC American Typewriter font, with which most typewriters are compatible. Watch the size. You may have to reduce your copy to integrate it into the newsletter.

Kall Publications offers a set of ready-to-print newsletters that it advertises as "a newsletter with an attractive 'I did it myself' look— without doing it yourself."

The American Homeowner, which Kall publishes, is designed to be printed on an office copy machine (better check at your shop to see if you are allowed to do this) on legal-sized paper, with typewriter-style type. The copy is professional, yet gives the appearance of being local. You can use your own masthead, with your own company logo, your name and picture, and nobody, but nobody, will know you didn't do it yourself.

Kall offers the best tip of the century for do-it-yourselfers. Or anybody. Have a quick-print shop make a 65-line screen made from your photo for $5 to $10. This way you can use any copy machine to enlarge or reduce your picture, you can reuse the same treated photo each month as you create a new issue and you can have it printed on your own or a copy-center machine. Bye-bye printers.

The same group also produces a ready-to-print newsletter that does not attempt to look homemade. It is slicker than the amateur effort, but not so slick as the professional national newsletters. It is easily personalized, and the publisher carries all kinds of "instant art" to use. Kall also continually develops excellent new farming tools. See "Resources," Appendix A, for the company's catalog.

When personalizing a ready-to-print newsletter, a printer can set type for you. The printer can design and print your heading or masthead or other personalization as part of the printing package.

All of this depends on how much personalization you want. You could just handwrite a personal note in one corner—"FLASH! O'Reilly's house on the corner of Elm and Oak just sold for the highest price in history." Simply adding the company colors, type style, logo and your own picture can make it yours.

One more way to personalize a ready-to-print or a preprinted newsletter is to develop a personal insert that is slipped into the newsletter when it is mailed. Some mailing services will do this for you and sometimes the printer will insert it while folding if the inserts are in his or her hands at the time. This is particularly important with company newsletters.

The Personal Marketer, a monthly newsletter for real estate salespeople to help them market themselves, which is produced by the Personal Marketing Company, devoted a whole issue to "Developing a Personal Advertising Insert," together with insert formats that you can use to paste your insert copy on. These insert formats are very sprightly and attention-catching. You could easily make this same type of insert format with your own computer, using a software program such as Print Shop (the computer graphics in this book were made with Print Shop; see "Resources," Appendix A, for more information).

The Personal Marketer provides precise directions for planning your insert ideas, getting tools you may need, doing your layouts, writing copy, putting it all together, getting it copied and inserting it into your newsletter.

The usefulness of its suggestions is illustrated by its instructions on placing the insert inside the newsletter: Have them both letter-folded (again, buy a folding machine) and then insert one inside the other. This way you could even add your personal insert *after* the newsletters arrive in the office already folded, if this turned out to be absolutely necessary.

Preprinted Newsletters

Sometimes the newsletter is produced by the real estate company itself. John L. Scott, Inc., in Washington state, distributes a marvelous newsletter. *Quality Street* is edited by Laura Reymore, now manager of the Kent office. A former real estate trainer, Reymore is a great sharer of ideas, and she has a ton of ideas.

Her letter is four pages in two colors, sometimes blue and brown, sometimes red and black, always on buff paper. The agents requested a businesslike letter with savable material rather than a folksy letter with recipes, so Reymore put together a lot of general real estate information about financing, home improvements, qualifying for a mortgage loan and so forth. She receives the information from a variety of sources, but most of it comes from Newsletter Services, a company that provides ready-made copy for newsletters (see "Resources," Appendix A).

Reymore's letter is divided into sections separated by rule lines; each department has its own heading. She has an advice column entitled "Ask Me" as a regular feature. The content is legal matters. I would have been tempted to call it "Legal Eagle," but, then, I am easily tempted.

One brilliant inspiration that appeared in one of the past year's editions was a children's coloring contest, an insert showing a drawing of a country cottage with a "sold" sign in the front garden. The insert could be slipped out of the newsletter for a child to color. The contest rules were on the back and the prizes were one Teddy Ruxpin doll for ages 5 and under; one Nintendo game each for ages 6 to 9 and 9 to 12. One hundred fifty-one responses were received. All contestants and their parents were sent to the branch office to submit their entries because the purpose was to encourage involvement between the agents and the homeowners in their areas.

The Scott Company newsletters are mailed from the advertising department. The newsletter, originally sent out to a printing company, is now a desktop publishing product composed by the advertising department with the help of the training department.

A supply of the newsletter is delivered to the offices and the agents. The usual way to personalize in cases such as these is simply to staple a business card to each copy.

The Gooder Group will rename its *Homeletter,* personalize it for a broker and deliver it preprinted to the broker's office—a lot less trouble and well done.

If your company provides you with a preprinted newsletter, you naturally will want to use it and your company will want you to use it. Certain circumstances arise, however, under which using the company newsletter may not be the best answer for either you or the company.

In areas where large companies are operating and farm areas are not protected, three and four of the company newsletters are sometimes distributed to the same farm area. Many managers have expressed their concern about this situation. I do not know if the Scott Company has this problem, but it is mailing 60,000 or more letters out in its region. Presumably, the company checks that there are no duplications in farm areas. This capability is one advantage of company control of newsletter distribution.

I can see the rationale behind unprotected farm areas (anyone in the company can farm anywhere), which is discussed in Chapter 2. It may be good company policy to allow any agent to farm any area, but the company newsletter should only be distributed once in any farm.

The duplication problem can be solved in two ways. If a farm already is being farmed by an agent, any new farmer must distribute a different farm letter: either a letter the agent produces or one he or she buys from the many companies who now make them available. Some of these newsletter companies offer a choice of several newsletters. All a farmer must do is to send for a catalog or sample copies.

FIGURE 7.3   Newsletters

Choosing a Newsletter

The variety of newsletters is truly staggering. See Figure 7.3 for a sampling of the newsletters available. Newsletters come in all shapes and sizes, from the normal 8½″ × 11″ size to a 5½ × 8½″ newsletter called *Home News Digest,* produced by Newsletter Services. Several one-page, legal-sized newsletters are available, one page both sides, two pages, four pages—anything you want.

Their content varies tremendously, too. *Homeletter* is a very professional, informational, response-oriented newsletter from Gooder Group. Getting a response is, after all, a vital attribute for a newsletter, especially in passive farming. If there is no follow-through *and* no response, what is the point of the whole exercise? Only institutional advertising. This is great for the company, but what does it do for the agent? It opens doors. Is this enough for most farmers? Unless it is, the choice of a response-oriented newsletter is vital.

Some of the newsletters are much lighter in tone, much less concerned with content and more with style. These are for active farmers who are not so worried about immediate response as they are about "warm fuzzies."

Some of the letters are printed in four colors (which makes them more expensive) and are extremely attractive. The Austin Group puts out two or three stunning four-page letters. Their content is not so informative and varied as that of *Homeletter,* for example, and contains recipes and cartoons. It is also not so densely written. They are simpler—more like a well-done cut-and-paste job. Remember, though, that in some places this type of newsletter may be better received, depending on the audience.

Personal Marketing offers a very interesting and different package of materials that includes a beautifully turned out four-page newsletter directed toward homeowners that, in fact, is called *Homeowners.* The newsletter combines a lot of valuable information with a stunning format. Another of its newsletters is directed toward corporations and, again, the layout and type are very clean and attractive.

The most interesting thing in Personal Marketing's package, though, is a large collection of material directed to the do-it-yourselfer. This includes not only the one-page masthead and graphics ready to type into it that were mentioned in the do-it-yourself section, but also a monthly marketing newsletter with all types of ideas for personal marketing.

Among the subjects covered in pamphlets provided by Personal Marketing are "Targeting Your Market," "Newsletter Distribution," "Summary of Market Penetration," "How To Manage an Effective Client Follow-Up Program," "Prospect List Development" and everything you ever wanted to know about marketing. This is a fabulous new approach.

Another exciting innovation that has made its appearance recently is the ghostwriter. Paul Christian Communications ghostwrites farming newsletters. It offers a ready-made series of five letters, or it will ghostwrite custom letters and newsletters. It also will rewrite yours on a personal arrangement basis (for a fee, of course) and might even consider taking your masthead, or one produced by Personal Marketing, and filling it in with some prearranged format.

Advice Columns

Ghostwriters also will write real estate advice columns for you, for your newsletter or for the local newspaper, whichever you prefer. Given the legal climate these days, it might be safer for you to use someone else's column than your own. You could give the wrong advice one day.

Miracle of miracles, companies exist that will take the entire burden of folding, inserting, stamping and mailing off of your shoulders. General Consulting Service, Inc., of Damascus, Maryland, a national firm, was one of this type of service. Local outfits also may provide similar service. Some real estate firms, such as Fox & Carskadon in San Francisco, perform this service for its agents through a direct mail company.

Some insist on a check up front, while others will charge your company account or your credit card.

The direction you can afford to take depends a lot on your stage of development as a real estate salesperson. Naturally, beginning agents, who are not yet well heeled, may want to start out slowly, doing as much as possible themselves or having their children work for them at minimum wage (all tax-deductible as a business expense). Some agents advocate putting aside 5 to 6 percent of your earnings from the beginning, to make your business grow by increasing your marketing effort. In a small company, the likelihood of running into the problem of too many sales associates farming the same area is almost nil.

Many large companies have solved this problem by producing a branch office newsletter. Sometimes this letter is produced by the office manager and sometimes by the whole office by working in concert.

Two or three branch office letters produced by a large Virginia company are on legal-sized paper in the company colors. They contain a lot of general real estate information and all are self-mailers with the branch office return address.

When asked where they got the material for their branch office newsletter they said all the agents contributed to it. An endless supply of material is available, they told me. *The New York Times Complete Manual of Home Repair,* for example, contains enough information on home repair tips to last you forever.

Quotations and Humor

The office humorist contributed such things as: "Today's Tip: Gravy stains can be easily removed from a silk tie with a pair of scissors." Everyone likes a touch of humor now and then, and the library contains shelves and shelves of humor, some of which is appropriate.

In one waterfront community each issue of the newsletter included a "Fishing Rule of Thumb"—12 of them, one for each month. They ranged from "Never drink beer in waders" to "Don't trust a fisherman with missing fingers."

It is possible to use quotations of all kinds, especially those that fit the occasion, such as "Call for a free market analysis today—remember the old Chinese proverb that a 'journey of a thousand miles starts with a single step.'"

This material is known as *filler.* A few fillers spark up a newsletter, but a whole newsletter of fillers defeats your purpose, which is to project a picture of yourself as a real estate expert.

Community News

The best news is news of things actually happening in your farm. The orientation of these branch office newsletters was toward the community itself. One newsletter contained the history of the town, information about local services, construction problems on town roads and community announcements, with only one column on real estate. A space was reserved for a picture and telephone number on the masthead, and if the subdivision was farmed by more than one agent, the manager's picture and telephone number appeared in that spot. If only one person was farming the area, that agent's name and telephone number were placed there. These branch office newsletters were supplied to the agents to use in their farms in addition to the company newsletter, which contained all real estate topics. An alternative was to use it as an insert to the company newsletter or by itself in subdivisions where the company newsletter already was being distributed by another agent. One office using this method had 110 agents who covered 60 subdivisions.

The selection of a newsletter can directly affect the success of a new farmer and it should be done carefully. Studies show that readers like variety and balance. A 70/30 percent ratio is considered a good mix, with 70 percent of the letter covering real estate topics and 30 percent with topics of general interest.

As to whether to use the preprinted or the do-it-yourself newsletter, two farming experts, Stipp and Underwood, have this to say in *The Farming Manual,* speaking somewhat from management's viewpoint on the advantage of the preprinted national newsletter: "If you choose a quality product, it will help educate the property owners in your farm with respect to the services which you have to offer, the advantages which property owners gain in dealing with a real estate professional like you. Moreover, it resolves the problem of you or one of your associates having to produce a monthly letter under stress of daily listing and sales transactions. Likewise, it obviates the necessity of finding a sufficiently trained individual who can ensure the professionalism of writing and the overall presentation."

P. J. Thompson in *Real Estate Farming* speaks for the individual salesperson:

> The most effective newsletter to use for your geographic farm is one which you plan and prepare yourself . . . least desirable for geographic farming, but suitable for other types, is a canned newsletter. These are

prepared for national consumption and their only personalization is the imprint of the agent's name, company and phone number. . . . You feel your effort may appear rather amateurish in appearance and/or content when compared to the slick (perhaps even four-color) newsletter that a large company underwrites. This contrast in itself is evidence that yours is a publication done by one individual especially for a particular area: recipients know that it is for them only, not for mass readership.

The compromise is the personalized ready-to-print newsletter. With the wealth of new products now on the market, maybe you can work it out so that you can have the best of both worlds.

Newsletter Distribution

You can distribute your newsletter at least six different ways. (There may be others.)

1. Deliver them to the homes in your farm yourself. (There is a $25 fine for putting them in a U.S. mailbox; get plastic door hangers if you deliver yourself.) Gives you a good excuse to ring the doorbell and say hello. Grab any excuse. (See "Resources," Appendix A, for plastic door hanger source.)
2. Hand them out in shopping centers or other local meeting places. This provides a way to meet people in your farm who are never home.
3. Have them delivered by a Scout, news carrier, neighborhood kid or one of your own children. This ensures the arrival of your newsletter on a Saturday!
4. Mail them first class or bulk rate. This is good especially when your company reimburses you for postage.
5. Have the company distribute them through the advertising department or a mailing service.
6. You pay to have them handled by a mailing service. "What, me worry?"

Depending on how rich or how poor you are, or how much time you have, select one of these methods to distribute in your geographic farm. In a target farm or to your sphere of influence, you probably are going to have to mail first class or deliver by hand. Ideally, for this group, you want a hand-addressed envelope. Use your home address for the return address.

If you do not have a computer to print labels, you can buy them in a stationery store by the ream with a master copy. They can be copied from the master on a copy machine. Not all copy machines do a good job, so you should experiment.

Unless you have them delivered by hand, expect to provide a list. The most important task ahead is compiling these prospect lists.

Compiling a list merely involves amassing the pertinent information if you are working a geographic farm. You can use the *Lusk Directory,* weekly computer disk subscription, year-end books on disk or their microfiche. At the assessment office you can hand-copy pages out of the record books or buy photocopies for about $1 a page in most areas. Some areas will sell you a computer printout for whole subdivisions for about the same price, but you may have to take the whole computer run: four or five subdivisions for less than $100. You also can use the courthouse records and cross directories. Title companies also keep records that they may sell you. See Appendix B for postal regulations.

For your sphere of influence, let us hope you have kept good records of past customers, friends, acquaintances, club and church memberships and anyone else you know from anywhere. Send all of them your newsletter, at least quarterly.

For target mailings, you sometimes may have to buy lists. Local businesses are good recipients of real estate newsletters, for they have employees coming and going. If you do not have a relocation department in your company, send newsletters to chief executive officers (CEOs) of local corporations and to personnel offices around town.

Right now, get out your yearly calendar and mark down the days and times that you plan to set aside for your newsletter. If you have charted how long the mailings take from the date of mailing to receipt, you should know exactly when to mail them to get them to the readers when you want them to arrive. The ideal day for a newsletter to arrive is the middle of the week. Open-house invitations should arrive on Saturday, if possible, when everyone is at home doing chores or sitting around reading and recovering from the workweek.

Whether you choose passive or active farming, newsletters are the leading means of communication for many farmers.

8

Creating a Personal Marketing Program

Spending Money To Make Money

Cost is the first consideration when choosing farming tools. Bear in mind that the most successful real estate people are those who are aware that they are running a business. Anyone who knows anything about running a business knows that businesses must be capitalized.

If you were opening a small storefront dry-cleaning business with a potential annual income of $60,000, you might need at least $50,000 to open your door.

It takes money to make money, according to the old saying. In real estate, a great many people apparently are still mentally back in their salaried days, when the "boss" took care of everything. They do not seem to understand that although this still is true, now they are the "boss."

Really successful real estate salespeople are not afraid to spend money. Les Boomer of The Prudential in Sacramento, California, for example, whom I previously mentioned as an unusually creative person, has been giving each of his clients a subscription to *Sunset* magazine at $16 per year. The main obstacle to success for many in real estate is the inability to switch from an employee mentality to a business-owner mentality. Les Boomer's ability to make this switch is one of the principal reasons for his success.

Huge incomes are being realized by real estate salespeople who have made this discovery. Although he may not by any means be at the top of the heap, a REALTOR® in northern Virginia annually nets at least $350,000, almost entirely through direct mail efforts. Each year he plows back into his farm a designated percent of his income to make his business grow.

Certified Residential Specialists, REALTORS® holding the designation offered by the Residential Sales Council of the REALTORS® National Marketing Institute, are among the most successful real estate agents in the country. Members concentrate on personal promotion with the help of the RS Council, which provides a series of "Pres Kits" containing camera-ready brochures, forms, checklists, charts, letters, ads and tables ready to personalize and "use for all aspects of your career from farming to creating a presentation book," says Randy Eager, CRB,CRS, one of the product researchers. Figure 8.1 shows an example of a personal promo by a CRS member.

Tools of the Trade

The new breed of real estate professionals who are making huge sums of money while the dying breed finds itself in the doldrums are distinguished by two characteristics: They run themselves like a business and they are up to their eyebrows in the new technology.

Sherie Broekema, GRS, GRI, of Tucson Realty and Trust Co., is an example of the plunge into technology. Her promotion piece in the annual National Relocation Directory has the following paragraph: "Special services: Have licensed personal assistant, 24-hour answering service, communication by car phone, beeper, answering machine, fax."

Until recently, no real estate agent had heard of doing what most other businesspeople do automatically: Hire a secretary. Sherie describes her assistant in terms of the value to her customers: "My licensed personal assistant helps to assure that every customer receives efficient, thorough service."

Our friend Les Boomer was one of the first agents to latch onto the "proactive" method of operation. While others in his hometown were still playing the old waiting game, Les was distributing a "Les Boomer" brochure. His business card is 5½" × 4¼" with his picture on the outside. He also has an informal with the same format, on which he writes a continuous stream of thank-you notes—at least ten a week.

Boomer believes in capitalizing his business. He has an IBM computer and all the tools of the trade: a stamp machine, an automatic paper folder, etc. He pays $600 a year for Metro Scan, a complete computer disk of the tax-rolls, updated monthly. Also, title companies

FIGURE 8.1   Personal Promotion by Certified Residential Specialist

Beware of Realtors® who owe their reputations to what they did on sunny days.

The climate has changed.

Todays real estate market presents unexpected challenges . . . and opportunities. Realtors® who have led in less challenging times, find themselves at a loss in current situations.

If you are buying or selling real estate, you need a seasoned professional who's capable of precise trouble shooting, someone like PAUL CARLOW.

Paul focuses his expertise on each challenge, drawing on his unique resources and marketing techniques. Today he ranks among real estate's successful professionals.

In today's market Paul is the way the wind is blowing. So study the climate and make the educated decision to call Paul Carlow.

Re/Max Tradition
3161 Solomons Island Road
Edgewater, MD 21037

956-3500

798-6148

Paul Carlow
Your South County Realtor®

Source: Reprinted by permission of Paul Carlow.

give him tax roll information on computer disks. In other words, he operates a business.

Would you want to work with this man? Well, I sent my son, Craig, to him when he and his new bride, Donna, moved to California. They couldn't seem to click with a number of other agents, but Les Boomer was as good as his word. The real point is that Les found a way to spread the word about his good service and he was willing to spend the money to do it. He didn't, as the saying goes, hide his light under a bushel.

Personal Brochures

A comparatively recent phenomenon, the personal brochure has become so popular that it has spawned a new industry. Camera Master, a firm in Boise, Idaho, will provide you with a camera-ready, response-oriented brochure. One Camera Master customer, Tim Cowles, president of Training Unlimited, says, "I found that buyers and sellers are not interested in how wonderful we are, or how many zillions of homes we have sold. They want to know what's in it for them . . . can we sell their home for top dollar, quickly and without hassle or get them into the home of their dreams?"

The brochures are very professional and attractive and cost a couple of hundred dollars. They are such a rage on both coasts that real estate salespeople with cards only are beginning to feel "out of it." They are especially useful in listing because studies have shown that owners are more interested in the experience of the salesperson than they are in any other factor, including the company name. They also make good direct mail pieces to include with other material. Tim Cowles lists 22 different uses for the personal brochure. It is not like a business card, which is often pitched five minutes after you hand it out, although people are less likely to pitch your card if it has your picture on it. These brochures have three pictures of you on them.

Farming Works

Les Boomer of The Prudential farms by mail with his own personal advertising campaign fliers. He provides his own brochures on every subject with his picture and his own ideas. In addition, he is part of a massive mail campaign by his company—30,000 pieces per promotion every three months. In this case, the company provides the mailouts and the agent pays the postage. Not only is he a perfect example of the creative mind, he is not afraid to spend money to make money. The beautiful gold sticker that he has affixed to *Sunset* magazine could have been a much cheaper variety. Les wants a "quality" image; he always goes for quality.

Referral Farming

Boomer also believes in referral farming: "Your past, present, and future business must all be worked all the time," he says.

Many members of the Northern Virginia Million Dollar Club agree. Top agents in all the large companies actively solicit business from in-house agents in widespread branch offices and through company relocation departments. They produce mailers and cards with their pictures and outline the areas they service and the referral fees they will pay. This varies from 15 or 20 percent to as much as 30 percent for a listing. For a joint listing, agents negotiate up to 50 percent.

Agents all over the country advertise for referrals in *Realty News.* There is a whole section devoted to exchanging referrals.

Some salespeople regularly send mailings to all realty board super-stars. Certified Residential Specialists (CRSs) have the advantage of receiving referrals from all over the country from the *CRS Directory* and promotions they and the RS Council do. The franchises and many large companies have thriving referral systems.

In Les Boomer's case, we are talking about a person who combines creativity with money to reach the optimum. Particularly with a person who is just starting out and does not have the funds to do everything he or she would like to do, creativity can be used as a substitute for large expenditures on farming tools.

Handouts

Some type of gift or handout is almost a necessity. Many possible handouts are available at a price. (See Figure 8.2.) Magnets are especially good because they are thin and lightweight and are easy to tuck into an envelope with a letter. Some companies like Progressive Specialty Co. in Maryland offer a whole catalog of magnets for your consideration. I like "house" magnets. In fact, I have had a house magnet that touts a friendly competitor on my refrigerator for 15 years. It reminds me of how effective these tools are in your competitor's hands.

I recall the problems I had in a farm many years ago when my major competitor had distributed pens that adhere to the telephone—no way to unstick those pens short of dynamite. I had to endure seeing my competitor's pens in every home I entered in my farm for many years.

FIGURE 8.2   A Variety of Handouts

Recently, I added a house magnet of a friend in our company. I never would throw out either of these. I use them to hold notes to the family, my diet plan, cartoons, etc.

If you can afford magnets, buy them. If you cannot, however, and you have an artistic bent, how about making up some attractive paper bookmarks to mail out with your monthly letters. Kall Publications' catalog offers inexpensive ready-to-print bookmarks featuring your logo (see "Resources," Appendix A). Or include a snappy index card with this month's recipe or repair tip. If you have a computer, you can make your own greeting cards or signs: "Did you clean your room today?" "No Smoking, Please," "No Parking," "Exit," etc.

Other Farming Tools

Several real estate promotion companies offer marvelous door hangers to place on your neighbors' doorknobs when you find they are not at home. One I especially like has your picture on it.

"Hello . . . I am _____." it reads. You write you name in the blank. These door hangers are inexpensive, and can be printed on one or both sides. It would save you time to just order them. If saving money is more important to you than saving time, you can design your own and have them printed on cover stock at the local copy center or run them off on your computer. Plastic bags are inexpensive to imprint and hold items you may want to leave the homeowner.

Seed packets, forget-me-nots, for example, cost 19 cents imprinted with your name. Or you can buy plain seed packets for 10 cents and stamp them on the back. Again, time versus money.

Ideas for inexpensive gifts in your farm include: four-leaf clovers, football schedules, tides schedules (for waterfront communities), silhouettes of birds to identify (call it "Birdwatch"), coloring sheets for kids, household and garden tips, wallet-sized calendars, 5½" paper rulers (small ones fit in the envelopes) to indicate the minimum "keeper" size for crabs or 6" rulers for knitting or crocheting. You can buy sheets of stickers: butterflies, smiles, birds, flowers, fish, pumpkins, wreaths, Easter lilies, shamrocks, hearts, flags, etc. People use them on the backs of envelopes or on holiday letters. Kids particularly love them.

You may even wish to establish some new community traditions in your efforts to serve your farm, such as the following:

- Annual crabfeast/picnic
- Spring sale/treasure hunt
- Directory or town guide
- Little League picnic, company balloons, sweatshirts, etc.
- Kids coloring contest

- Spruce-up photo contest
- Pet show
- November turkey raffle; spring azalea raffle
- Town parade
- Beach party
- Halloween-costume contest or party
- Pumpkin door delivery (pie recipe? pie recipe contest?)
- Brainstorm other ideas for next year's planning session
- Newsletter or monthly letter campaign themes
- Community service ideas: free classified ads in newsletter
- Listings: services offered: elder care, adult day care, grass cutters, window cleaners, car washers, etc.
- Real estate advice column
- Congratulations: weddings, graduations, birthdays, Valentine greetings, promotions, awards and recognition
- Flash! Announcing special news or send flash cards: Wow!

Neighborhood Appreciation Awards

One of the ingenious tools Les Boomer uses in his farm is his annual "Civis Superior" award to the most improved home in the area. The certificate itself is now a coveted classic (see Figure 8.3). Signed, sealed and beautifully lettered, it proclaims that the owners: "Successfully overcame untold obstacles in order to generate an atmosphere of excellence, increasing in the process not only the value of their own home, but also those of the entire neighborhood. Truly outstanding pride of ownership is a contribution to the whole community." Similar award certificates are available commercially (see "Resources," Appendix A).

Information

The cheapest gift is information. You can buy or make up bulletins of information that will prove more valuable to the recipient than expensive handouts: local events calendar, street construction schedule (Oak Street will be closed Tuesday, Pine the following Monday) or "What To Do about a Wet Basement."

Professionally Printed Information

The Gooder Group produces the most thoroughly researched and professional-looking material I have seen. Their handbooks for homebuyers, homesellers and people who are relocating are a fat 24 pages and come with standard or imprinted covers, featuring your own name

FIGURE 8.3 Award Example

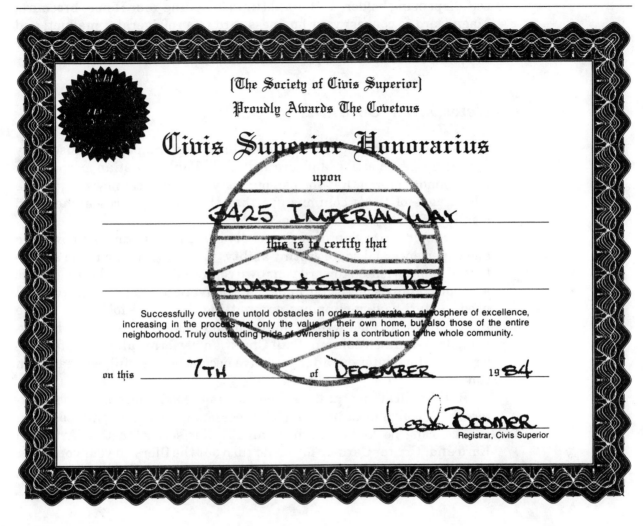

[The Society of Civis Superior]
Proudly Awards The Covetous

Civis Superior Honorarius

upon

3425 Imperial Way

this is to certify that

Edward & Sheryl Roe

Successfully overcame untold obstacles in order to generate an atmosphere of excellence, increasing in the process not only the value of their own home, but also those of the entire neighborhood. Truly outstanding pride of ownership is a contribution to the whole community.

on this **7th** of **December** 19**84**

Registrar, Civis Superior

or your company name and logo. They also offer two very informative brochures, "Tax Reform, How It Affects Your Home" and "Free and Easy Fix-Ups To Sell Your Home for the Best Price." Duplicating this material would require many hours and much talent. This material is particularly appropriate in areas around universities and in high-tech areas where the level of sophistication requires in-depth approaches to informational offerings.

Promotion Specialties

At the other end of the spectrum are items such as wanted posters, huge $10 bills giving termite or other discounts, shopping calendars and a raft of objects put out by Sanzo such as a "Welcome to Our Open House" doormat; balloons, banners and streamers for open houses; key tags (I am #1); seeds (imprinted packets); real estate terms brochures with self-dispensing holder; a "Helpful Hints in Selling Your Home" brochure; Magnacard to convert your business card to a refrigerator magnet; and other items too numerous to mention here. For more information or how to obtain these products, see "Resources," Appendix A.

Newspaper Columns

Real estate newspaper columns have high impact because they appear to be objective and are soft sell. Paul Christian prepares a ready-made column that you can buy for your own local newspaper. The advantages of these columns are that they are well researched and legally safe. They also are time-saving.

You could write your own, especially if you have a fund of knowledge and experience and some writing ability. Your own letter has the advantage of being oriented toward your own community rather than a generic audience. Many sources for material are available to use, and you will need to start saving clippings and putting them in a folder for future issues. You also could write a question-and-answer column or a handyman, do-it-yourself column. Paul Christian performs all kinds of ghost-writing, which later on, after you have become successful, will save you time.

Kall Publications catalogs nine farming tools: it offers two newsletters (both look almost homemade), a personal advertising kit, seasonal ads, coloring books for children, an EZ flier series, Instant Art, Kall Kard and "Critter Cards." You could turn out the fliers on your computer and, if you are artistic, you might be able to create children's coloring books.

Cards

The best-looking cards with the greatest variety I have seen are produced by Harrison Publishing and Carole Kelby. The Harrison catalog displays a variety of cards: "Thank You," "May I Serve You," "Your Home Is Special," "A Friendly Reminder," "In Appreciation," "Congratulations," "Announcing" and others. Holiday cards and real estate cards appear in countless variations. It would be hard to design more effective cards than these, but if you have a lot of artistic talent, turn it loose and save yourself some money.

Personal Marketing sells good-looking parchment notes and personal stationery with handsome custom-made sketches of the homes your customers have purchased that you can use as closing gifts in your farm. They also offer a series of market newsletters for agents that they give away if you order its newsletter. Its ADMail series of self-mailers for your farm allows you to conduct a direct mail campaign without doing the work.

Keeping Direct Mail Costs Down

Keeping costs down, according to Dan Richards, president of the Gooder Group, writing in *Real Estate Business,* is a matter of establishing a tracking system.

What you are interested in knowing is the efficiency of your mailings, that is, the ratio between cost and response. The least expensive mailing in the world is no good if you generate zero response. The response record for most real estate farmers is disgraceful. This low response discourages them and often makes them give up.

Establishing a Tracking System

Keep a record of responses so you know what works and what does not. Coupons or direct-call responses are easiest to keep track of. If you have a computer, you can use a program such as Smart Agent to track responses. An alternative is to keep a manual account in your farming notebook. A form for this kind of recordkeeping is shown in Figure 8.4.

Testing

"Different target prospects will have different 'best offers,'" says Richards. In other words, it is fruitless to offer recipes to engineers or slide rules to chefs. The incongruity, of course, is never so blatant as that.

You need a figure for the cost per response. Keep testing. Conduct a split test: Send half your farm one offer and half another and then check the response. Send half, for example, the questionnaire you devised and the other half the questionnaire you bought from Sanzo. Remember, it is not just a question of total cost, but *cost effectiveness* that counts. Eliminate the offer that resulted in a high cost-per-response figure. On the other hand, use the good offer over and over, as long as it produces. Reuse it, change the heading, give it a new twist, combine it with a different offer, update it, change it. Do not stop using an offer that brings response.

FIGURE 8.4   Direct Mail Tracking Form

Mailing #	Date	Destination	Offer	Premium	Response

Conclusion: _____

Cost Analysis

To determine the cost per response, simply divide the dollar amount spent to promote an offer by the number of qualified responses. What are "qualified" responses?

Qualified responses are those received from people who are prospects for some kind of a real estate transaction.

For example:

Mailing A

To a farm of 200 homeowners, send an offer to provide a pamphlet on the cost of the new sewer system.

Printing:	$22.50	6 responses
Address Labels:	6.29	Cost per response, $10.63
Postage:	21.50	3 lots listed at $20,000 each
Return Cards:	12.00	Commission, $1,500
Return Postage:	1.50	(Split 25% or 10% total commission)
TOTAL:	$63.79	Net proceeds, $1,436.21

Mailing B

Offer to send a comparison of the market for 1994 and 1995 and to conduct a free market evaluation of the home.

Printing:	$10.00	2 responses
Labels:	6.29	Cost per response, $39.14
Postage:	21.50	One house listed at $104,400
Evaluation Card:	40.00	Commission, $1,827
Return Postcards:	.50	(Split 25% of 7% total)
TOTAL:	$78.29	Net proceeds, $1,748.72

You can see that many factors must be considered. First is the cost per response. Unless you have a track record to go by, this factor is paramount. If you have sales and listings as a result of the mailing, the actual return to you can be used to select the most profitable offer. The return, of course, depends upon your real estate skills.

Another intangible is the permanence of the approach and its timing. Mailing A worked this time because of a new sewer system installation in two years that will cost lot owners about $2,500. Those who sell now can avoid this cost. This mailing can be used only until the new sewer is installed. It was productive enough to make the mailing well worthwhile, and since the opportunity to use it will soon end, you may well decide to concentrate on this offer even though the second mailing has obviously produced better. Here again, the result depends on your real estate skills. Can you continue to produce a listing out of every other response?

Mailing B was effective because of a sudden upswing in housing prices in this area caused by a shortage of waterfront property and the new sewer system. Turnover had been about ten houses per year (5 percent). Now, however, it may spurt ahead because people are aware of the doubled prices and will want to cash in on the new values.

Because both these offers were productive, you can use both, but do not stop experimenting because you may be able to devise even better offers.

Based on the evaluation of a number of possible offers, you can decide what offers to make in future mailings. Track results through cost per *qualified* response. Naturally, if you offer two tickets to dinner in a local restaurant, you will be swamped with responses, but how many will list or buy a home? Work constantly to improve responses and cut costs and set aside funds for your promotions.

Analyzing Target Groups

Discovering what groups are most amenable to your promotions and what approaches are best for the particular targeted group are other ways to cut costs. Know your target groups and know their "hot buttons."

Who fits better in your area—young marrieds or empty nesters? How do you approach each? Test.

Other Factors

Naturally, bringing in responses does not help if the agent is not skilled in general real estate skills.

Turnover rates, general market conditions, the demographics of the area, what the competition is doing, whether the area is burned out by too much of a good thing (same newsletter received four times, same approach—"Wanna free market analysis?"), whether your market timing is correct, all these things and others affect your response rate and your income from farming. Be aware, don't just blindly follow what everyone else is doing.

Whatever tools you decide to use, remember that your objective is to make your business grow.

PART 3

Marketing Yourself in Your Community

Cultivating Your Farm: Contacts = Contracts

Right here is where we separate the farmers from the gardeners. Confusion about the objective and a lack of commitment are the two main roadblocks that new farmers encounter.

What is your overriding objective? You want to cultivate and nourish a long-term association with your farm friends and neighbors. How do you accomplish this? By selling yourself to people.

I never really began to think seriously about the true goal of a real estate farmer until that day I mentioned in the first chapter when I picked up *REALTOR News*® with the advertisement that had a headline two inches high: "I NEVER HAD ANY SUCCESS UNTIL I STOPPED SELLING REAL ESTATE . . ." (That made me look at the fine print.) "and started selling myself."

It suddenly hit me that although most farmers do not see it that way, of course it is true: Your first objective in your farm is to *sell yourself*. You should not do anything to jeopardize this objective.

Agreed, you may want to conduct research and make surveys, set up appointments, keep in touch with clients and customers, qualify prospects, follow up referrals, increase direct mail response, plus a hundred other things. But you should take heed of a phrase in the doctors' creed, "First, do no harm."

Don't Make Cold Calls!

Refusal to make cold calls in your listing farm has nothing to do with a well-known obstacle to success in real estate labeled *call reluctance*. Call reluctance is the refusal to make a sufficient number of contacts to make success possible. This reluctance is "a career-threatening condition," according to Dick Wilson, president of the National Institute for Sales Training and Consulting. In an article that appeared in *Real Estate Business* in the fall of 1988, Wilson said that identifying this trait is not so easy as one might suppose: "Insufficient prospecting alone is not proof of call reluctance."

Call reluctance, which is curable, is something that happens to salespeople who otherwise would succeed. Wilson stresses that "First, sales associates must be motivated. You can't plug 110-volt agents into 220-volt careers. They must be internally energized, and really want to succeed." But even if they really want to succeed and are powerhouses, there still are 10 or 11 kinds of call reluctance that can act as circuit breakers to success.

The point is that people may tell you that because you are not making cold calls in your farm area you are suffering from this disease. Nonsense! It is counterproductive to make cold calls in certain circumstances, especially when it is neither necessary nor desirable. The early stages of active farming is one of these circumstances.

Farmers constantly receive advice from people who do not understand the dynamics of successful farming to cold call. Nothing could be more detrimental to your long-range objective than to start out this way.

Precede all calls by:

1. An introductory letter,
2. A door hanger with your picture on it, and
3. A small favor or gift.

The people should know who you are when you pick up the telephone or drop by.

Before making calls, remember the four seasons of farming (plus one more):

		Time Frame
Season One	Getting acquainted	3 months
Season Two	Building trust	6 months
Season Three	Becoming the neighborhood real estate specialist	12 months
Season Four	The harvest	18 to 24 months

Obviously, these are time estimates. They depend on the skill of the farmer and the ripeness of the farm to a certain extent. Even after four successful seasons of farming, one stage may be the downfall of many farmers:

		Time Frame
Season Five	Defending your territory	Ad infinitum

Remember what season you are in because your calls always should be appropriate to your seasonal goals. Hard sell that might be acceptable in the "harvest" season is totally out of place in the "getting acquainted" season.

First, Build Rapport

Before you can start asking people for business, you have to answer the questions in their minds: "Do I like and trust this person?" and "What can this person do for me?"

First Impressions

Building rapport is a fundamental principle of good selling. In any selling situation, the first impression is vital. Develop the art of creating a good first impression by following these suggestions:

1. Be careful about your appearance. Make people in your farm feel comfortable by dressing as much like they do as you can and still be businesslike. Always be appropriate.
2. Be conscious of your facial expressions. Always look glad to see your friends and neighbors. Be ever pleasant and friendly!
3. Modulate your voice. Don't shout or whisper. A relaxed manner will help give you a soothing voice.
4. Watch your body language and that of others. Observe other people and what their posture and gestures give away about them. Be guided by these observations. Many books on this topic are on the market.
5. Exhibit humor and empathy. Seeing things from the other person's point of view helps to determine how he or she would like to be treated. Humor, particularly lighthearted good humor, is an icebreaker.
6. Make people comfortable with you. Be able to relate to all types in your farm: tinker, tailor, soldier, sailor, rich, poor and in-between.
7. Bathe them with approval. Accept people. Acknowledge the worth of everyone. Don't look down on anyone. People detect the slightest breath of disapproval.

8. Study people and learn how to read them. Learn how to cope with difficult people and how to influence the decisions they make.
9. Acknowledge the capabilities and accomplishments of others. Make them feel good about themselves; then you will be welcome everywhere.
10. Make people feel important. If you have the choice between making yourself look good and making the client look (and feel) good, choose the latter.

If you live in the community, be a good neighbor. Cut your lawn, pick up your trash and keep your pets in your own yard or on a leash. Fit in. Better than that, contribute. Join the life of the community so that you become "one of us." During the first stage of farming you are searching for a good way to get a foothold in the community.

Riding the Farm

Get to know the farm by driving your car through the farm, looking for all kinds of clues. Be on the watch for home improvements such as a new coat of paint, an addition, a new front door or new shutters. Use that information to create goodwill by quickly sending a note to the homeowners about how great their improvement makes the house and the community look. Mention the new azaleas or the pink dogwood. After you break the ice with a letter or note, your reception when you drop by should be friendly. If you want to make it more casual, walk your dog about and chat with whomever you encounter.

Make it a high priority to go and see every property the moment it comes on the market. You want to be able to discuss it if it comes up and become known as an expert. Be *the* neighborhood expert. Remember, they say someone has to see you 6 times to remember your face and 12 times to remember your name.

One thing is certain, you cannot sell yourself without some form of communication. You must talk to the people. You can talk to them in person or you can talk to them on the telephone, but trying to farm without talking to the people is like making love with a ghost—very unsatisfactory.

Ideally, farming should consist of a mix of personal visits, telephone calls and letters. You need to find the most efficient and effective mix for you through experimentation.

Attitude is everything. If you look on sales as a means of helping people realize their own dreams, then you will have the right touch when you communicate.

Communicating is not always so easy as it sounds, because people often come from tremendously different backgrounds, with varying points of view. Even the words they use to express themselves may be strange to others. Have you heard the saying: "I know that you believe you understand what you think I said, but I'm not sure that you realize that what you heard is *not* what I meant." I keep this saying over my desk telephone to remind me that I need to speak in a simple, conversational, even chatty, manner. Use warm tones. Concentrate on the listener. Speak his or her language. Skip real estate jargon—use plain English. What does it mean to a homeowner if I say that I am going to "run comps"? The novice in real estate probably would be completely mystified by "Is your house listed?"

With whom? Dunn and Bradstreet? The Housing Office? "Do I have what? A wraparound? I think my wife has a wraparound skirt." Clear and simple, but not patronizing or superior, is the way to reach people.

You must appear competent and knowledgeable about real estate financing, present home values, local development, interest-rate patterns and so forth if you are to reach your goal of being seen as *the* town real estate specialist. You must project confidence, so people will be confident in you. But a certain amount of humility, courtesy, empathy and genuine concern for people will keep you from sounding arrogant. Also using their names a lot and avoiding a stream of *I*'s will humanize you.

The Golden Triangle

Methods of working your territory fit into a triangle (Figure 9.1). At the base is direct mail, the foundation for all you do. Next is your sphere of influence: community leaders, old customers and clients, organizations and clubs, bird dogs and friends and neighbors who will give you their endorsement. Third is your telephone campaign. Because of the rise of two-wage-earner families and the mobility of today's population, telemarketing may have superseded door-to-door canvassing as the preferred method of communication in your farm. In some areas it has even superseded mailing in the latter stages of farming. Because telemarketing is the fastest growing sales trend of the decade, it is being advocated for use in the beginning stages of farming. In my view this is a mistake. Unless it is used very carefully, telemarketing can be counterproductive to your goal. If the people who live in your farm see you as a genuinely caring person, sincerely interested in them and their families, forget the competition, you are in like Flynn. A cold call from a stranger trying to sell them a proposition in which they have not the slightest interest is likely to be seen as an invasion of privacy rather than a sincere concern for their welfare as might a tactful inquiry from an old friend.

FIGURE 9.1   The Golden Triangle

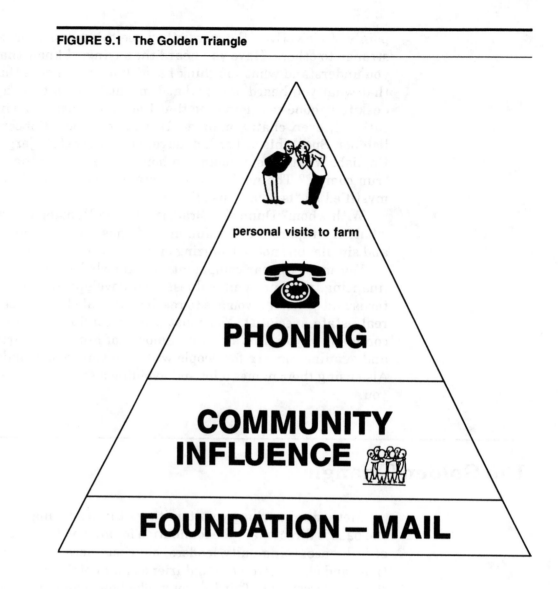

personal visits to farm

PHONING

COMMUNITY INFLUENCE

FOUNDATION – MAIL

Telemarketing

In the fourth stage of farming, after you have succeeded in becoming a trusted friend, the techniques of telemarketing described in Steve Kennedy's book, *Successful Farming by Phone,* will make the difference between your being a tenant farmer or a rich landowner. If you contemplate doing a lot of telemarketing, you will no doubt be much better off with a computer program like Smart Agent, a modem and automatic dialing with a telereport.

Person to Person

The apex of the triangle is held by person-to-person encounters that you have in your farm. This can be done by chatting daily with your neighbors as you walk your dog, by systematically canvassing your neighborhood on a regular basis, as advocated by Alan Jacobson in his book, *Cultivating Your Listing Farm,* or through working social gatherings and clubs.

Whatever mix you plan, do not let your ambition exceed your energy. You only have so much time and energy. It is better to work a small farm well than a large farm badly.

Jacobson and all the other expert farmers urge you to develop a careful plan and follow it. This is easier to do if you have not bitten off more than you can chew. Once you master your farm, you always can add to it. Or you can find another plot to move your growing families up to or your empty nesters down to.

Reverse Contact

One suggestion Jacobson makes that I like is to first mail to everyone. Then divide your farm in half and contact half by telephone and half in person. With the next mailing, reverse the procedure. Telephone those you visited, and visit those you telephoned. You can even break your farm into smaller segments, thirds or quarters. The key to success is a planned, specifically detailed program that is followed religiously.

The decision about the exact mix to use—telephone versus door—depends somewhat on which most successfully projects your personality. Don't forget that over the telephone your prospect is one step removed from you. This may be an advantage or disadvantage depending on your strengths and weaknesses. If your voice is enchanting and you are ugly as sin, grab the telephone. If the telephone intimidates you so that you come off stilted and distant while in person you are warm and charming, forget the telephone.

For many, the telephone eliminates the personal prejudices that poor body language, annoying mannerisms or strange personal appearance arouse in some people. With a melodic voice and a pleasant personality, you can reach people on the telephone who might have rejected you on their doorstep.

Remember that whatever you decide, you are faced with the undeniable fact that contacts do make contracts. If in the final analysis you shrink from that personal contact, there is no way you can make it in real estate.

Telephone Contacts

The main advantage that telephone contacts have over face-to-face contacts is the number of contacts that can be made in the same time frame. You probably can reach at least 15 prospects per hour by telephone, while on the street you could not contact more than 15 a day, if that.

Telephone interviews will be successful about half as often as face-to-face interviews. Your impressions also will certainly be more lasting in person than your telephone impressions. You can use the telephone to cut out the deadwood in your farm, however, and then contact the live wires in person, thus speeding up the whole process.

When you first start farming, unless you have lived in the community a long time and know everyone, you are going to need to ferret out a lot of facts.

Certain information will make cultivating your farm easier:

- Who stays at home during the daytime? Who does not?
- Of those who do not, are they in business, volunteers, etc.?
- Who are the senior citizens?
- Are there singles? Young marrieds? Retirees?
- Who belongs to the garden club, women's club, political clubs, church groups, PTA, civic associations?
- Who would make a good bird dog (someone who will flush out prospects)?
- Who is friendly? Unfriendly? A hermit?
- Who rents the home? Lives there by leave of a relative?
- Who has an extra lot? Adjacent? Separate in same community?
- Who owns a pet? Is a bird-watcher? Hunter? Fisherman?
- Who is an environmentalist? Antivivisectionist?

Two ways to obtain this information are consistent digging in person or over the telephone (phone is better) or by mailing a questionnaire or conducting a survey. Or a mix of both.

It is easier to ask questions over the telephone. Also, you receive immediate feedback. You can form an instant impression of the person and attune your message to your audience before you have sent out a mailing of 500 pieces.

It would take you months to dig up this information on foot. Eventually, however, you are going to have to appear in person. Writing a contract over the telephone is really tricky.

Keeping in touch by phone is a good practice to continue. Studies show that almost 70 percent of business customers drop off because they feel neglected. Your chances of digging up a prospect are good, too, for the *Los Angeles Times* has reported that more than half of the homebuyers buy within 15 miles of their old house. This is one reason open houses in farm areas are so productive.

Naturally, if you have a sphere-of-influence farm, the telephone is your method of choice. (Handwritten notes are good, too.) Referral-building by phone is a natural.

Other target groups also are easier to reach by telephone: all the waterfront properties, all the historic homes, etc.

Dealing with Rejection

The main detriment to dependence on the telephone is the inability of many to cope with the high rejection rate. Because you are able to cover so many more people in the same time, you will receive that many more rejections. It is easier to reject someone forcefully on the telephone than it is in person. Think of this as a numbers game. If you called on 15 people in an eight-hour day, you might receive three rejections. After telemarketing for eight hours (you reach 15 multiplied by 8, or 120 people), using the same ratio, you would receive 24 rejections. Twenty-four! In one day! I couldn't stand it, you say. But think, with the 15 house calls, suppose one homeowner agrees to sell. With the 120 telephone calls, eight homeowners mention plans to sell in the near future. Could you stand those rejections after all . . . for eight good leads? Of course, in most cases the eight hours of telephoning would be spread out over three or four days. It is not necessary to stay glued to the telephone all day. Two hours usually is enough. Three hours is for gluttons. While many experts say to spend absolutely no more than one hour a day on the telephone, once you gear up for a telephone session you probably will persist for at least two hours just to make the session worthwhile. Experiment.

Rejections also occur because you bother people when they are busy at mealtimes, before they get up or after they go to bed, while they are out in the garden or watching a favorite TV show. You can head off some of this potential rejection by being very careful about the hour you call and by asking immediately when you sense annoyance, "When would be a better time to call you?" or "Do you have a moment?" Don't insist on talking to a reluctant dragon. Remember, this is a long-term relationship you are building. Better later than never.

Warm Calls

Most of these rejections will not materialize, however, if you have properly prepared the soil. Write a nice, warm introductory letter enclosing a little gift such as a paper bookmark or football schedule. Then a week later, place door hangers on each doorknob that say: "Hello . . . [beautiful smiling picture of you] I am Jannette Joanes.

I would be happy to answer any real estate questions you may have . . . [Below that] Please phone me anytime. Business 555-8200. Residence 555-6138."

Now they know your name. They know your face And when you call them, you are going to offer them something of value—a calendar of community activities or an illustrated map of the town. Why should they reject you?

Your approach is crucial. On the telephone (as everywhere, but magnified on the telephone) your attitude seeps out around your words. Cold and abrupt is the kiss of death. Pushy is murder. Think of the telephone as a handshake—a friendly introduction to someone's inner sanctum.

Smile all the time you are talking, even if you have to put a mirror over your desk to remind you. Paste smile stickers on the telephone. Pretend you are talking to your best friend. Woo the voice at the other end.

The first 15 or 20 seconds of a telephone call makes or breaks it for you. Brainstorm your opening words. *Jump* immediately into your listener's shoes. Remember, very few people can coolly let a telephone ring. People are excited by a ringing telephone. Don't disappoint them. Make your first words exciting.

Your Telephone Center

Where will you make most of your phone calls from—your home or the office? Wherever you are most comfortable. Peace and quiet are important. Access to your records is important. If you have a small den at home all to yourself, wonderful. Even a little corner, with a screen. Where are you going to get the fewest interruptions? You need to concentrate.

If you have contact management software and have attached a modem to your system, you can mark, or tag, all the names on your target list and elect to have the automatic dialer call each one in sequence. During this process, the computer keeps track of the date, time, who was called and issues a report after the telemarketing operation is complete.

If you don't have a prospect management computer system, get a touch-tone telephone with a repeat button so you can redial a busy number easily. Also, if you have only one phone, order Call Waiting, provided you can handle the etiquette of it (see "The Etiquette of Call Waiting and Hold Buttons," later in this chapter. An absolute necessity is telephone answering machine, voice mail or a new service offered by the telephone companies called Answer Call. Answer Call receives messages even while you are on the phone. You can retrieve messages from virtually anywhere, you can use an optional busy greeting, it can be activated without being turned on and there is no installation or maintenance. It has a multiple mailbox feature, which gives you up to eight separate message boxes, so everyone in the family can get his or her own message.

Attention! Return calls like greased lightning! Nothing impresses prospects like instant response to their calls. A car telephone in your farm would be wonderful if you can afford it. Imagine being able to stop in front of a house and call the owners to tell them how great their new paint job looks. Or to ask to see their new landscaping. Or to make a listing or showing appointment.

Telecommunication Tools

The following tools will facilitate your telemarketing; have them at your fingertips:

- Your farm records
- Your call-out lists
- Your appointment book
- A large wall calendar
- Pens, pencils, eraser, sharpeners, calculator, sticky notes, interest-rate book, financing data, general information
- A folder containing all your script outlines

If you are really serious, you could rent your own reverse telephone directory or your own MLS terminal or you might even input your own laptop computer with your farm program. Set up everything so you can reach anything you need without stretching or knocking things over.

Make a Commitment

Plan to make a certain number of calls for a certain number of hours. Keep your goal achievable. You could eat an elephant, if you took small enough bites.

Make at least six attempts to reach each number. Carry over any unanswered calls to the next day.

Keep track of messages left, telephones unanswered, busy signals never reached, calls completed and appointments entered. Make an oath in blood never to skip anyone on your list (REALTORS® and listed properties excepted). Don't stop during the session. Take your cola with you when you sit down. Go to the bathroom before you begin. No radio or TV. If something is not working out—the script, the time, the offer— make a note to change it. Note objections to overcome or to avoid by using different phraseology. Use sticky notes for callbacks, busy signals, people not home.

Keeping Records

Before undertaking any telephone campaign, your first chore is to make sure that your farm records are up-to-date and the telephone numbers are correct. Cross directories do not have unlisted numbers and some are not consistently up-to-date. The directories of your local telephone company are more likely to be accurate than those of private directory firms. You often can find local directories in the library if your office does not keep them on hand. Renting them costs anything from $40 to $150, depending on the telephone company and the size of the community. Some subdivisions also have local directories.

With unlisted numbers, you are going to have to compile these laboriously over time or be very inventive. One idea is to give away raffle tickets on a Thanksgiving turkey. Place the tickets in a plastic bag on the doorknob of each person who has an unlisted number. On the ticket note, "Winners will be notified by telephone where to pick up their turkey." Leave a place on the ticket and stub for a telephone number. Be sure to mark it *free*. The only alternative is to telephone the unlisted numbers you have collected and keep plugging away at the rest.

As noted in Chapter 4, I have designed a form that can be converted easily into a telephone report form. Cole Publications form is shown in Figure 9.2. See "Copy It," Appendix C, for this fold-up form. Set up these forms in your telephone center before you start calling. If you are using a computer farming program, file the computer data form instead. Keep your tickler file up-to-date, at least weekly. Daily is better!

Once you start calling, take notes on your farm records. Schedule an additional half hour for chores resulting from the telephone session— mopping up. Follow through the same day whenever feasible. Enter appointments on your calendar immediately.

When you get into season four (which, by the way, could arrive much earlier than you plan), you should start tracking the results in terms of the monetary worth of each call. You make ten calls an hour for two hours, three times a week. You average one commission from appointments made for every 60 calls. A $100,000 house listed or sold with a 6 percent commission. For a co-op that would mean at least $1,500. In-house, $3,000.

So each call is worth $25. Those rejections are looking better all the time. The more rejections you receive, the closer you get to that commission.

Use your voice to create an image of self-confidence, intelligence, sincerity, competence and concern for others. Speak directly into the telephone so that your voice is not muffled. It is best to talk at the same speed and volume as the other person. If you talk too slowly, you will give the impression of stupidity. If you talk too quickly, some people will not trust you. Be relaxed, optimistic, outgoing and friendly.

You should follow a pattern for your call, which, when you are making a number of calls, should last only three or four minutes. Start

FIGURE 9.2   Real Estate Listing Form

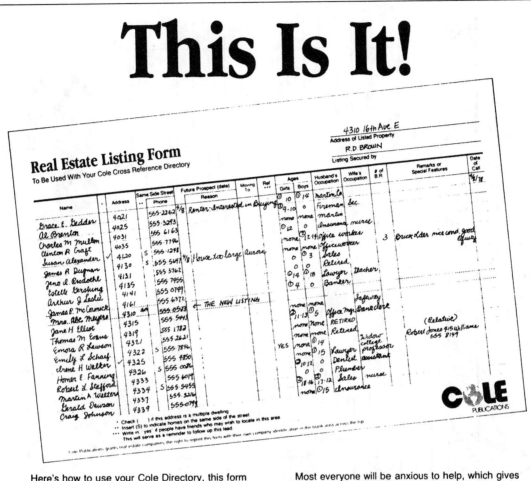

This Is It!

Here's how to use your Cole Directory, this form and the telephone to:

- ASK FOR PROSPECTS FOR THE LISTED HOME
- GET INFORMATION TO HELP A PROSPECT MAKE A DECISION
- SELL HOMES FASTER
- GAIN ADDITIONAL LISTINGS

Follow this simple, effective technique!

1. Put the information about the new listing in the center, shaded space.
2. Working each way from the listing, use your Cole Directory to secure the names, addresses and phone numbers of the neighbors on the same and opposite side of the street.
3. Telephone each one. Here is a sample of how the conversation might go:

YOU: "Hello, (Mr., Mrs.) _____ name _____?"
NEIGHBOR: "Yes..."
YOU: "Thank you, (Mr., Mrs.) _____ name _____
This is _____
of _____ Realty.
We have just listed the home (next door, across the street, down the block, etc.) for sale. I'm sure you're interested in it being sold to someone who will become good neighbors...and we would very much like to find new owners that would make you happy. Would you mind if I ask you a few questions that will help me do that?"
NEIGHBOR: "All right, what would you like to know?"

Most everyone will be anxious to help, which gives you an opportunity to get all the information you need. Here are some suggested questions you can tactfully ask.

Questions to get prospects for the listed home...
"Have any of your friends or relatives ever mentioned locating in this neighborhood? Wouldn't this be a good time to let them know about this home? May I call them to arrange a time to see it?"

Questions to get information to help a prospect make a decision...
"I hear children in the room...how many do you have? How old are they?" (Knowing the ages of neighbor children may overcome the prospects' fears that their children won't like the new home.)"What kind of work do you (does your husband) do?" (Knowing that there are two attorneys on the street, for example, may sway a prospect who is also an attorney.)

Questions to gain additional listings...
"Your home is a three bedroom, isn't it? Are you considering a smaller (larger) home as the children grow up?"

Managers, please note:
Your directory representative will be happy to show your sales staff how to use this form and the telephone technique described above. This is just one of the many additional services you receive at no additional charge by being a Cole Directory subscriber. Please call if you feel this service will be helpful.

Source: Reprinted by permission of Cole Publications & Information Services Division of Metro Mail.

FIGURE 9.2   Real Estate Listing Form (Continued)

Real Estate Listing Form
To Be Used With Your Cole Cross Reference Directory

Address of Listed Property

Listing Secured by

Name	*	Address	Same Side Street ** Phone	Future Prospect (date) Reason	Moving To:	Ref. ***	Ages Girls	Ages Boys	Husband's Occupation	Wife's Occupation	# of B.R.	Remarks or Special Features	Date of Call

*   Check ( ) if this address is a multiple dwelling.
**   Insert (S) to indicate homes on the same side of the street.
*** Write in "yes" if people have friends who may wish to locate in this area.
     This will serve as a reminder to follow up this lead.

F1331

COLE
PUBLICATIONS
& INFORMATION SERVICES
DIVISION OF METROMAIL

Cole Publications grants real estate companies the right to reprint this form with their own company identification in the blank area across the top.

off the call with the call recipient's name and yours and then your company name. State your reason for calling. Ask if the recipient has a moment to talk. Then make your offer, answer any questions and ask any that you have. Wrap up and hang up after the recipient does.

Telephone Tips

First, know why you are calling, and what you are trying to accomplish. Keep in mind what you have to offer this person. Write all this down in front of you when you start telephoning so you are clear in your own mind what you are trying to say and do.

Remember, the more natural and human you sound, the warmer responses you will get, and the fewer rejections you will garner. It is those empty mechanical voices that get sworn at. Who wants to talk to a robot?

The following are "don'ts" to keep in mind when calling:

- Don't cold call.
- Don't sell real estate over the telephone.
- Don't fear failure.
- Don't waste time.
- Don't try working a day at a time. Plan ahead.
- Don't neglect to use the listener's name.

To make an impression on the telephone, you have no more than 15 seconds (via voice approach). Just by listening to those first few words, the call recipient can tell how you feel toward him or her.

The Etiquette of Call Waiting and Hold Buttons

It is best never to put any customer or client on hold—ever. If you must do it, say: "Excuse me, Sir (or Madam), let me take the number of this caller. I will be right back to you." Then, when you come back on the line, say, "Sorry for the interruption, Sir (or Madam)." Then repeat the last sentence of the interrupted phrase. It is very rude to the first caller to carry on an extended conversation with the second caller. Tell the second caller that you will return his or her call.

Telephone courtesy is a must, not only for you, but for all members of your family. If your family cannot remember to be courteous, it is best to get a second line. "Who is this?" and other such abruptness should be avoided. "May I tell him (or her) who is calling?" is the accepted phrase. Sounding bored, uninterested, angry or hurried; monopolizing the conversation; not paying attention; arguing; hanging up first; and using slang or obscenity all are no-no's.

Develop a Script

The major difficulty is staying on track. Script outlines will help you do this. You are looking for clear, logical communication. The script will help you organize and clarify your thoughts, make you sound smoother and give you self-confidence. You can plan ahead how to handle objections, so that if any come up you are prepared for them.

I cannot emphasize enough that your farm telephoning goal is not to get a listing or a sale at this stage, or even an appointment (although you certainly wouldn't turn one down if the opportunity arose). Your goal is to leave an impression of competence and concern for others. You want everyone in your farm thinking of you as the person to turn to when they need real estate help.

The script sequence usually is as follows:

- Opening
- Rapport-building
- The offer
- Questions and responses
- Handling objections, if any,
- Close

In his book on telephone farming (see "Resources," Appendix A), Steve Kennedy suggests using index cards for scripts, color coding them according to the script section so you can easily see where you are in the outline. He also suggests practicing your script with a tape recorder, critiquing it and asking friends for their opinion of it. Practice with a partner; find any weaknesses in the script and correct them.

One thing to remember is that most of the time it is not so much *what* you say as *how* you say it that matters. In the beginning you don't have to worry so much about objections, but in stage four, when you will be doing more in-depth telemarketing, it may pay to list common objections and ways of handling them.

Keep working on the script until you feel comfortable with it. The following offers an example of one side of a conversation:

"Mrs. Brown? This is Mary Jones. I live on Hickory Lane and I am with ABC, REALTORS®.

"I understand you are a fellow member of the PTA. Are you familiar with the School Profiles that REALTORS® are using to give newcomers school information?

"You're not? Well, it occurred to me that perhaps the PTA might like to have some input in these profiles, and I was wondering if you would like to have one of them to look at.

"Not interested? Perhaps you could tell me who in the organization might be the one to talk to? Have I caught you at a bad time or do you have a moment?

"I see. Well, I hope to see you at the next PTA meeting. I think your Suzie and my Pammy are in the same class.

"Great. Look forward to meeting you in person. Good-bye."

This demonstrates that even a nominally unsuccessful conversation can end on a friendly note. Next time will be better. You are *building* trust.

Let's examine and critique each of the parts of the script.

Opening: Her name	No problem in the opener.

Rapport-building:
  I live on Hickory Lane.
  Fellow member of PTA
	No problem in rapport section.

Offer:
  School profile
  PTA input
	Offer is weak and confusing.

Benefit to listener:
  Listener saw none.
  Speaker gave none.
	Benefits never were explained.

Close:
  Common ground
  Set up meeting.
	Close rescued the call.
	Strong
	Time and place agreed.

You can see from this analysis how scripts can be amended and improved through the feedback received.

One of the problems with this call was that it was a cold call. How much easier it would have been if the caller could have started out like this:

"Hello, Mrs. Brown. My name is Mary Jones. You may have gotten my letter last week. I am with ABC, REALTORS®.

"You did? I also left a door hanger with my picture on it. Because we are both in the PTA, I thought we might know each other.

"Oh, you do remember me. I know your Suzie and my Pammy are in the same class.

"I've put together a calendar of local events and I wonder if you would like to have one.

"Great, I'll just drop it by one day this week. If you are not home, I can slide it under your mat. Are you usually there in the daytime?

"Well, perhaps I'll see you then. Bye-bye."

Make them an offer they can't refuse. Find out information for your files each time you make contact. Build rapport and trust. Use a nice, relaxed tone. These are the things demonstrated by this call. Starting off too directly is a mistake. Remember, at this point you are planting seeds that will bear fruit later.

Let me demonstrate call closes at various stages of the farming season:

Stage One: Getting Acquainted

"Nice talking to you, Mrs. Brown. I hope I'll get to meet you in person one of these days."

Stage Two: Building Trust

"It will be wonderful meeting you at last, Mrs. Brown. Be sure to call me if I can bring anything else along."

Stage Three: Becoming the Neighborhood Specialist

"I thought you'd be thrilled to know, Mrs. Brown, that I was able to help your friend, Mrs. Anderson, out of the tough situation she was in. Give her a call one of these days; she speaks so highly of you. She gave me permission to advise you of her new phone number."

Stage Four: The Harvest

"Suzie's off to college, I hear. It won't be long until you can zero in on that condo on the water that you have been dreaming about. No more raking leaves or shoveling snow for Mr. Brown. How soon can we get together and discuss it? Would tomorrow night be good? Between eight and nine? Great, see you then, eight at your house. Bye-bye."

When you arrive at stage four you can use a little higher pressure. For example, you can use descending interest rates as a reason to call all the people in your farm who have high-interest loans and suggest that they move into larger, better quarters for the same monthly payment. Use the *Lusk Directory* to find out which people have the high-interest loans. Steve Kennedy offers a script for this in his book on telephone farming. It is so good there is no doubt in my mind that many people would look on the offer as a "service" to them, rather than as a sales pitch.

Stage Five: Defending Your Territory

"Sorry I missed you yesterday. What a view from your deck! I know you have settled in for the rest of your days. Just stopped over with a little housewarming gift, a pair of binoculars to watch those spinnakers on Sunday evenings. I also dropped by to see the Gossamers. They love your old place. Said to tell you 'hi!'"

Hot Buttons

Reading people will help you find their "hot buttons." People seldom act logically. Decisions generally are based on emotions. People will deny this, but watch them. In order to be able to persuade people, you must learn to look beneath the cold bare facts to find the psychological reasons why they do what they do. No matter how splendid the home, for example, you will never get a person who has a basic motivation of "seeking status" to buy on the wrong side of the tracks. Observe people and listen closely, so that you can find these so-called hot buttons. You will have an opportunity to do this in your farm. Keep your eyes and ears open.

If you approach cultivating your farm in the right spirit, you will find that getting to know all these wonderful people in your neighborhood is an exciting adventure. People will seek you out and sure enough you will find "contacts equal contracts."

Listing in Your Farm: The Harvest

During the past six months to two years, you have been preparing the soil, planting the seeds and cultivating the plants. Now you are ready for the harvest.

The techniques needed for the first stages of farming are systems of continuous communication. Those needed for the second stages are real estate selling skills.

Selling Yourself

Selling yourself is involved in both of these skills. REALTORS® generally, and inexperienced salespeople particularly, do not place enough emphasis on the ability to sell themselves in real estate. Most new agents start out trying to sell the company, and most companies encourage this.

Of course, telling your story and what services you and your company have to offer is an important part of a listing presentation. It is a fundamental of selling, however, that before you can sell anything, you must be able to sell yourself. The public will not believe anything you say until they trust you.

A few years ago a large East Coast real estate firm conducted a survey among its past clients. It used a very large sample. Clients were asked why they chose to list their property with the company. The overwhelming majority of the clients replied that they listed with the company because they liked the salesperson.

One reason farming works so well is that it gives you an opportunity to become acquainted with people before they have to make a decision about choosing a broker.

Even if you are involved in passive farming, sooner or later you are going to have to meet face-to-face with the client. It is impossible to list and sell any other way. The sooner the better. It smooths your way to listing if you are already an old friend.

Your Marketing Plan

According to Carole Kelby, one of the most sought-after real estate seminar speakers and trainers, writing in the *Real Estate Professional,* the best way to sell yourself in a listing presentation is through your marketing plan.

There are as many marketing plans as there are people and companies. Some agents' idea of marketing a listing is to throw it into MLS and go home. Others spend hours creating elaborate fliers, brochures, door hangers and glossy advertisements that will appear in glossy magazines. Some companies rely completely on classified ads. Others employ advertising departments that produce home magazines that rival *House Beautiful,* tabloids as big as *The Wall Street Journal,* plus a stream of promotional items for the use of salespeople. Some produce hour-long television shows that sell as many as one out of four homes advertised within a week of the show.

Carole Kelby has come up with an idea to make you competitive with anybody. And my 20 years of experience in real estate tells me that she is right on target with this idea.

Exposure to Real Estate Professionals

Kelby's written marketing plan starts with a *key* pronouncement: "My experience in marketing homes successfully has been based on total exposure to real estate professionals."

This statement requires some explaining to clients. Clients think that classified advertisements sell real estate. We know from ongoing studies that only one person in 64 calls on the house he or she ultimately buys. Most callers have no idea what they can afford. They usually call on houses they cannot or would not buy, either because they cannot afford the house or it really is not suited to their needs. What happens is, as we all are well aware, good real estate salespeople know the market like the backs of their hands. They also know how to determine people's needs and wants, how to qualify them financially and personally and how to match them to the very home they need. So they direct them from the unsuitable house they called in on to the suitable home they need. On the 64th time, salespeople may sell clients the home that they called on, but how many houses are advertised that often to make the odds great enough that an advertisement will sell the house?

The people who show and sell houses are the professional real estate salespeople in an area. According to Kelby, "My role is to make sure that every agent is aware of your home."

Attracting Salespeople Is Vital

An important aspect of this approach is the negative aspect. Anything a homeowner does wrong or refuses to do that keeps salespeople from showing the home will decrease the chances of selling it at the top of the market. Using the Kelby approach will encourage homeowners to use a lockbox or give you a key, because they understand that exposure to qualified buyers sells homes and that REALTORS® are the ones who expose qualified buyers to homes. Why is condition so important? Because professional salespeople are reluctant to lose meticulous buyers by showing them untidy homes. Why is price so important? Because salespeople qualify buyers and know what they can afford. They do not take them to overpriced houses unless they are desperate, and by then the prospective buyers have seen so many houses that they are well aware that this one does not measure up to others with the same price. Why not cut the commission way down? Because salespeople, being human and being given the choice between a small commission and a larger one, inevitably will choose the larger one. Of course, you, as the listing agent, would show the house regardless of the amount of the commission. But what of the 2, 4 or 10,000 other real estate salespeople?

Increasing Exposure to the Real Estate Community

The marketing plan that you present should list all the things that you plan to do to increase exposure of the home to the real estate community: fliers, inspections, lockbox, MLS, open houses, agent's coffees—anything you can create to attract the other brokers to your listing. Some sales associates have cards printed up to send other associates with similar listings that say something like "while you are showing your listing on _____ Street, why not show mine on _____ Street?" Some agents will go to great lengths to aid cooperating salespeople to sell the agent's own listings. Some listing specialists' available listing inventories are larger than that of many small companies. If a contract that comes in on one of their own listings is not accepted, they attempt to switch the buyer to another of the agent's own listings. Some help the selling agent with complicated financing plans, contract writing or anything else that is needed to be sure that one of the listing agent's own listings is sold.

This whole approach is just the opposite from the dog-in-the-manger attitude that still prevails in some areas. People who try to hog their own listings are behind the times. Cooperation is the watchword of success in today's market.

Do not misunderstand me. I am not saying you should not sell your own listings, particularly in your own listing farm. What I am saying is that the more of your listings that sell quickly, the more listings you will receive and the more opportunity you will have to sell many of your own.

Your Competitive Advantage

Your marketing plan naturally should include all your competitive advantages. If your company is one of those with a sophisticated promotional program, including TV, relocation or other marketing advantages, you should emphasize this (see Figure 10.1). If you, personally, have a leading edge in your community, of course you will explain that you arrived at this point because of the wonderful service that you give your clients. Then list the services. If you are a Certified Residential Specialist, explain *how* this helps your client.

Genuine concern for the clients' needs is the secret to developing the trust you need. The only thing the seller is interested in is "What can you do for me?" Sellers do not want to hear a long litany of your past successes. They do not want a recitation of your company services unless these particular services have bearing on their personal situation. Pick out the ones that do and leave them a list or brochure of the rest.

Personal Commitment

The one thing sellers are dying to hear is your own personal commitment to getting their homes sold at prices that they can cope with, in a reasonable amount of time.

Don't be afraid to face superstars who are competing for your listing in your own farm. Remember you, the farmer, have two tremendous advantages:

1. You know everything that has been going on in this farm for a long time. You know all the people by name. You know that 222 Park

FIGURE 10.1   Sample Marketing Plan

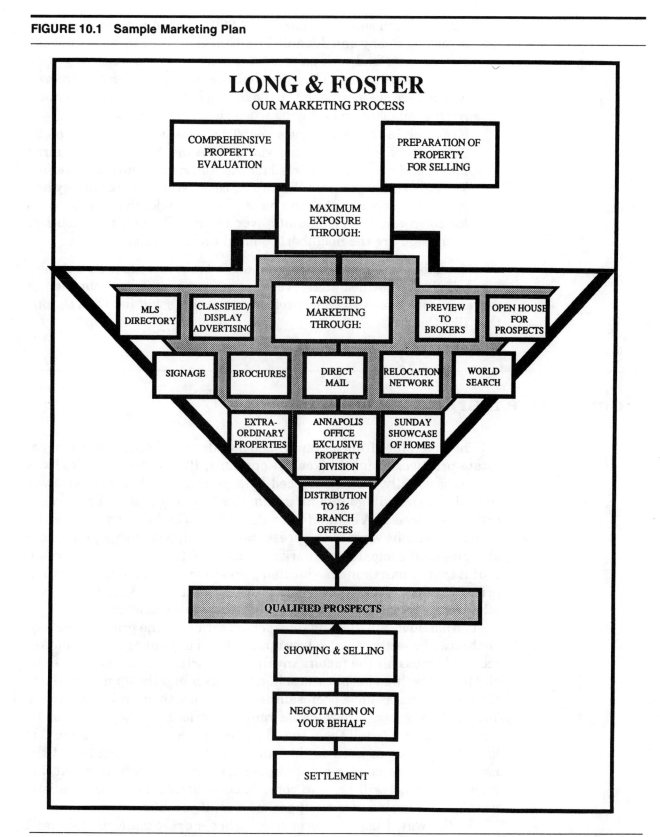

Street, which sold last year for $2,000 over the market price, was owned by Bobby and Jeannie Fox, that they paid $2,500 of buyers' closing costs and took back a second mortgage because they were so desperate to sell. They also left the washer, dryer and freezer, which were not mentioned on the listing form or computer printout. Aren't you going to look good when this sale is discussed?

2. Everyone in the farm knows you. They have seen your face on 24 newsletters. They have met you at PTA meetings, at the church bingo, and when you collected for the American Heart Association. They also know you sold White's house after another company had it listed for six months. You have rendered a dozen small services for them and the community over the months or years. You live there. You are the neighborhood real estate specialist.

Remember that establishing rapport is *the* critical factor in obtaining a listing. Provided that everyone who makes a presentation is perceived as a knowledgeable professional, sellers will list with the one they like the best.

Competitive Market Analysis

The PFA (pluck from air) appraisal has almost disappeared from real estate practice. Thank heaven! At one time, PFAs were the rule. Even now, occasionally, an experienced salesperson who has drifted away from the basics will go into an unfamiliar territory and make a drastically overpriced PFA estimate of value, only to be brought up short by a competitor who went to the presentation equipped with a professionally prepared comparative market analysis (CMA) that demonstrated that it takes more than an educated guess to arrive at a realistic listing price. One star recited a tale of woe to me, quoting the seller, "Well, the other agent seemed to know much more about *our* market."

I do *not* advocate that the salesperson establish the price. Those who do this can be setting themselves up for a fall if any change in the market occurs. Discuss all the factors involved in pricing, including the necessity to please three people: the seller, the buyer and the appraiser. Show them what houses have been selling for and ask them to select a price. You could suggest a reasonable range of prices. If they will not be realistic, be sure to tell them that no house has ever sold for a price this high, but you are so keen on their home that you are willing to test the market: "In a couple of weeks, however, if the market indicates that this price won't fly, I will have to come back to arrive at a more realistic price—or we could order an appraisal now, if you like."

By the way, I use the term *competitive market analysis* because I want to alert the sellers to the fact that they are in competition with other sellers. I also find that there is a tendency on the part of some sellers to bridle when "comparables" are mentioned: "I don't give a darn what the Joneses got for their house, I need umpty-ump dollars." They do not understand, at first, that buyers buy by comparison. The crucial nature of price in the sale of a home is something that has to be carefully explained. Other agents may be telling them, "I can get you this and I can get you that." While it is true that the more exposure to qualified buyers a house receives, the more likely it is to sell at the top of the market, point out that *there is a top*. If the house is listed more than 5 or 6 percent above that top, it may negatively affect the sale. The house becomes shopworn. People wonder why it has been on the market so long and start to make very low offers.

You have a tremendous advantage in your listing farm by being able to find the top of the market because you know the homes so well. You know how the condition, terms and market of the homes that sold in the past affected the price. You understand the many emotional factors that were involved in the sales.

You should not have to do much research to produce an accurate CMA because you already have all the records.

If you are using a computer to keep farm records, you can keep comparable files for your entire farm area in your data base. These can be entered from sales information selected directly from your sources or from the competitive market analyses you conduct for sellers as you produce them. CMAs can be customized for the particular situation with your name, your company name, your seller's name and address and other information you might want to include (Figure 10.2). Attach a sheet showing the seller's estimated net proceeds (Figure 10.3) and a brochure of your company services to your personal marketing plan—it makes a very impressive package.

You also can use your computer data base to print out other relevant statistics. For example, if the sellers can see in black and white that it takes 120 days for a home to sell in the current market, then they will be prepared to wait that amount of time.

If you can also use the computer to prove that the For Sale By Owners (FSBOs) are coming out short on the bottom line, you can include this fact in a prepared list of reasons why sellers should not attempt selling their own homes, in case you encounter someone so inclined. You could use the flier "The Key To Selling Your Own Home," "Copy It," Appendix C.

After the property has been on the market for 50 to 60 days, you may want to prepare a second market analysis, particularly if the market has changed. Take the occasion to reevaluate the whole listing experience.

Because you have been going to see every property in your farm on the first day or so that it was put on the market, you have information about what features and condition these properties had to offer. You also know what listings expired because they originally were put on the market at prices that drove away the backlog of eager buyers who

FIGURE 10.2   Competitive Market Analysis Form

_____
(Firm's Name)

Competitive Market Analysis

Name _____ Address _____ Date _____

Subject Property Facts: Rooms _____ Bedrooms _____ Baths _____

Lot size _____ Finished Sq. Ft. _____

Garage _____ Fireplace _____ Air cond. _____

Extras: _____

_____

Area Homes For Sale

ADDRESS OF COMP	SQ. FT.	BEDRMS	BATHS	DAYS ON MKT.	PRICE	EXTRAS

Comparable Sales Analysis

ADDRESS OF COMP.	DATE	PRICE	SQ. FT.	±DATE	±SIZE	±EXTRAS	±AREA	ADJ. PRICE

Buyer Appeal Rating
1. Location .... _____%
2. Extras .... _____%
3. Financing ability .... _____%
4. Street appeal .... _____%
5. Interior appeal .... _____%
                    Total Rating _____%
Graded on basis of how market views property.
Each item rated 0% to 20%.

Marketing Position
1. Why are they selling .... _____%
2. How soon must they sell .... _____%
3. How well will property finance .. _____%
4. Proper pricing .... _____%
                    Total Rating _____%
Graded on basis of desirability or urgency.
Each item rated 0% to 25%.

Marketing suggestions and comments _____

_____

Estimated market range $ _____ to $ _____ top competitive market value $ _____

_____ Date _____

FIGURE 10.3   Sellers' Estimated Net Proceeds Form

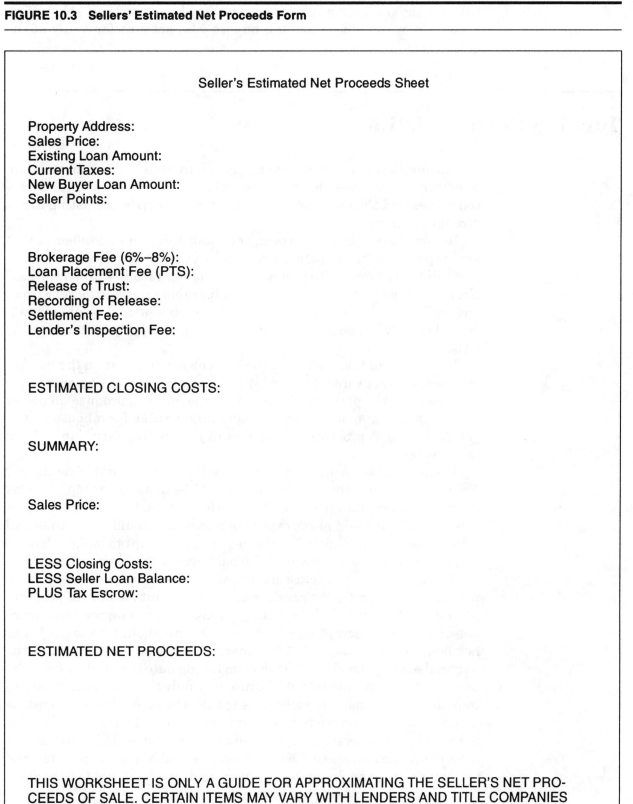

Seller's Estimated Net Proceeds Sheet

Property Address:
Sales Price:
Existing Loan Amount:
Current Taxes:
New Buyer Loan Amount:
Seller Points:

Brokerage Fee (6%–8%):
Loan Placement Fee (PTS):
Release of Trust:
Recording of Release:
Settlement Fee:
Lender's Inspection Fee:

ESTIMATED CLOSING COSTS:

SUMMARY:

Sales Price:

LESS Closing Costs:
LESS Seller Loan Balance:
PLUS Tax Escrow:

ESTIMATED NET PROCEEDS:

THIS WORKSHEET IS ONLY A GUIDE FOR APPROXIMATING THE SELLER'S NET PRO-
CEEDS OF SALE. CERTAIN ITEMS MAY VARY WITH LENDERS AND TITLE COMPANIES
AND ARE SUBJECT TO CHANGE WITHOUT NOTICE.

will pay the most for a house because they have not been able to find what they want. These are the buyers who account for many of the quick sales.

Turning Down a Listing

Turning down a listing anyplace but in your listing farm is *not* something I recommend. I have seen this done too many times by my colleagues and then watched while a competitor rode the listing into a nice fat commission.

In your listing farm, however, the main thing to remember is that your reputation for competence is at stake every time you take a listing.

Ordinarily, would I turn down a listing because it was overpriced? No, I would not. I would present the comparable sales and be very frank and up front about the chances of getting such a price. I would make it crystal clear why I believe that pricing a home properly is crucial to the owner.

Even if I could not convince the homeowner to put it on the market at or near market value, I would take it anyway. One thing I would never do anywhere, but particularly in a listing farm, is to promise an owner that I can "get him or her" more than market value for a house just to get the listing. A practice such as this in your listing farm can kill you in the long run.

Would I turn down a listing because it is not in salable condition? No. I would advise the owner what should be done to get top price for the home and explain "fixer-uppers" to the owners. I would explain how house condition could affect exposure and how it could affect time and price; if the owners resisted to the death any attempt to make a "cream puff" out of their "dog," however, I would accept the listing.

Successful listing practice means properly servicing a listing. A large part of servicing a listing consists of turning it into a salable property during the first term of the listing. If the average owner were more reasonable about accepting professional advice about how to get his or her house sold at the top of the market, we easily could reduce the national average for the duration from listing date to sale date from the present 90 days to about 20. Unfortunately, only the passage of time will convince a great many homeowners to take the steps that a real estate professional knows have to be taken in order to sell the house. It helps to be a good salesperson: i.e., trusted and persuasive. This will shorten the time it takes to make the owner understand his or her position and prevent expirations. In any case, I have made it a habit not to turn down listings without an exceptionally compelling reason.

The Unmotivated Seller

Is there *any* reason to turn down a listing? The only one I have discovered is the unmotivated seller. If the seller has no real urgency to sell the house, then even the passage of time will not influence the seller to do what is necessary to bring the listing into line.

Ordinarily, the result of taking this kind of listing is not drastic. You end up with an expired listing and wasted time and money, but this is not fatal.

Keep Your Eye on the Ball

In your farm area, though, keep your eye on the ball! What is your objective? To be known as the real estate specialist of the area. Don't forget that your reputation for competence in your listing farm is at stake every time you list a home. You cannot afford to have people asking themselves what is wrong with you because you cannot seem to sell the home. Remember, they do not realize the house may be overpriced or that there may be no way to show the home because you have no key, no lockbox and the owners are never home because they work all day and leave town on weekends. Others are unaware that although the outside may be well kept because the man of the house is anxious to take a new position in Chicago, the inside may be a disaster area with beds unmade, dishes unwashed and clutter everywhere. The lady of the house may have moved six times during the past ten years and may have no interest whatsoever in this move. You cannot afford wrong impressions in your listing farm. A motivated seller is a must.

Years go, in my old farm area, a certain family placed their house on the market every spring for six years. Each year the price was about $5,000 (10 percent) above the market value of comparable homes, and each year after 120 days the listing expired and they sat tight until the following year, when prices had risen about 15 percent, at which time they put the house back on the market at 25 percent above the previous year's price. I watched this whole process from afar. Many times I could have obtained the listing, but at what cost? They never listed twice with the same broker and they always blamed the lack of a sale on the poor service and chicanery of real estate brokers, specifically and in general.

Neighbors Influence Choice of Brokers

Recently, a friend of mine who had a house for sale in Charleston, South Carolina, for over a year changed REALTORS® on the advice of her neighbors, who blamed the lack of a sale on the original listing broker. As it turned out in the end, the house was more than $100,000 over-priced. My friend, who was not at all in need of money and not at all sure she was doing the right thing in moving back to Ohio, backed out of the sale at the last moment. Even though the failure to sell the house had nothing to do with either real estate sales associate, the neighbors still are telling each other to avoid these two REALTORS® in their own farms. Obviously, the influence of neighbors in the choice of a real estate agent can be considerable.

If the neighbors' perception of your competence is influenced by your failure to move properties of owners who are not really serious, your reputation will suffer. It behooves you to do a little digging to determine the seller's urgency. Many times a few questions will unearth the true situation. Why are they moving? When must they move? Does everyone in the family agree on the move? Who is the decision maker in this family and where does he or she stand? Sometimes the decision maker is a 12-year-old kid.

The Motivated Seller

With a motivated seller, mountains can be moved.

I once had the world's worst listing. First, it was $10,000 overpriced. The owner insisted that the same model had sold at the listed price, although I could find no record of it. I did find an identical model that sold for $10,000 less. The comparable was on a nice, level, wooded lot, while my listing perched on top of a cliff. The lot was perpendicular. It was terraced down the hillside with railroad ties. A mountain goat would have had to mow the lawn. The house was a two-story with a basement and a subbasement. I always claimed the subbasement had a balcony. Actually, it was a deck. In a recreation area in the valley below, the kids playing ball looked like ants.

If a house has problems like these, what will make it sell? As trainers tell rookies, "Price cures all." This one was $10,000 over the market.

That wasn't all. The owners would not give me a key or a lockbox and had to be called two hours before a showing so that they could drag their German shepherd snarling out of the house. No sign, they said. Signs are tacky. (No matter that 50 percent of our buyers in that area were calling from signs.) No open houses, they said. Open houses just attract "lookers." (No matter that I had open-house guest books for three years and not a single person could be reached at his or her original telephone number, although all had been verified and all prospects contacted shortly after the open houses.)

Why in the world did I want this listing? Because it was June 1 when they contacted me and they had to be at the new job halfway across the country on August 1. They had previously tried to sell it themselves. "Nothing to it," they said, "we actually sold it twice." (They didn't know how to qualify and financing fell through each time.) In the existing market it was taking an average of 80 days to sell a house and 60 days to get a buyer approved, so time was of the essence.

The wife made no bones about it: If the house wasn't sold by August 1, no way was she leaving her husband alone in a strange city . . . she would be going along . . . they needed their money . . . in fact, they were short of cash for this move . . . etc. In other words, I had a motivated seller who would do whatever was necessary to sell once I was able to make them understand their position.

Servicing the Listing

I listed the house on a Friday afternoon. On Saturday morning, I appeared on their doorstep about 11 A.M. "I'm a little worried about your situation," I said. "In fact, I had a hard time sleeping last night because, as I mentioned yesterday, it is taking a rather long time to get the financing through and I don't think you should have this house vacant a long time with all those kids down in the valley playing ball."

Ordering the Appraisal

They invited me in. "Here is what I am thinking. If this house has not sold in three weeks, we will know we have overshot the market and we are going to have to take some steps to get in line. It takes about three weeks to get a VA appraisal through the lending institution and if we have one in our hands we will be in a position to know the market value and to prove it. Also, if we order the appraisal from an approved lender and we do get a veteran buyer, it will save us 20 days in approval time. What do you say to ordering it right away? I could have it at the lenders by Monday." They said OK and I got a check from them made out to the lender.

Getting the Sign Up

Sunday afternoon about 1 P.M. I appeared on their doorstep again. "Did you see the ad the developer ran yesterday for those contemporaries he is selling at the end of your street?" I asked them. They had. "I came out to see what kind of action he was getting, and the place was mobbed. There were prospects riding all around the neighborhood taking down the numbers on our competition's signs . . . and we don't even have a sign on the property!" I reached into my trunk and got one. Fifty percent of our sales up there have been from signs and now I understand why. They stood there and let me pound the sign into the ground in front of their house.

Two weeks later, not one single co-op agent had shown the property. I had shown it twice. Same response each time: the price was too high.

Scheduling Open Houses

I scheduled an evening appointment with the sellers. I showed them the nice flier I had sent out to surrounding brokerages. I explained that I had telephoned several agents I knew to find out why it wasn't being shown. Too hard to show, too much trouble to work their prospects around it or to get them to wait two hours, especially out-of-towners who had a limited time to decide. We needed to get the dog out and get a key.

Choices

"We have two choices," I told the owners. "We can put the dog in a kennel or we can just start holding an open house every weekend. You could take the dog over to your folks when you go."

Always give people a choice between something and something, not something and nothing. Naturally, they chose open houses over a kennel.

Three weeks passed. No takers. The appraisal came in and we reduced the price to the appraisal. I had heard that if you have a hard time with a problem house, advertise the problem. I ran an advertisement with a headline "California Cliff-Hanger," held the open house twice running and sold it within the listing period. Motivated seller.

There are two lessons here: the importance of a motivated seller and the importance of servicing and marketing your farm listings.

The Listing/Selling Cycle: Open Houses

Double Your Income

If you can establish a listing/selling cycle in your farm, you are in clover!

You accomplish this feat when you always have a backlog of prospects waiting for your next listing in your farm.

Your backlog of buyers must match the houses you have to offer; that is, the kind of buyers you have are looking for the kind of houses you list. The best way to accomplish this is through open houses.

Why People Tour Open Houses

Why do people come to open houses? Undoubtedly, a few people happen into open houses by chance. I happen to believe, however, that most of us are too busy today to spend our time aimlessly wandering around open houses. In my opinion, "lookers" are a myth. Most of the people who come to open houses have a very good reason for being there. Perhaps it isn't to buy the open house but rather to get an idea what houses are going for in case they decide to sell their own. In other words, listing prospects go to open houses. What "lookers" are there, mostly nosy neighbors, often are wonderful candidates for bird dogs. They should be warmly greeted and pumped for neighborhood news: Who is expecting a transfer, whose kids are moving out, leaving the empty nesters with a huge house and even who is having marital problems and may split up?

But back to buying prospects—why are they at your open house?

A great many of those touring open houses already have decided that they want to live in that area for one reason or another. Maybe because it is a prestigious neighborhood and they are looking for status. Maybe because the style and price range of homes that they are looking for can be found in this neighborhood.

Maybe because the train station or subway stop is near or because this is the most attractive neighborhood close to town that they can find.

The reasons are myriad: The high school specializes in science and they have a budding science genius in the family; they were brought up in a mammoth frame house in New England with a wraparound veranda and this is the only community they have found where these old homes in marvelous condition are found on tree-lined streets; they love the idea of living alongside a golf course, where they can just walk over and start playing after work.

Whatever the reason, these folks beat it out every Sunday and go through every open house. Whether you ran an advertisement or not, they would be there. Whether you sent out open-house invitations or not, they would be there. Whether you had distributed door hangers around the neighborhood or not, these people would be there. Any convenient day you could just pound in a few open signs, place a few strategic open arrows and a certain number of people would arrive. The more open arrows, the more of these regulars you will have.

You must ask yourself, though, why hasn't some enterprising salesperson sold them something? In some cases the answer is that nobody has found their hot button. But believe it or not, the main reason is that nobody has ever followed up. Nobody has ever called these people. In fact, in most instances nobody has even obtained their telephone numbers.

The Perils of No Follow-Through!

Incredible, you say. Well, listen to this story. I was holding an open house in a local community of three-bedroom brick ramblers and four-bedroom brick Cape Cods that were the perfect style and price for rental properties. A couple came through and we chatted a bit, and I found that this was exactly what they had in mind. They already owned a couple of rental properties and were looking for another. Several days later, I called them back and they offered absolutely no resistance at all. In fact, it was the easiest transaction I remember. Afterward, the woman said to me, "You know we have been looking for a rental unit for more than six months. We saw several we were interested in. We could never understand why no one ever called us, although we let the agents know we were interested. You were the first person in all those months who ever followed through!"

Maybe this is the reason why it is possible to keep a backlog of prospective buyers in a farm area. If you just keep in touch and keep letting them know you haven't forgotten them, you should be able to hold many of them until you can get a house listed that suits their needs. On the other hand, some prospects are so eager to buy that if you do not contact them the very next day, they already will have bought.

Open Houses: A Waste of Time?

The ideal open house is priced right, shows well, has curb appeal and is in a good location. Not every house you hold open can fill this description, especially in your farm. In your farm you should hold open *every one of your listings* in order to build up your backlog of potential buyers. I had a friend who listed a problem house in a nice subdivision. The house was backed up to an interstate with a rise right in front of it that caused trucks to shift gears, with an ensuing roar night and day. The house was a housekeeping nightmare and no amount of counseling with the owner could change a 20-year habit. The agent held it open 21 times and finally sold it. By that time she knew the name of every potential buyer for that subdivision for miles around. She sold so many homes in that community that she made Rookie of the Year.

Agents sometimes complain that they held an open house and nobody came. When you dig into it a little, you find they didn't invite anyone. No open-house invitations, no fliers, no door hangers announcing the event. The agent just moseyed out there about ten minutes late, opened the place up and watched the ball game.

In the past I have witnessed a mysterious occurrence. I would have a house I couldn't seem to sell and finally in desperation, I would hold it open to please the seller. Nobody came. A week later, the house was sold. After this happened six or seven times, I began to ask what was going on. Then one day, I happened to read that the kind of advertising that the public would like to see REALTORS® doing is advertisements that give the price and the address. How many struggles have real estate sales associates had while on floor duty with prospects who want "just to drive by"? Well, open house advertisements are the ones sure to have the price and address. Easy to drive by and look it over. If later on you want to see it, you can call any agent and go to see it. If you are busy that day or on your way to the beach, do it when you get back. Open house advertisements call attention to the existence of houses. For that reason alone, some sell. They call attention to the existence of your farm area. People drive out and look around and think to themselves: "This is a nice area. I never knew this was here."

Subsequently, I sold the investors I mentioned previously three other houses—two rentals and a personal residence (priced at $300,000).

Don't ever let anyone tell you open houses are a waste of time. In one open house I held in my farm, I sold the house, I sold another house in my farm and I listed two homes in outside communities. How could you spend a more productive Sunday? During 20 years of real estate experience I can count on the fingers of one hand the times I have not managed to reap at least one transaction from a house I was holding open.

Not only are open houses *not* a waste of time, they are the greatest single source of transaction chains that I have encountered.

Selling Your Own Listings

It is impossible to find a better vehicle than an open house for selling your own listings. And consistently selling your own listings is an extremely lucrative practice, anytime, anywhere, but especially in your own farm. In your own listing farm it guarantees your objective of becoming the neighborhood specialist. Word gets around.

One other aspect of holding open houses should be mentioned. It takes a long time to make a farm productive. Meanwhile, you need money, and holding open houses well is a surefire way to make it.

I dwell on this because I do not want you to get so wound up in getting your backlog of buyers together that you forget the main purpose: to sell the house. Most agents do lose track of this objective. If you were to conduct a poll among real estate people regarding the objective of open houses, I wager 85 percent or more would reply that the objective was to obtain prospects. The average agent has no intention when he or she goes to the open house to sell it. In fact, in one of my classes a new agent told the group that he held a house open the previous week and could have sold it, but he didn't have a contract with him. Agents have asked me: If the objective is to sell the open house, why don't more agents do it? The answer is that it is almost impossible to do anything you do not have the clear intention to do. I know many agents do not have this clear intention because I see them go to the open house late without the necessary information with them regarding financing the house, tax information, boundaries, etc.

Not only that, but before they leave their own home, they slide a roast into the oven. Obviously, they intend to go home and have dinner after the open house. They have no intention whatsoever of staying out until midnight to sell the house.

Often it is hard to determine why they go at all, because they do not get people's names and telephone numbers, do not find out what people are seeking or do not get any information that would help them sell or list a home. These are the very people who say it is a waste of time to hold a house open. For them, it is.

The Listing/Selling Cycle

If you learn to hold open houses properly, however, and keep records of everyone who comes through the homes in your farm, with a description of their needs and motivations, and if you keep in touch with these people on a regular basis, you eventually will get your listing/selling cycle going.

When you advertise, promote and market the homes in your farm, you will attract the kind of people to whom you can sell these homes as they come on the market.

Target Your Advertisements

Targeting is especially important if you want your advertising to get to the essence of the appeal these homes have to the buyer. Ask your sellers why they bought the home. Others will buy it for the same reason. Why would you buy a home here or why did you? What kind of people are attracted by the homes you have to offer and where do these people live? Statistics show that 60 percent or more of buyers buy within 70 miles of their present home. So you may need to promote the homes in your farm within a 70-mile radius of the farm. Special situations may mean that these statistics do not apply to your area. Retirement communities attract people from colder climates. Resort communities attract people from crowded urban areas. Find out where your buying prospects are coming from and design promotions to attract them to your open house.

Why Hold an Open House?

Among the reasons for holding open houses are the following:

1. To *sell* the house! (You owe this to your client.)
2. To find buyers so you can sell your own farm listings

3. To find prospective sellers, so you can properly exploit all your opportunities to make income out of your farm

4. To use in conjunction with TV shows—REALTORS® who are associated with shows such as "Sunday Showcase of Homes" have found that holding simultaneous open houses gives them a tremendous market advantage; sometimes these shows generate so much traffic that two or more salespeople are needed at the property

5. To identify bird dogs—people who will keep you abreast of what is happening in the neighborhood

6. To keep yourself and your company visible and to demonstrate your skills and the company services

Preparing for an Open House

Preparation for an open house includes many steps for the agent:

1. Arrange the date and time with the owner. Check conflicting activities such as sports events and local events. Hold it early or late if necessary, or on Saturday instead of Sunday.

2. Lay the groundwork by knowing all about the area: schools, churches, shopping facilities, child care, etc.

3. Research financing: Bring information on possibilities for owners to hold financing, first or second mortgages, assumptions, new financing, variety of adjustable-rate, fixed-rate or local low-cost financing opportunities, current interest rates and market trends.

4. Run comparables on the area and visit any listings that you have not already seen. Two reasons for this are: (1) People come because they are looking for something in this area. Be the one to show them the new listings coming in, even if they are not your own. Let them know that *you* are the area *specialist,* and that if anything comes on the market you often know about it in advance. (2) Many of your visitors will have houses to sell, some in the same area. Be prepared to list a home the day of the open house if the opportunity arises.

5. Select open house material from the following items: A leather guest book with gold letters saying "guest register"; house location plat; a copy of the listing; computer printouts for other agents who may drop in unexpectedly with or without their customers; a good-looking flier, brochure or fact sheet to hand to your own prospects, with your name, picture, telephone numbers and a short biography; monthly utility bills (receipts in an envelope with a total monthly figure written on the outside); community profile sheets and commuter schedules; company open house welcome mat; pennants; balloons; "Open" sign with your name and home

telephone number on it; open arrows; and toys and coloring books to keep the children busy. A handout—a ballpoint pen with your name and telephone number—is a good idea.

6. Write addresses on open invitations ready to mail or use door hangers to be distributed the day before the open house; have your kids leave fliers at homes around the house to be held open; or insert the fliers inside the local newspaper, if possible.

7. Notify your sphere of influence, prospects and people who have attended previous open houses (see your guest book) either by invitation or by telephone. If it is your second open house, send fliers to other real estate salespeople who specialize in the area or the price range or type of house, and to superstars.

8. Write an advertisement that is carefully targeted to the group most likely to buy and make sure you meet your office's advertising deadline for open houses. Carefully inspect the house and suggest to homeowners that they put their best foot forward. Make it a cream puff, if you can. Spotless, flowers inside and out. Pay special attention to the front entrance, open garages and stacked carports. Make sure the grass is freshly cut, and park old and extra cars elsewhere. If the house is cluttered, try to get the sellers to pack some of their possessions in boxes and place them in the basement; even move some furniture to the basement if there is so much it makes the rooms seem small.

9. Ask the owners to make plans to visit friends. Explain that one reason people come to open houses is because they expect the owners to be gone. Do not, unless the owner is ill or handicapped, conduct an open house with the owners at home. Selling the house that day is immensely complicated by having owners underfoot. Children and pets also should not be present. I remember once trying to sell a house that always had a sleeping teenager in every bed. Advise the owners not to leave money, checks, valuable jewelry, knickknacks or objects d'art in plain sight. For a home filled with valuable antiques we once hired a policewoman to take names. It was wonderful; people volunteered age, weight and mother's maiden name. I wanted to do it every time. Another alternative is to ask a new agent to come along to keep an eye on everything.

10. Be sure you bring all the tools of the trade: calculator, tape, rate book, listing and sales contracts, seller's net sheets—everything you need to list or sell a house should always be close at hand.

Showing the Home

To show the home, you might want to use the following as a checklist:

1. Arrive at least 15 minutes early to set the stage. Eager beavers (the best kind of buyers) come early.
2. Wear a name badge so people will know and remember you.
3. Turn on every light and open up the draperies.
4. Put all your materials as far from the front door as possible so you will have time to develop rapport before asking for prospects' names. Leave trays of your cards in several rooms. Label chandeliers and other things that unexpectedly do not convey and leave notes around to point out special features or possibilities, such as "a spa would fit beautifully into this sun room." If the house is vacant, be sure to bring a card table and two chairs. It is hard to write a contract while standing up.
5. Greet people at the front door. Give your name. Often they will reciprocate.
6. Usher them through the house in a relaxed, friendly and helpful way. For safety's sake, let them precede you! Answer questions, give vital information and ask unobtrusive and natural qualifying questions. Try to find some common ground so that they can identify with you.
7. When you get to the area where your materials are spread out, ask your prospects if they would like to see the utility bills or the house location plat. If they say no firmly, they may be saying no to the house. Hand them a flier and ask for their name. *You* write the name in the guest register. Since I began doing this instead of asking them to sign, I can read all the names, I have fewer wrong telephone numbers and more people give me their names. When you are standing there with the book in you hand, they have to insult you to refuse, and most people don't like to do that, especially if you have successfully established any rapport in your trip through the house. Some, of course, would insult the Pope, but those are unlikely buyers. Once you have their names, you can suggest that they walk on through the home while you greet the newcomers and you will get back to them later. Somewhere, sometime in the conversation be sure to ask them if this is the type of home they are looking for. If not, what do they have in mind? You need the response to this question to be able to follow through properly later.
8. If there is not a constant stream of visitors, then you can concentrate on the one prospect. You might find that they don't care for the house, but would like to see others in the neighborhood. See if you can show these houses later that day after the open house or make an appointment for another date. If they like the home you are holding open but have a home they would need to sell before buying, then try to get them to let you come by after the open house and inspect their home and give them some idea what they might

9. After each family leaves the open house or as soon afterward as you have a free moment, jot down notes about the prospects you have qualified, either on the back of the sign-in page of your guest book or in your appointment calendar or in a separate notebook. By qualified I mean as to their needs and wants as well as their financial position. This is vital. When you get back to them, you must show your interest by remembering your conversation. Unless you have a terrific memory, you will need notes.

10. At the end of the day, turn off the lights, lock up the house and leave a note for the sellers telling them as much as you can about the way it went. "We had ten people, two couples with another agent (I will call the agent to get their reaction). One family seemed quite interested. I will follow up. I think we ought to schedule another open house next Sunday. Two in a row sometimes results in a sale. Thanks for the coffee and brownies. I will call you Monday." On Monday, inform the sellers of positive and negative comments. Repeated negative comments on a feature may encourage the sellers to remedy a problem or understand why they receive low offers. The reason you are leaving a note is that you are going to be showing another house in your farm or talking to one of the day's prospects about listing their home. Pick up all your signs as you leave.

Follow Up

On Monday morning, sit down at your desk in the office and analyze all your prospects. For example, one couple said the house was much too big for them. What they were looking for was a small Tudor. The Tudor didn't necessarily have to be in that neighborhood, but in a similar one. Search for this house: Try your own office listings, and look on the MLS and in your local homes magazine. Ask in the office if anyone knows where there is a small Tudor in a nice, reasonably priced area. If you find something comparable, fill out a prospect card with all the information. Take the next name on the list. These people seemed to like the house. It was the right type of home for the family. However, they have a home to sell. Do some research on their home. Figure out the finances as far as you can. Look up their present home in the *Lusk Directory* if you have one in your area or use whatever source you have. Find out what they paid for it, what kind of a loan they have and for how much. Figure out their equity if possible. Look up the tax assessment. Put all your information with the prospect card for these folks.

The next couple on your list has a problem with location. One of them works in a city 35 miles north of the town and the other works in a city 45 miles south of the town. Also, the houses in your farm are a little high-priced for this couple. Is there a neighborhood to the west of town, midway between the two workplaces, where there are some nice town houses suitable for this young couple? Start searching. You find just the thing! Put all the information with their prospect card. I find that using prospect cards psychologically affects my inclination to regard them as real customers and my inclination to follow through.

When you have finished the research, sit down and call each one you can reach. You may have to call some in the evening. Say exactly the same thing to each:

"Mr. or Mrs. Blank, this is Mary Jones of Upp and Addam Real Estate. I was in that open house in Oakton you came through yesterday (or Sunday). Do you remember me?"

"Certainly, Mrs. Jones."

"I was just wondering if you would give me your reaction to the home, Mrs. Blank."

"Well, as we said . . . it is much too large a home for just the two of us, but it is very nice, except for that wet basement."

Now, what the Sam Hill am I doing here? I know perfectly well what these people think of this house. Well, out of loyalty to my seller, before I propose another home, I must be sure that the prospects have turned down this one. One of my associates once had a homeowner call her and read her the riot act because the client's sister-in-law had gone through the open house and the associate had tried to turn her on to another house. The seller was furious. I vowed to get a rejection of the house being held open before suggesting another. I now am free to propose another home.

"Yes, Mrs. Blank, I remember your saying that you were looking for a small Tudor. They are terribly hard to find, aren't they? But guess what? I've found a little gem. It's in the Rosedale community. Would you and your husband like to look at it tomorrow or would you rather go on the weekend?"

You cannot compare the effectiveness between proposing to show a specific house and suggesting that "We look at 'some' houses." The response to this latter suggestion often is "Oh, I'm working with an agent from ABC Real Estate." But if ABC Real Estate were doing a good job, these people wouldn't be wandering around in open houses. The fact is that the prospects have not been shown a house that they would buy. If you have the house they are seeking, they will go with you to view it. After that, it is a matter of demonstrating excellence.

Send thank-you notes to anyone you cannot reach immediately, with a comment that you may have something they would be interested in seeing.

Newcomers to real estate often don't call back because they feel that they shouldn't "pester" people. People who really are avidly hunting for a property are not pestered by being shown a house that answers their needs. Don't show just any old house just to be showing something; that will waste your time and lose you customers. Keep in touch by telephone and tell your prospects about the houses you have previewed for them and rejected because the houses did not meet their needs. Send them newsletters. Let them know they are not forgotten.

Let them know that what they want is not easy to find and if you do locate it, they should be ready to drop everything and go. Lay the groundwork in advance.

Remind them again that you are the specialist of your farm area and that if anything at all becomes available, you will be the first to know it. Then keep in touch!

If the price is lowered on the house you held open or the terms bettered, be sure to call back your entire list of viewers. I was holding an open house once when the prospects mentioned that the house they really wanted was the one next door, but that the price was just too much for them. I happened to know that the price on that house had been substantially reduced before the sale. The listing agent had not called these people to advise them or she would have had a sale much sooner.

After you have been holding houses open in your farm for a number of years, you gradually will acquire a stockpile of prospects for the area. Sometimes certain communities will become almost seed areas for people moving up to your farm. New home subdivisions and high rises often are reservoirs from which to draw buyers for your listings. Local employers also may provide a stream of people transferring in who are naturally attracted to the type of housing you have. Once you have your listing/selling cycle going, you can stop the tour-bus service you have been running to supplement your income while you were building up your farm, your gas mileage will drop off and your efficiency will increase threefold.

12

The Tortoise and the Hare

If you do not view farming as a long-term campaign, do not waste your time and the company's money starting out. This is not a hit-or-miss undertaking. *Frequent, consistent, persistent contact* is the name of the game.

Frequent means every home receives something in the mail or hand-delivered, or a telephone call *at least once a month.*

Consistent means month after month, year after year, just like clockwork.

Persistent means follow through by phone or in person, forever.

Rewards are as certain as the tides for persistent farmers.

Calvin Coolidge had this to say about persistence:

> Nothing in this world can take the place of persistence. Talent will not; nothing is more common than unsuccessful men with talent. Genius will not; unrewarded genius is almost a proverb. Education will not; the world is full of educated derelicts. Persistence and determination alone are omnipotent. The slogan "Press On" has solved and always will solve the problems of the human race.

When conducting the research for this book, I encountered several real estate professionals who voiced opinions about highly successful farmers such as: "She has no personality at all," or "He's a real nerd." If, by sheer persistence, people described in these terms are succeeding through systematic farming, what could *you* do?

Add to organized attention to detail a pleasant, friendly personality and well-honed selling and listing skills—and the sky is the limit. Bringing in responses to your various farm activities will not help you reach your potential if you are not skilled in closing sales (listing is selling), do not know how to hold a good open house and generally are incompetent in real estate practice.

Quite often, efficient people are great at the mechanics of farming and ignore the people skills.

To reach your peak you need training to handle the business you stir up. If you feel wobbly about how to go about listing a house or how to qualify people as to their needs and wants or their financial capacity, while you are working on building the foundation for a long real estate career in your farm, also launch a lifetime of perfecting your skills. The better your real estate skills, the better your farming results.

Wheel of Success

Carl Clayton of Clayton Enterprises, Mount Prospect, Illinois, writing in *Real Estate Today*®, describes the "wheel of success." He says your success is like the spokes of a wheel. If a wheel is out of balance, you can destroy your tire, and the same thing can happen to your career if it is out of balance.

He names the seven spokes of a successful career:

1. Product knowledge
2. People skills
3. Sales skills
4. Listing and farming skills
5. Customer relations (keeping in touch)
6. Office/time management
7. Self-development

Of these seven skills, Clayton thinks the last, self-development, may be the most important. Agents often plateau. They reach a certain income level and cannot seem to rise above it. I've heard it said that this is a sort of self-imposed ceiling inflicted by their self-images. Others say it is a normal case of working up to your level of incompetency.

Whatever causes this phenomenon, it can be averted by a continuing-education and self-improvement program. This is true no matter how experienced you are. We never grow too old or too smart to learn. My own father began learning the "new math" at the age of 85.

As Clayton says in his article, "Remember, you're at the hub of your success wheel." In other words, it is up to you how far you go.

If you need a brushup of your general real estate skills, read Danielle Kennedy's book, *How To List and Sell Real Estate in the Nineties,* a good, well-balanced, entertaining and original work.

P. J. Thompson's book, *Up and Running in Real Estate Sales,* is good, too. An entire list of possibilities appears in "Resources," Appendix A.

Professionalism Versus Amateurism

As you become a seasoned professional, you should be aware that there is such a thing as being too businesslike, particularly in your farm, where a warm personality is an asset. You can use too much real estate jargon. Your speech can be too canned. You can become too cold and hard, too shiny and slick. As Paul O'Donnell says, "Your success will be entirely dependent on your ability to win the confidence of property owners in your market area."

Real professionalism means being dependable and ethical. According to O'Donnell, "You sell service . . . you do not sell real estate. You neither possess nor control real estate. Your product is service. As professionals, you offer your services to your clients; you proffer your knowledge, training, experience, judgment, prudence and skill to further their aims and protect and promote their interest." For an example of how one real estate salesperson highlighted these qualities in her personal brochure, see Figure 12.1.

It works best to maintain your amateur standing as a human being— a caring human being, interested in helping others. There is an old saying in real estate that you should take to heart: "Nobody cares how much you know, until they know how much you care." This approach works best in the neighborhoods of our nation.

I recently received a letter from one of the most successful farmers I know addressed to the people in his community. The quality of humanness and caring that this letter demonstrates raises this man way above the strictly professional and even superbly competent real estate agent. Of course, this quality in itself will not be enough without the competence. But if you can achieve both, and add persistence, there will be no stopping you.

When you have your farm running like clockwork, there is a tendency on the part of many to sit back and say "Ahhhh . . . " This is a mistake. Remember season five: *Protect your territory.* If you neglect your original farm, you may find it slipping away. Because of constant change, a new kid on the block or a rising company in the region, you can be pushed out quickly. Rapid turnover can work against you as well as for you, and you can fade away if you do not keep in touch. Persistence is forever.

FIGURE 12.1   Response-Oriented Brochure Highlights

You get

Professional Service

with

Ann Honda

Ann Honda

BISHOP GROUP REALTY, INC.
98-1277 Kaahumanu Street
Aiea, HI 96701

Your Formula For Success

When **BUYING** you want...

• **A Smooth Transaction** - fast, honest and accurate communication • **Your Needs Addressed** - a sincere agent who understands your unique situation • **No Surprises** - the result of meticulous attention to detail.

When **SELLING** you want...

• **A Fast Sale** - the result of an experienced agent handling your transaction • **The Right Price** - achieved by an accurate analysis of the market • **No Problems** - attained by total commitment to you.

Yes, I'll call Ann now!
Ann Honda
BISHOP GROUP REALTY, INC.
98-1277 Kaahumanu Street
Aiea, HI 96701
Office (808) 483-5000
Pager 525-9259
Fax 483-5020
Home 536-6691

Source: Reprinted with permission of Training Unlimited and Ann Honda.

FIGURE 12.1   (Continued)

You gain tremendous advantage with Ann, Plus...

Quality

"Ann... We were very pleased and impressed with your proficient manner in the marketing and sale of our condo. As we were not in Hawaii during the time it was for sale, your frequent communication kept us up to date. From the moment the listing agreement was signed to the final closing, you handled every detail with the most professional and personal care."

–Pamela & Jack Stanford
Aspen, Colorado

You want and deserve quality service. Ann provides you with personalized and professional service to meet your unique needs. She gives you the attention to detail, the experience and knowledge that spells quality. Ann Honda understands she needs to stay on top of your transaction and enjoys the challenge of providing you with quality service.

"Ann...Selling our home was one of the most important decisions of our lives. Your expertise, thoroughness and compassion made that decision the right one!"

–Ed & Lyla Dang
Honolulu, Hawaii

©Training Unlimited. 1992
Box 8206, Boise, ID 83707 800-777-7657

Communication

You want an open channel of communication. Ann knows the importance of your needs and wants. Ann keeps in constant communication with her clients. Much of her job satisfaction comes from her love of helping people. You benefit from Ann's hard work and dedication.

A word from Ann...

" You want an agent who works hard for you in achieving your real estate goals. You can count on my honesty, integrity, and sincere desire to help people. You are very important to me!

My commitment is to provide the highest degree of professional real estate service possible. You will benefit from my communication skills, meticulous attention to detail, my professional and personalized service and my dependability and diligence. I hope that this commitment and concern for your satisfaction will create a life time real estate relationship.

When you want quality service from an agent who sincerely cares about you, **call me at 483-5000, office or 536-6691, home.** "

... Ann Honda

"Ann... You are an individual that gives 300% in all your endeavors! You are a wealth of information to anyone considering buying or selling their property. By going that extra mile for us, we were able to purchase our dream home. Thanks!"

–James & Stacy Caswell
Kaneohe, Hawaii

Camera Master – Ready for your printer!

Till Your Fields and Reap the Rewards

Remember, though, this *is* a business, and you are a small businessperson. You are the boss. Every business has to be capitalized. Every businessperson knows you have to spend money to make money. Plan to plow back into your farm every year a percent of the harvest. Consider farming tools as the fertilizer that makes your crop grow. Check "Resources," Appendix A, for the names of companies that sell these tools. See Chapter 4 about creating some of your own tools. Above all—market yourself!

It is said that real estate is the best-paid hard work and the worst-paid easy work available. If you are a hard worker who would like to be paid what you are worth, real estate farming is for you. If your idea of real estate is "get-rich-quick" (and easy), forget farming. In fact, forget real estate. Fortunes have been made, and are being made today, in real estate, but not by shirkers. As in the old story of the tortoise and the hare, the hare took off like gangbusters, but the tortoise was in there for the long race . . . and won.

The thrill of real estate is that the sky really is the limit, but it doesn't come easily. It takes real commitment. In a recent article in *Real Estate Today,*® Jack Gale writes about some farmers who "go whole hog and move into their farms." Now that takes commitment and long-range thinking. But Gale says that it "could be an important step." He does warn to postpone this step until "after you've farmed an area six months and verified its income potential."

Gale also says, "Successful real estate farming is just another name for well-paid hard work."

It is also the only job I know where you get exactly what you are worth, no more and no less. Both failure and success in real estate can be described in one word: For failure the word is *inertia* (Don't do anything and you won't be paid anything); for success the word is *commitment* (Your reward is in direct proportion to the depth of your commitment).

The greatest reward is that when you are making a success of anything, it is no longer work. It becomes a way of life. You enjoy every minute of it because you feel happy to be of service to others and to be realizing your own potential.

Successful farming is simply being a good friend and neighbor; providing service and expertise to the community; giving back to the community; and keeping the dollar signs out of your eyes. A successful program is based on good human and public relations. Establish a genuine basis for mutual respect and understanding between yourself and the people in your farm . . . my friend, my real estate agent.

Appendix A

Resources

CHAPTER 1: **Farming: A Systematic Way of Prospecting**

Books: *The Service Road to Success.* Hanover, Mass.: Hall Institute of Real Estate.

Recruiting Sales Associates, by Ken Reyhons. Real Estate Brokerage Council of the REALTORS® National Marketing Institute of the National Association of REALTORS®.

The Best Seller, by Ron Willingham. Englewood Cliffs, N.J.: Prentice-Hall Inc. Integrity selling.

Articles: "The Listing Farm," by Merlin B. Coslick. *Real Estate Today.* National Association of REALTORS®.

Computer software: Smart Agent Contact Management System, the Cole EasyList data disks for faster, more effective direct mail and tele-marketing.

CHAPTER 2: **Leadership: The Company Approach**

Article: "Which Is the Right Hat for You?" by Laurence K. Janik. *Real Estate Today.*® Chicago: National Association of REALTORS®. Independent contractor regulations.

Publications: The Trisler Company, San Jose, Calif. Programs, books, video and audiocassette learning systems. 800-448-4416.

Directories/Programs: *Cole Cross Reference Directories,* Cole Publications and Information Services, a Division of MetroMail. 402-473-9715, 800-228-4571.

CHAPTER 3:   On Your Own: Plan Your Work and Work Your Plan

Directories/Programs: Real Estate Data, Inc. (REDI). Tax books, microfiche. 800-327-1085 nationwide; in Florida, 305-432-3115.

Rufus S. Lusk and Sons. Tax books, maps, microfiche. 301-683-6677.

Haines Directories, North Canton, Ohio. Cross directories, 89 cities. 216-243-9250.

Stewart Directories, Inc. Cross directories. 410-628-5988.

Cole Directories, members of the International Association of Cross Reference Directory Publishers. Publish in more than 150 markets. For catalog of directories call 800-228-4571.

For more than a thousand other local cross directories see your local library.

Computer: Multiple Listing Communications Services Realty Systems. Sunnyvale, Calif. Map Solutions, automated maps for real estate, GeoLocator 2.0, a professional mapping tool, reduces the time to locate properties and allows you to create professional-looking street maps for your clients. 408-744-0290.

Products: Myron Manufacturing Corp., 205 Maywood Ave., Maywood, NJ 07607-9988. Date log, one of the most compact and convenient appointment booklets on the market. Imprinted in quantity at very low prices; a great gift! Keep one for yourself.

Real Estate Planner, 21609 N.E. 4th St., Redmond, WA 98053. Daily, weekly, monthly schedule forms. Other forms: prospective seller, listings and sales in progress, buyer-seller communications, goal and production charts. Address/phone section. If you are not computerized, this is the way to go.

CHAPTER 4:   The Computer Revolution

Services: Digital Diagnostics, Inc., Sacramento, Calif. MetroScan, updates of assessment rolls on computer disk. 913-921-6629.

Some county tax offices also sell rolls and updates, and Cole's EasyList has names by census tract on disk and label formats.

Courthouse Records, Inc., Aurora, Colo. Access up to 520,000 properties on a single compact disk. 800-950-3232.

The Computer Connection, Frederick, Md. DOS-Help, immediate help with computer problems, designed for the newcomer.

RightSoft. Right Writer 3.0 is an intelligent grammar and style checker. Examines documents and cleans up usage, punctuation and style.

Power-up Computer Software, San Mateo, Calif. Certificate Maker: creates awards certificates, winning messages. For catalog, call 800-851-2917.

Supplies: Deluxe Computer Forms and Supplies, St. Paul, Minn. Data maintenance, continuous labels and index cards. 1275 Red Fox Rd., P.O. Box 64181, St. Paul, MN 55164-9848.

Stationery House, Hagerstown, Md. Continuous postal cards, yellow, white, blue. 899-638-3033.

Software: Smart Agent software, 100 real estate letters written by Joyce Caughman for agents and brokers. Capacity to create own letter-writing campaigns and direct mail pieces. Referral, client, customer data base, mail merge, address labels and envelopes, telemarketing with report. Perfect farm system. Computer disk provides power to carry out programs outlined in *Real Estate Prospecting*.

Smart Agent support services: John Newlin, NEW-WARE, San Diego, Calif. 619-455-6225; or Tony Bray, PC Answers, Inc. 919-274-7773. To order disks, specify 5¼″ or 3½″ disks. Call Cole Publications, MetroMail, 800-228-4571. $149.00.

Top Producer Systems, Inc. This Residential Sales Council–recommended software contains client records, word processing, business scheduling, farm and phone canvass, MLS connection, income and expenses, housekeeping functions. 800-444-8570, ext. 227. $495.00.

Stride Software, Real Estate Agent. Master menu includes calendar and appointments, to-do list, address book, farm data base, seller and buyer data bases, referral data base, memos and letters, loan amortization, income and expenses. 800-828-0970. $198.00.

Saletrac 2000. The Real Estate Specialist: QE2 time management, target marketing, prospect management telemarketing, case management, expense records. 714-499-6003 or 818-952-1000. $555.00.

Realty Works and Microsoft. An unbeatable combination; for DOS, Windows and Mac. WorksWare. 818-989-2298. $149.00

Go Computer Systems. Realty-8: Desktop organizer, word processor, spelling corrector, thesaurus, graphics, address book, calendar, to-do list, spreadsheet. Data base: farm, customer, REALTOR®, personal, fill in the blanks to be ready for mass mailing. Communications, with Hays modems, auto-dialing. Access to most MLS services. Lease of 286 Laptop available. 214-733-5630. Complete system, $595.00.

Comparative Market Analysis: Realty Tools, Inc. MLS Toolkit, for personal access to local multiple listing service. CMA Package. 800-828-0970.

MATRIX r.e.p., Inc. "Easy Step CMA." Agent or company program, 15-page package. 800-695-1158.

Graphics: Broderbund Software, San Rafael, Calif. Print Shop. Helps you design and print your own greeting cards, signs, letterheads and banners quickly and easily. Call 800-EGGHEAD.

Epic Software, Task Force of New Vision Technologies, Print Magic; Lotus Smart Pic; graphics programs can be found at Egghead, Babbages or other local software suppliers. Call 800-EGGHEAD for the name of the nearest Egghead store.

Clip-Art Company, 351 East Hillcrest Boulevard, Monrovia, CA 91016. Clip and paste graphics, available in art supply stores.

Dynamic Graphics Catalog. Includes clipper, camera-ready illustrations, packaged theme art, four seasons artwork, borders and mortices, humor, farm graphics, promo themes, coupons, desktop art. Books such as *Editing Your Newsletter, Copywriter's Handbook, Writing for the Media,* and addressing letterheads, creativity and many other pertinent subjects. 800-255-8800.

Desktop Publishing: First Publishers. Desktop publishing and graphics. PSF Software Publishing Co. 800-647-7403.

Springboard Software, Newsroom. Desktop publishing. Graphics. 612-944-3915.

Microsoft Publishing. If you have Windows, this is super. Ready-made templates. 800-426-9400.

Hardware: Moore Personal Terminal. Portable terminal that will allow you to hook up to computers (MLS or time-sharing or data-base services) any time you have access to a telephone outlet. Also to lender's quick qualifying systems such as Citicorp. 800-876-6367.

Printers: Texas Instruments, Inc. Micro-Marc ink jet is quiet, weighs about 12 pounds and measures 16″ × 13″ × 6″. It uses PCL 3 emulation, which makes it compatible with about any application. Inexpensive. It is ideal for portable use. List price, $419.00.

Vertisoft Systems Inc. Emulaser will upgrade a present printer that does not give you letter-grade quality. It has about 70 scalable fonts, and prints in bold and italics. Gives you graphics and color. To order, call 800-824-1284. $49.95.

Computer Publications: Clark Publishing. *Computer Digest,* 703-525-7900.

Omega Press. Computer texts. 800-222-2665.

Technology Transfer Institute, Santa Monica, Calif. Desktop Publishing Seminars. 310-394-8305.

Time-Life Books. Time-Life Computer Series, *Understanding Computers.* 800-621-7026.

P.C. World Communications, Inc., *PC World,* published monthly. Up-to-date information about every phase of computers, new products and resources. 800-825-7595, ext. 501.

PC Novice, 24 issues for $42, and well worth it when starting out new. Articles like "How To Install and Use Modems," "What Is Desktop Publishing" and "How To Upgrade Older Computers." 800-262-8500.

International Data Group. *DOS for Dummies* and other computer books and magazines. *New York Times:* "An irreverent primer for the perplexed." Available in bookstores and computer chains.

REALTORS® National Marketing Institute, Residential Sales Council, Chicago, Ill. *Real Estate Business,* a quarterly magazine for residential sales professionals, call Matt Lombardi, 312-670-3780.

CHAPTER 5:   **Farming by Mail: Direct Mail**

Books: Calculated Industries, Inc. *Successful Farming—by Mail. Successful Farming—by Phone,* by Steve Kennedy, 800-854-8075.

Crain Communications. *Successful Direct Mail,* by Bob Stone. Touhy and Lincolnwood, Chicago, IL 60646.

The Jacobson Corporation. *Cultivating Your Listing Farm,* by Alan Jacobson and Jack Gale. 305-253-1110.

Real Estate Farming: Campaign for $uccess, by P.J. Thompson. P.O. Box 91832, Santa Barbara, CA 93190. The best and most complete letter-writing campaign to a farm to be had. Simple and clear. Complete directions for cut-and-paste newsletter.

Mailers: Val-Pak Direct Marketing Systems, Inc. 813-579-8100.

Money Mailer. Each office independently owned and operated money saving coupons from area business. 301-263-0400.

ADVO, Inc. Penetrate your market area: Call for local branch information. 203-285-6100.

Cards: Harrison Publishing. Proven winners! Real estate cards for every occasion. Send no money. Examine your cards, return or keep choice. With or without name imprinted. 800-438-5829.

Carole Kelby Winner's Workshop. Kelby's real estate cards are as bright and perky as she is. P.O. Box 629, Glen Ellyn, IL 60138.

The Gooder Group, Inc. Postcard Prospecting Program: NewsCards. Jumbo one-panel card; double two-panel card; triple, three-panel card. For free sample or to order call 703-698-7750.

CHAPTER 6:   Farming by Mail: Active Farming, the Personal Touch

Newsletters: Gooder Group. Preprinted and ready-to-print newsletters, brochures and booklets. All quality, professionally done materials. Will personalize *Homeletter* for your company and deliver preprinted. 703-698-7750.

Books: Tom Hopkins Champions Unlimited. *Breakaway,* by Danielle Kennedy, 800-428-0446.

CHAPTER 7:   Farming by Mail: Newsletters

Newletters: The Personal Marketing Company, Houston, Tex. AdMail, direct mail that sells; self-mailers, fliers, cards, ads. Personal advertising inserts for company or ready-made newsletters; camera-ready copy. A newsletter for real estate farmers. Marketing and distribution tips. 800-458-8245.

Newsletter Services, Inc., Littleton, Colo. Newsletters, three choices. Advance proofs. Two months' trial. Preprinted and ready-to-print. Sends undated master proofs that you or your printer can personalize with explicit directions about ways to do it. 800-231-1579.

Kall Publications. Bright ideas in residential farming. Send for catalog. "I did it myself" newsletters, preprinted and ready-to-print newsletters. Imaginative and sprightly fliers, cards, brochures—formats to personalize. Instant art, seasonal ad kit, coloring sheets for kids on safety themes. Bookmarks. Thrifty gifts. 800-345-5255.

Paul Christian Communications, Taylorsville, N.C. Paul Christian's Ghost Writers. Unique marketing programs including "ghostwritten" newspaper columns, "on-the-air" radio scripts, camera-ready postcards and image advertising, master letter library, and personalized buyer/seller marketing brochures. Also, series of five camera-ready farming letters: introduction, seasoned farmer, FSBO, tenant, investor letters. Contact Paul Christian at 800-234-1481.

Austin Group. Professional-looking newsletters in color with tips for "landing more listings and increasing your income"; addressing service. 800-234-0143.

Services: National Association of REALTORS®, Fax-on-Demand Information Service. Free to members, for real estate practitioners only, not available to general public: public-policy summaries, brief updates on current topics suitable for newsletters. Call 202-383-1014 from touch-tone phone. Key in your fax and membership numbers.

REALTORS® National Marketing Institute, Residential Sales Council. PRES Kit. RS Council's new series. Each module contains camera-ready brochures, forms, ads, letters, ready to personalize. Three-package set. To order, call RS Council Product Order Center, 800-852-7592. For further information about the RS Council, call 800-462-8841.

CHAPTER 8: **Creating a Personal Marketing Program**

Products: Superior Real Estate Supply. Free catalog. Fresh new farming tools for FSBO follow-ups and open houses. Twenty-six power-packed door hangers, farming videotapes. Computer software catalog. 800-234-0592, ext. 5. Fax orders to 602-285-1803.

Sanzo Specialties, Endicott, N.Y. Real estate postcards; open house balloons with logo or name; pennants; welcome to our open house mats; buyers' questionnaire (paint us a picture) to pass out at open houses; new neighbor cards and many other real estate cards; forget-me-not and other seeds imprinted with your name and company; recipe cards; books. 800-222-4041.

Miles Kimball. Business book catalog features photolabels, labels, stickers, personalized tape, stamps and ink pads, home sketches on memos, note cards, stationery, name badges, awards and certificates and newsletter kit. 800-558-0220.

Print-Mart, Minneapolis, Minn. Door hangers, three styles; send camera-ready copy, logo and photograph for personalized hanger. Stunning self-stick labels, return cards, brochures, certificates. Send for samples. P.O. Box 21533, Minneapolis, MN 55421.

Progressive Specialty Co. Creative magnets. Design your own or use your business card. Becky Schumacher. 301-929-0011.

Omnipak Corp. Doorknob flier bags. Worth their weight in gold to an active farmer! 800-433-2328.

CHAPTER 9: **Cultivating Your Farm: Contacts = Contracts**

Articles: "Understanding the Fear Of Prospecting," by Dick Wilson, *Real Estate Business*. Call reluctance explained. "Is Call Reluctance Limiting Your Success?", by Linda and Bill Grimes, *Real Estate Today*®. National Association of REALTORS®.

CHAPTER 10: **Listing in Your Farm: The Harvest**

Article: "Selling Yourself Through Your Marketing Plan," by Carole Kelby. *Real Estate Professional*, Needham, Mass. How to win by putting your own plan together and embracing your competition in a bear hug.

Products: Carole Kelby's Winner's Workshop. Open house stands, super-sized house magnets with important numbers, tapes: "How to Hire, Train and Maintain a Personal Secretary." 800-243-3003.

MC Enterprises. MAGNACARD: Convert existing business cards into a permanent billboard. "Nobody ever throws away magnetic business cards." Simply remove liner and apply to card. $29.95 per 100. Less in quantity. 800-634-5523.

CHAPTER 12: **The Tortoise and the Hare**

Articles: "New Frontiers of Farming," by Jack Gale and Alan Jacobson. *Real Estate Today.*® Chicago: National Association of REALTORS®.

"Wheel of Success." by Carl K. Clayton. *Real Estate Today.* Chicago: National Association of REALTORS®.

"The Condominium Specialist," by P. J. Thompson. *Real Estate Today.* Chicago: National Association of REALTORS®. Finding a niche and mining it.

Books: *How To List and Sell in the Nineties,* by Danielle Kennedy. Kennedy International Productions. Videos, cassettes and manuals. 714-498-8033.

Barron's Real Estate Handbook. A & M College Station, Tex.: Texas A&M, Real Estate Center. Bibliography of 500 real estate books and articles.

List for Success, by Jim Londay. Chicago: Real Estate Education Company. Professional Real Estate Selling Skills. *Power Real Estate Listing* and *Power Real Estate Selling,* William H. Pivar. Chicago: Dearborn Financial Publishing, Inc.

Products: Training Unlimited. Camera-ready master of personal brochure, SPECIAL real estate prospecting reader discount. Call Tim Cowles, 800-777-7657.

Miscellaneous: *Realtor News,* National Association of REALTORS®. REALTOR® Resource: Products & Services for the real estate industry. REALTOR® Referral Section. Received by all members of NAR. Nonmember subscriptions available. Circulation manager: Chicago, 312-329-8200; Washington, 202-383-1000.

Appendix B

You and the Post Office

Your first step in preparing a mailing is to make friends with the post office. This is like any other real estate transaction: first, build rapport. This is a lot easier to do than it used to be. Years ago, most post offices were manned by crusty old dragons who never smiled. Today, I find the post office personnel helpful and pleasant. If yours aren't, kill them with kindness.

Get acquainted with the clerk or clerks in the bulk-mail department of the post office where your permit will be held. Only at this post office will you be able to use that permit number.

Pick up a copy of the U.S. Postal Service publication 24: *A Guide to Business Mail Preparation.* Get a current copy (they change) of the Rates and Fees Schedule. Also get a copy of the *U.S. Postal Domestic Mail Manual (DMM).*

Get the clerk to give you all the items you need for a bulk mailing: forms, rubber bands, colored stickers, mailbags and instructions. Usually the clerk is very patient and specific the first time you do a mailing, especially if you don't act like you already know everything there is to know. After that, you may be on your own. These clerks are very busy and may take a dim view of explaining all this to you 12 times a year.

The U.S. Postal Service also has a "Postal Answer Line." an automated telephone service that gives information on various subjects. Publication 349 gives you the topics and instructions on using this service. Each topic has its own message number. Number 333, for example, gives you postage rates and classes of mail and discusses what class of mail you should use for your purposes.

The first thing you will learn is that there is first-class through fourth class mail, and the cost is commensurate with the service. It costs nearly twice as much to mail a piece first class as at the third-class bulk rate. So you have to decide what type of mailing is appropriate for what type of mailing.

Sphere of Influence: First Class Mail

Mailings to all the people you know (friends, relatives, colleagues, organizations, church circle, etc.) who are spread out around various ZIP codes and with whom you usually have something of a personal relationship is best sent first class.

The same goes for a demographic list (professions: all teachers, nurses, lawyers, doctors, chiropractors, geologists, computer specialists, ad infinitum); politicians; the Ethiopian community; the Class of '74, etc. Commercial list brokers sell them by the thousands. Usually send first class to these people.

You can mail at the regular rate. You also can mail 500 or more pieces at a reduced rate. They must be presorted and ZIP-coded and are limited to a weight of one ounce per piece. The first-class weight limitation may persuade you to send heavier pieces at the third-class bulk rate where the limit is currently 3.667 ounces, if you can find a way to meet the other requirements.

As you can see, the more work the service is, the cheaper it is, so this is like a lot of other decisions in real estate: Is your time more valuable than your money?

For first-class bulk rate, you have two options:

1. Presorted by ZIP code
2. Carrier route first class, presorted by carrier route

Again, 500 pieces is the minimum number of identical, printed pieces that you can send first-class bulk rate. Printed means not handwritten, not typewritten, not hand-stamped. Computer copy, however, is considered "printed."

There is also a per-piece discount for ZIP + 4, for which there is an annual fee. ZIP + 4 first class, nonpresorted rate requires no annual fee, but the rate is higher. Precanceled stamps are available. There are many attractive commemorative stamps you can use to dress up your mail.

First-class mail usually is faster and more personal. You can use a typewritten address if you want clear, professional-looking mail. If you want it to appear warmer and more personal looking, you can use a handwritten address. Unless you are using the first-class bulk rate, you can even send handwritten notes. But if you send first-class bulk rate, the contents must be "printed."

If you are pressed for time you can use address labels, turned out on your computer, and delegate the task of affixing them (to your kids?).

Cleaning Lists

Even if you plan to send your mailings third-class bulk rate, the cheapest way, you may want to send your first mailing first class and clean up your list.

You can put an "endorsement" on first-class mail to indicate the type of service you want. There are six endorsements, each offering a different service.

Authorized endorsements include:

- *Address correction requested.* Pieces will not be forwarded. The sender will receive an address correction or reason for nondelivery and get mail back with no charge. "Do not forward" endorsement will be handled the same way.
- *Forwarding and address correction requested.* Mail forwarded at no charge and the sender will be sent a separate address correction for a fee. Undeliverable mail will be returned to the sender at no charge, and a reason given.
- *Return postage guaranteed.* Mail is forwarded or if undeliverable returned to sender with reason, both at no charge.
- *Do not forward address correction requested/return postage guaranteed.* Mail will not be forwarded and will be returned to sender with address correction or reason for nondelivery.
- *Forwarding and return postage guaranteed/address correction requested.* Mail will be forwarded unless undeliverable, in which case it will be returned to sender, with reason for not delivering. Both services at no charge.
- *Insured.* Mail will be forwarded at no charge. If it is not delivered, it will be returned to sender with reason at no additional cost.

Business Reply Mail Increases Response Rate

If you expect homeowners in your farm to respond to your promotions, enclosing a business reply card is very important. It makes it easy and cheap for your prospects and is well worth the cost to you in terms of response rate.

It is a waste of time to put stamps on return cards for you can only expect a return of 1 to 4 percent; the rest of the cards are thrown away.

If your company already has a return-mail permit, you can use it. If not, you should set it up for yourself

You apply to the post office for a permit, pay an annual fee and arrange for the replies to be sent to the address where you want to receive them.

Before having these return cards printed, be sure to check postal regulations carefully, as there are specifications about where the permit imprint and required bars go on the card and the exact wording of the various endorsements and how far from the bottom they can be printed.

Business reply postcards, like any other postal cards, may not be smaller than 3½″ × 5″ or larger than 4½″ × 6″. Double reply cards are permitted. The address side of a business reply card or letter may not be handwritten, typewritten or hand-stamped. No borders are allowed on cards or letters, although they are allowed on labels. Any color card or ink is permissible if it is readable.

Senders guarantee payment for the returned cards and the post office will set up an annual account to cover payment of business-reply fees, in addition to the regular first-class rate per piece returned.

Geographic Farm: Bulk Rate Pays

Some farmers make great sacrifices in order to mail everything first class. Because it costs twice as much to do this it would have to be crucial to make it worthwhile. These farmers are under the impression that people "just throw out all this junk mail."

You may be surprised to hear that most people *love* to receive mail. Any mail. This fact has been confirmed by many market studies conducted by advertisers and the post office.

According to P.J. Thompson in *Campaign for $uccess,* a leading direct mail house queried 30 million prospective purchasers and gave them the option of having their names deleted from that mailing list. Of the 30 million, only 424 took the opportunity to cut back on their junk mail. Obviously, it is true that one man's junk is another man's treasure.

Go ahead and send the mass of your mail third-class bulk rate. This way you can send twice as much.

Isn't It a Nuisance?

At first it seems like a lot of trouble, but once you get the hang of it, there's nothing to it. It just takes a little time. The only alternative is direct mail services from a company such as General Consulting

Services, Inc., which advertises "no sweat mailing." You complete the order form, attach payment, send in the order and "this turnkey operation does all the work."

Until you get rolling, you may have to do it yourself. So here's how, courtesy of GCS 301-670-0100.

PAYMENT OF POSTAGE

Each bulk rate mailing requires payment of postage.

METHODS OF PAYMENT

There are three methods of postage payment for your bulk mailing. They are:

1. Precanceled Stamps
2. Permit Imprint
3. Postage Meter

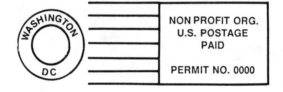

5-DIGIT PRESORT SACKING/LABELING REQUIREMENTS

Before you begin, read over the general requirements for sacking and labeling which appear in Chapter 3 and apply to all bulk mailings. After performing all general requirements you may proceed with the following step-by-step directions. These steps will qualify you to mail at the 5-digit presort rate.

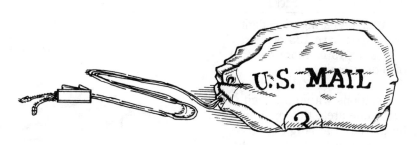

GENERAL

To qualify for the 5-digit presort rate, packages of 10 or more pieces to the same 5-digit ZIP Code destination *must* be placed in a 5-digit or 3-digit sack containing a minimum of 125 pieces or 15 pounds of mail.

The following abbreviations may be used on the contents line of the sack label for 5-digit presort mailings:

Letters	LTRS
Flats	FLTS
Mixed	MXD
Digit	DG

STEP ONE: 5-Digit Sacks

If you have 125 pieces or 15 pounds of mail packaged to the same 5-digit ZIP Code destination, they must be placed in a 5-digit sack. Each sack must be labeled as follows:

EXAMPLE:

Destination → ARLINGTON VA 22202
Contents → 3C LTRS
Office of Mailing → BOSTON MA

5-DIGIT PRESORT SACKING/LABELING REQUIREMENTS (Continued)

STEP TWO: 3-Digit Sacks

If, after preparing all 5-digit sacks, you have 125 or more pieces (or 15 or more pounds) of 5-digit mail going to different 5-digit ZIP Code destinations within a 3-digit ZIP Code area, this mail must be placed in a 3-digit sack. Only 5-digit packages may be included in this sack. The sack must be labeled in the following manner:

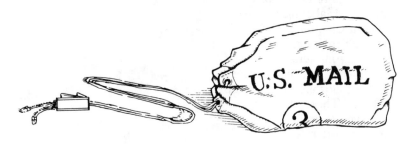

EXAMPLE:

Destination —
Contents —
Office of Mailing —

BINGHAMTON NY 137
3C LTRS MXD 5-DG PKGS
PHILADELPHIA PA

LINE 1–City, 2-Letter state abbreviation, and 3-digit ZIP Code Prefix.

LINE 2–Contents followed by the words "MIXED 5-DIGIT PKGS"

LINE 3–Office of Mailing.

NOTE: The appropriate top line of the sack label may be found by referencing the listing of 3-digit ZIP Codes which is available from your Bulk Mail Acceptance Unit or account representative.

STEP THREE: Residual Pieces

After completing Steps 1 and 2, you may package and sack all remaining pieces in accordance with the Basic Sort Instructions found on pages 18 through 22. Remember, you must have a minimum of 200 pieces or 50 pounds of *qualifying* 5-digit mail to be able to claim the 5-digit presort level rate. Residual pieces subject to the basic rate of postage, may be mailed with the qualifying 5-digit discount rate mail. However they do *not* count towards the minimum quantity required.

NOTE: Basic Rate sacks should be kept physically separated from the mail sorted to qualifying 5-digit presort rate destinations. Otherwise, a listing of the number of qualifying 5-digit pieces to each ZIP Code destination must be provided.

CARRIER ROUTE PRESORT

GENERAL REQUIREMENTS

Each mailing must consist of at least 200 pieces or 50 pounds of mail presorted to qualifying carrier route destinations.

Only packages with 10 or more pieces to the same carrier route, rural route, highway contract route, post office box section, or general delivery unit may qualify.

WEIGHT AND SIZE LIMITATION

Weight: Each piece must weigh less than 16 ounces.

Maximum Size Standards: Pieces must not exceed 11 3/4 inches in width, 14 inches in length or 3/4 inch in thickness.

Exception: If you are mailing merchandise samples with detached labels, contact your local Mailing Requirements Office for additional information.

LISTING REQUIRED

At the time of mailing, mailers must provide the post office with a listing indicating the number of qualifying carrier route presort pieces and the number of residual pieces mailed to each 5-digit ZIP Code.

MARKING REQUIRED

In addition to the endorsement BULK RATE (or NONPROFIT ORG.) the identifying words CARRIER ROUTE PRESORT or the abbreviation CAR-RT SORT must be incorporated in the permit imprint, or it may be printed or rubber stamped above the address in the area to the left or below the permit imprint, meter stamp, or precanceled stamp on pieces entered at the carrier route presort level rate.

EXAMPLES:

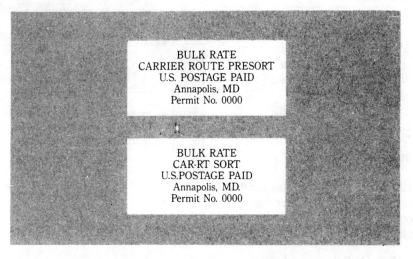

If the endorsement CARRIER ROUTE PRESORT is not printed in the postage area, the endorsement may be located in the address area on either the line above the address or two lines above the address. (The preferred position is two lines above the address.) See samples of formats below:

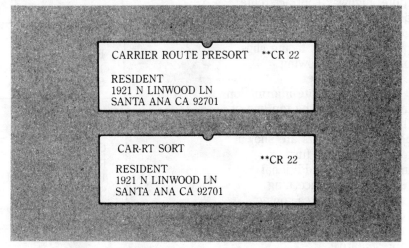

PACKAGE LABELING

CARRIER ROUTE PACKAGES

Packages not placed in a carrier route sack must be labeled in accordance with one of the following methods.

METHOD 1:

The mailer may prepare packages with a facing slip. When using facing slips they must be affixed to the front of the package and marked as shown below:

LINE 1–City, State and 5-digit ZIP Code of the address.

LINE 2–Carrier route, rural route, highway contract route, post office box section, or general delivery unit.

LINE 3–Office of Mailing.

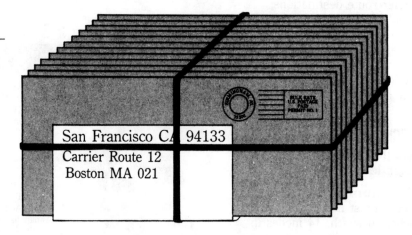

METHOD 2:

Packages made up to an individual carrier route, rural route, highway contract route, post office box section, or general delivery unit may be prepared without facing slips provided the following conditions are met.

The carrier route information must appear on the top line of the address. Samples of acceptable formats are shown to the right. For further instruction and additional requirements concerning labeling procedures contact your Mailing Requirements Office or local account representative.

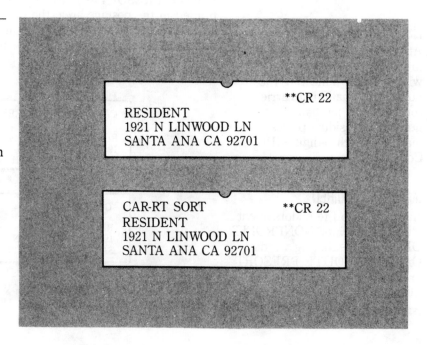

STATEMENT OF MAILING—RED FORM

Form 3602, (red form)
*Statement of Mailing With
Permit Imprints*, is used with
permit imprint mail only.
   Below are instructions for
each section of the form,
labeled 1 through 18.

1. Your permit number.
2. Location of the post office of deposit.
3. Date of deposit.
4. Class and rate of mail. Check the appropriate box.
5. Processing category. Check the appropriate box.
6. Weight of a single piece (in pounds). Contact your Bulk Mail acceptance unit for instructions on how to compute the weight of a single piece.
7. Total number of pieces.

8. Weight of entire mailing.
9. Number of sacks or other containers used.
10. Name and address of permit holder.
11. Telephone number (including area code).
12. If authorized for nonprofit rates, check this box.
13. Name and address of the person or organization for whom the mailing is prepared if it differs from the permit holder (i.e., if you are "lending" your permit to someone else).
14. Complete if the name and address of the organization which prepares the mail differs from the permit holder.

15. Compute postage on the line or lines appropriate for your rate category or categories. Note: There is only one discount per form. (Basic rate is not a discount for this purpose.)
16. Complete if necessary. Call Bulk Mail Acceptance Unit for additional instructions if necessary.
17. Enter total amount of postage.
18. Signature of the permit holder required before mail acceptance.

PS Form 3602, Apr. 1988   **FOR ZONE RATED MAIL USE FORM 3605**   Side B

| U.S. Postal Service **STATEMENT OF MAILING WITH PERMIT IMPRINTS** | MAILER: Complete all items by typewriter, pen or indelible pencil. Prepare in duplicate if receipt is desired. Check for instructions from your postmaster regarding box labeled "RCA Offices." | Permit No. ① |

Post Office of Mailing ②   Date ③   Receipt No.   Mailing Statement Sequence No.

Check applicable box ④

3rd Class
- ☐ Carrier Route
- ☐ Basic ZIP+4
- ☐ 5-Digit ZIP+4
- ☐ ZIP+4 Barcoded
- ☐ 5-Digit
- ☐ Basic
- ☐ Single Piece

4th Class
- ☐ Library Rate
- ☐ Special 4th Class Single Piece
- ☐ Presort Special 4th Class

Processing Category (See DMM 128)· ⑤
- ☐ Letters
- ☐ Flats
- ☐ Machinable Parcels
- ☐ Irregular Parcels
- ☐ Outside Parcels

Weight of a single piece ⑥
__ . __ __ __ lbs.

RCA Offices: ⑨

TOTAL IN MAILING / **NUMBER OF**

| Pieces ⑦ | Pounds ⑧ | Sacks | Trays | Pallets | Other Containers |

Name and Address of Permit Holder (Include ZIP Code) ⑩   Telephone No. ⑪

☐ Check if nonprofit under DMM 623* ⑫

Name and Address of Individual or Organization for which mailing is prepared (If other than permit holder) ⑬

☐ Check if nonprofit under DMM 623*

Name and Address of Mailing Agent (If other than permit holder) ⑭

POSTAGE COMPUTATION

Pound Rate	1. Pound Rate Postage Charge	No. Pounds	Rate/Pound $	Postage
Piece Rates ⑮	2. ZIP+4 Barcoded	No. Qual. Pieces	Rate Per Piece $	Postage
	3. 5-digit ZIP+4	No. Qual. Pieces	Rate Per Piece $	Postage
	4. Basic ZIP+4	No. Qual. Pieces	Rate Per Piece $	Postage
	5. Carrier Route	No. Qual. Pieces	Rate Per Piece $	Postage
	6. 5-digit	No. Qual. Pieces	Rate Per Piece $	Postage
	7. Basic	No. Qual. Pieces	Rate Per Piece $	Postage
	8. Rate Category	No. of Pieces	Rate Per Piece $	Postage
	9. **SUBTOTAL (1 through 8)** ▶			Postage

10. Additional Postage Payment (State reasons for additional postage payment on reverse side under "Comments") ⑯   ☐ See reverse side   No. of Pieces   Rate/Piece $ Postage

11. ☐ Check if applicable third-class bulk piece rate is affixed to each piece. (Form 3602-PC required)

12. ⑰ **TOTAL POSTAGE** (9 plus 10) where applicable ⟶   Total Postage $

* The signature of a nonprofit mailer certifies that: (1) The mailing does not violate section 623.5 DMM; and (2) Only the mailer's matter is being mailed; and (3) This is not a cooperative mailing with other persons or organizations that are not entitled to special bulk mailing privileges; and (4) This mailing has not been undertaken by the mailer on behalf of or produced for another person or organization that is not entitled to special bulk mailing privileges.

The submission of a false, fictitious or fraudulent statement may result in imprisonment of up to 5 years and a fine of up to $10,000. (18 U.S.C. 100!) In addition, a civil penalty of up to $5,000 and an additional assessment of twice the amount falsely claimed may be imposed. (31 U.S.C. 3802)

I hereby certify that all information furnished on this form is accurate and truthful, and that this material presented qualifies for the rates of postage claimed.

Signature of Permit Holder or Agent (Both principal and agent are liable for any postage deficiency incurred) ⑱   Telephone No.

(THIS SECTION FOR POSTAL USE ONLY)

PS Form **3602**, Apr. 1988   **FINANCIAL DOCUMENT — FORWARD TO FINANCE OFFICE**

CHECKLIST QUESTIONS FOR BULK MAILINGS

GENERAL

- Is the mailing deposited at the correct acceptance unit during the established acceptance hours?

- Have you included the correct mailing statement, properly completed and signed? (Note: If you require more than one drop to complete a mailing, a separate, complete mailing statement must accompany each drop.)

- Are your annual bulk mailing fee and permit current?

POSTAGE

- Are sufficient funds on deposit to cover full postage for permit imprint mailings?

- Is the amount correct on mailings with postage affixed?

PREPARATION

- Does the mailing consist of at least 200 pieces or 50 pounds?

- Are all pieces in the same processing category (e.g., letters or flats)?

- Is the mail sorted according to the packaging/sacking requirements described in this publication?

- Does all mail in the packages face in the same direction?

- Are all sacks under 70 pounds (preferably under 40 pounds)?

- Are all packages preferably under 4 inches thick?

- Are all addresses within the United States and the United States territories?

- Are all pieces in the mailing identical in weight if the mailing is by permit imprint?

- Is the correct date (month and year) of deposit shown on dated mail? (Note the reference to dates in the section on metered postage in Chapter 1.)

Appendix C

Copy It

This entire section and only this section may be copied for your use. All rights are reserved for the remaining material in *Real Estate Prospecting: Strategies for Farming Your Markets.* Copyright 1994 by Real Estate Education Company, a division of Dearborn Financial Publishing, Inc.

ACTION PLAN OF _____ for 19_____

Geographical farm area   _____

_____

_____

# of Homes _____   Turnover Rate_____   Share of Market_____

Goals: Annual dollar volume _____   Market Penetration _____%

# of Listings   # Sales   #Mailings

Targets

Community Influence: friends, family, & acquaintances   _____

clients and customers   _____

officials and well-known individuals   _____

organized groups: _____

_____

_____

_____

_____   _____

absentee lot owners   _____

absentee single family owners   ___ ___

renters   _____

commercial landowners   _____

builders   _____

CONTACT SCHEDULE	Jan	Feb	Mar	Apr	May	June	Jul	Aug	Sep	Oct	Nov	Dec	Total
Newsletter													___
Personal Letters													___
Informals													___
Cards													___
Calendars													___
Door Hangers													___
Handouts													___
Mailback Cards													___
Others													___
Telephone													___
Face to Face													___
Newspaper Column													___

DAILY FARM PLANNING SHEETS

Date:_____Day of the Week_____

APPOINTMENTS   Mailing Activities

8:00 _____   _____
8:30 _____   _____
9:00 _____   _____
9:30 _____   _____
10:00 _____
10:30 _____
11:00 _____   Phone Calls to Make
11:30 _____
12:00 _____   _____
12:30 _____   _____
1:00 _____   _____
1:30 _____   _____
2:00 _____   _____
2:30 _____   _____
3:00 _____   _____
3:30 _____   _____
4:00 _____
4:30 _____
5:00 _____
5:30 _____   Personal Calls To Make
6:00 _____
6:30 _____   _____
7:00 _____   _____
7:30 _____   _____
8:00 _____   _____
8:30 _____
9:00 _____
9:30 _____   Records to Keep
10:00 _____
                                            _____
Target #   Mail   _____
Target #   Phone   _____
Target #   Face to Face

LISTING FARM DIRECTORY/ACTIVITY REPORT

Name(s)_____   Phone _____

Address_____ City _____ Zip _____

Children	Age		Handouts	
1 _____	_____	A _____	F _____
2 _____	_____	B _____	G _____
3 _____	_____	C _____	H _____
4 _____	_____	D _____	I _____
5 _____	_____	E _____	J _____

Pets (Name) _____ Anniversaries _____ Sports & Hobbies _____

_____ _____ _____

Referrals:

Name _____ Address _____ Lister/Buyer

_____ _____ _____

_____ _____ _____

_____ _____ _____

_____ _____ _____

MAILOUTS	CONTACTS
January _____	_____
February _____	_____
March _____	_____
April _____	_____
May _____	_____
June _____	_____
July _____	_____
August _____	_____
September _____	_____
October _____	_____
November _____	_____
December _____	_____

TRANSACTIONS

LISTED	SALE
_____	_____
_____	_____

Kept in 3-ring binder -- in the order you would work your farm.

Sunday	Monday	Tuesday	Wednesday	Thursday	Friday	Saturday
		1	2	3	4	5
6	7	8	9	10	11	12
13	14	15	16	17	18	19
20	21	22	23	24	25	26
27	28	29	30	31		

A COMPUTER FARMING SYSTEM

1. A personal computer* (possibly laptop) and a decent printer.

2. Farm record software.

3. Customer management software.

4. Competitive market software.

5. Graphics software.

6. Word-processing software.

7. Owner information software, if available, or computer printouts.

8. Continuous-feed letterhead, envelopes, address labels, postcards, index cards, etc.

9. Modem to MLS or data banks (optional).

10. The right attitude. This is a skill, like playing the piano.

*For a branch office farming system to be used by all salespeople, the computer should use 3½ inch disks, not the older style 5¼ inch disks.

TIPS ON DIRECT MAIL DESIGN

Here are some "tips" about writing and designing direct mail we have condensed from a flier sent out by A. B. J. Marketing, a firm that does custom real estate mailings.

1. Emphasize your unique service
2. Stress benefits
3. Make the mailing piece cohesive
4. Offer a premium
5. Use a letter
6. Use a P. S.
7. Include a response mechanism
8. Back up your claim
9. Be personal
10. Be simple
11. Have a strategy
12. Review the copy
13. Use standard paper sizes
14. Make copy inviting
15. Consider visual appeal
16. Grab your reader
17. Use enclosures
18. Use stamps
19. Watch design
20. Test . . . test . . . test
21. Choose words carefully
22. Appeal to emotions
23. Show action
24. Long copy works
25. A picture is worth 1,000 words

RESPONSE CHARTS

MAILING #	DATE	DESTINATION	OFFER	PREMIUM	RESPONSE

Conclusion: _____
_____
_____
_____
_____
_____
_____

NEIGHBORHOOD INFORMATION REQUEST

NAME_____

ADDRESS_____

Dear (Mr. and Mrs. Seller)
Marketing your home will be much easier if we know everything
there is to know about your neighborhood. Any tips you can
furnish us will give us a competitive edge over the other homes
for sale in the area.
Please complete this form to aid us in attracting people to (name
of town, subdivision). If you need more room for pertinent
information, write on the reverse side.

1. Why were you attracted to this neighborhood?

2. Do children take a bus to school, if so how close does it
stop?

3. Names of schools, including private schools that neighborhood
children attend.

4. Youth activities available?

5. Senior activities available?

6. Public recreation (pools,playgrounds,parks, tennis etc.)

7. Transportation: Public. Where?   When?

    Carpooling. Bicycle paths, walks etc.

8. Closest shopping center:
          hospital
          community center
          senior center
          places of worship

9. Professional groups represented in the community:

10. General information about your immediate neighbors:

11. Services available (babysitters, eldercare etc.)

12. What about your home most attracted you and might also
     attract a new buyer? What type of family or person
     would be most likely to buy your home?

13. Why?

14. Other useful information:

Call me when you are ready and I will drop by to pick up the
completed form. Your help is greatly appreciated.
YOUR REAL ESTATE SPECIALIST,

Questionnaire of Interests

What to do with your completed questionnaire:

If you are interested in having information on any of the following topics, please check the ones you desire.

___ How To Fight Your Tax Assessment

___ Do-It-Yourself Alarm Systems

___ Figuring the Real Return on Real Estate Investments

___ Tax Information on Second Homes

___ Over-55 Tax Break on Your Last Home

___ Planning a Low Maintenance Yard

___ The Pluses and Minuses of 15-Year Mortgages

___ Reverse Mortgages: Get Your House To Pay You

___ Your Home Business

___ Home-Buying Tips

___ Home-Selling Tips

___ How To Check Your ARM Loan Payment

___ How Much House Can You Afford

___ Which Home Improvements Pay Off When You Sell

___ Community Services: Elder care, babysitting, grass cutting, window washing, snow removal, sewing, boat cleaning, housekeeping

___ Leisure Activities: Garden club, bridge club, bowling, Scrabble club, chess club, sailing club

___ Senior Citizen Activities

___ Family Activities: Little League, soccer and field club, picnics, fairs, etc.

___ Other: _____

_____

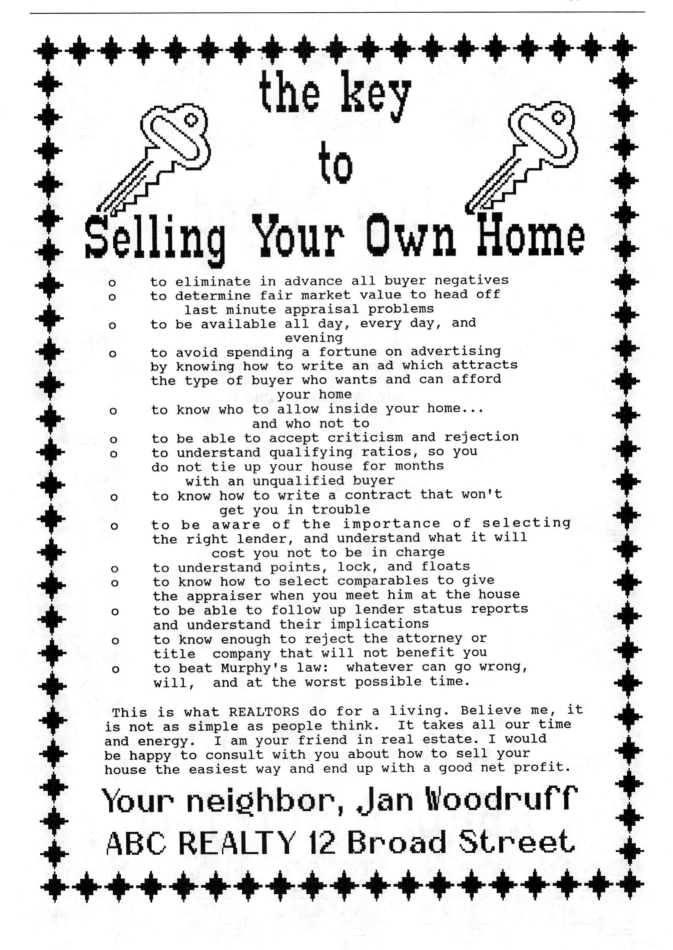

the key to Selling Your Own Home

o to eliminate in advance all buyer negatives
o to determine fair market value to head off
      last minute appraisal problems
o to be available all day, every day, and
                  evening
o to avoid spending a fortune on advertising
   by knowing how to write an ad which attracts
   the type of buyer who wants and can afford
                  your home
o to know who to allow inside your home...
              and who not to
o to be able to accept criticism and rejection
o to understand qualifying ratios, so you
   do not tie up your house for months
      with an unqualified buyer
o to know how to write a contract that won't
              get you in trouble
o to be aware of the importance of selecting
   the right lender, and understand what it will
              cost you not to be in charge
o to understand points, lock, and floats
o to know how to select comparables to give
   the appraiser when you meet him at the house
o to be able to follow up lender status reports
   and understand their implications
o to know enough to reject the attorney or
   title company that will not benefit you
o to beat Murphy's law: whatever can go wrong,
   will, and at the worst possible time.

This is what REALTORS do for a living. Believe me, it
is not as simple as people think. It takes all our time
and energy. I am your friend in real estate. I would
be happy to consult with you about how to sell your
house the easiest way and end up with a good net profit.

Your neighbor, Jan Woodruff

ABC REALTY 12 Broad Street

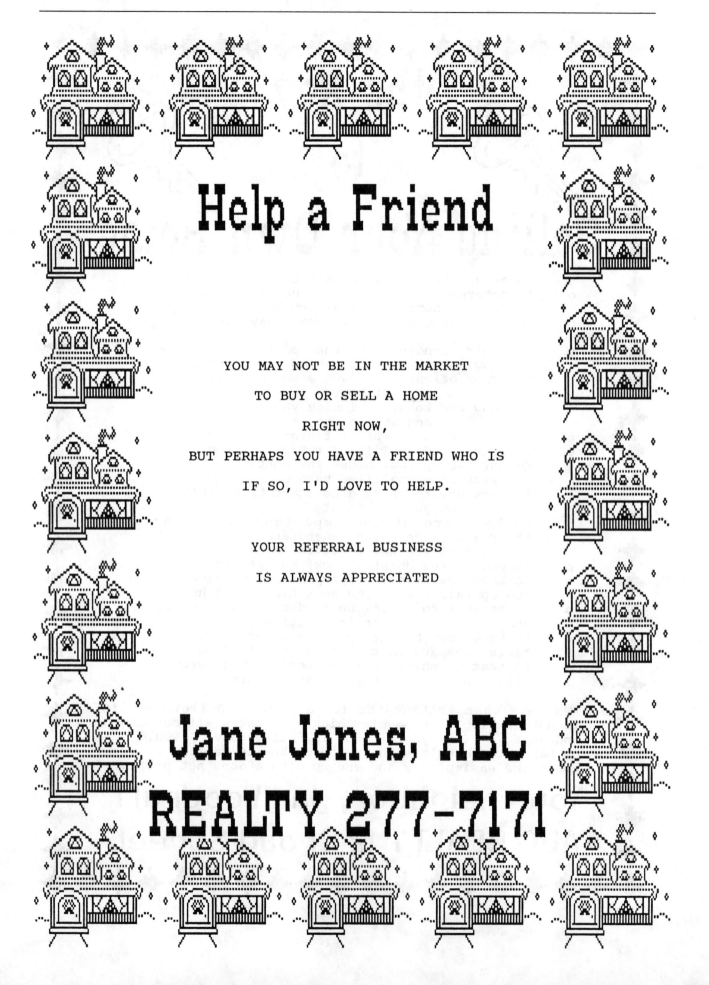

Help a Friend

YOU MAY NOT BE IN THE MARKET

TO BUY OR SELL A HOME

RIGHT NOW,

BUT PERHAPS YOU HAVE A FRIEND WHO IS

IF SO, I'D LOVE TO HELP.

YOUR REFERRAL BUSINESS

IS ALWAYS APPRECIATED

Jane Jones, ABC
REALTY 277-7171

There are 2,000,000 Real Estate Licensees in the Country!

How do you Select

one

to assist you with your real estate needs?
Consider a Certified Residential Specialist.

- I will take only the time necessary to solve your real estate problem–I won't waste your time!

- My knowledge of the market will assist you in determining accurate value for your property so that will mean–more money for you!

- Today's financing choices may help determine your success, whether you are buying or selling property so–let my financial knowledge work for you!

- An experienced agent has the education to solve any problem that may arise in a real estate transaction and– my real estate education and experience has been nationally recognized!

Fewer than 2% of all Real Estate Licencees have received the CRS® Designation!

I'M PROUD TO BE ONE OF THEM.

JOYCE CAUGHMAN
IF YOU WANT THE BEST – CALL ME!

410-956-0364
METRO MR REFERRALS

PEN IN HAND

Your Neighborhood Real Estate Specialist
303-6767   LINDA CARTER   303-7185

THINKING OF SELLING? Two new videotapes give sellers tips on how to prepare for the buyer's eye. One by Barb Schwarz is called "How To Prepare Your Home for Sale," and the other by Pam George, "House Sense: Setting the State for the Sale." If you would like to borrow one of these tapes, give me a ring at 261-7777.

Peter Dickinson, author of the *Retirement Newsletter,* has come up with a booklet on the best retirement havens in the world. He also has one called the *Book of Great Retirement Discounts*. If your retirement is coming up, consider getting these books with a subscription to the newsletter.

WET BASEMENTS! One of the greastest causes of decline of property values can often be solved inexpensively. Quite often the problem is as simple as grading away from the foundation. This could be a do-it-yourself project that would save you lots of money in the long run. Check your grade around the house to be sure that it is not carrying water toward your basement wall.

MONEY WAITING FOR YOU? If you ever sold a house with an FHA loan on it, FHA may be holding your lump sum mortgage insurance refund. Many borrowers fail to claim their refunds. Call 202-755-5616 if you think you might be owed money.

Babysitters: Mary Ann Rodgers, age 16, 302-2344
               Granny Forman, experienced, 302-7893

Tutoring: 25 years' experience teaching math and science. Call
          302-7854.

Local News: The Rosedale Lion's Club Annual Grapefruit Sale will be held on Saturday, March 30, from 8 a.m. to 3 p.m. at the Armory. Call Don at 302-7291 for information and orders.

Upp & Addam, REALTORS
266-5505   261-7665

Call anytime for an answer to any real estate question.   Source information courtesy of the REALTOR® Library, National Association of REALTORS®.

Telephone Report Form and Follow-Up Guide

File these sheets in address order, so that as you walk a street or make telephone calls you have the information in the order of your progress through the neighborhood.

Number:_____Street: _____   Contacts

Family information: _____   Dates   Phone/Pers.

_____

Home phone:_____Office: _____   1.

Subdiv.:_____Style: _____   2.

Prev. sales price:_____   3.

Amenities: _____   4.

Target group: _____   5.

Farm stage: 1 2 3 4   6.

- -

_____

Comments:

Date: _____   Pets, anniversaries, hobbies

_____   _____

_____   _____

_____   _____

Your computer can't be with you at all times, but information from your computer can. Pictured in Chapter 3 is an example of a tickler file that holds a letter-size sheet folded in four, making a 5½″ × 4¼″ record for each home in your farm. It can be carried in your briefcase, coat pocket or purse as you walk about your farm or make phone calls. Copy pages from your farm book or print records out of your computer and use the back of them to keep notes about personal visits or telemarketing sessions in your tickler file.

Penetrate your market area. . . .

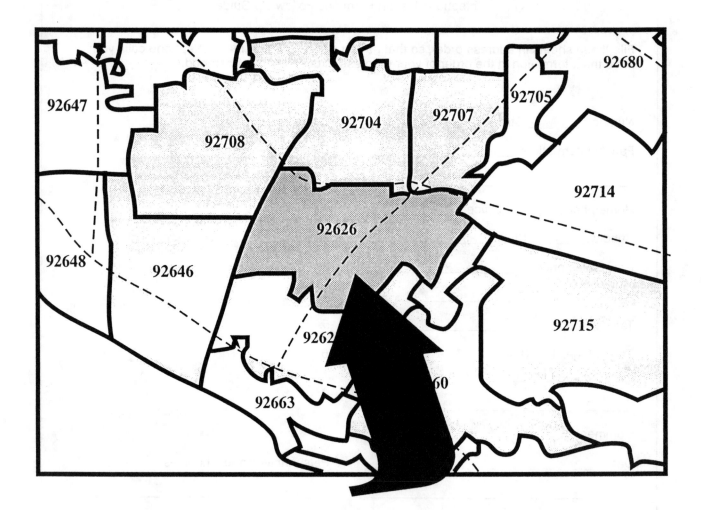

"Target-In" on Your Customers
Mail one Zip Code or the Entire Market

ADVO, Inc.

Index